LOYALTY

NOMOS

LIV

NOMOS

Harvard University Press

I   *Authority* 1958, reissued in 1982 by Greenwood Press

The Liberal Arts Press

II   *Community* 1959
III   *Responsibility* 1960

Atherton Press

IV   *Liberty* 1962
V   *The Public Interest* 1962
VI   *Justice* 1963, reissued in 1974
VII   *Rational Decision* 1964
VIII   *Revolution* 1966
IX   *Equality* 1967
X   *Representation* 1968
XI   *Voluntary Associations* 1969
XII   *Political and Legal Obligation* 1970
XIII   *Privacy* 1971

Aldine-Atherton Press

XIV   *Coercion* 1972

Lieber-Atherton Press

XV   *The Limits of Law* 1974
XVI   *Participation in Politics* 1975

New York University Press

XVII   *Human Nature in Politics* 1977
XVIII   *Due Process* 1977
XIX   *Anarchism* 1978
XX   *Constitutionalism* 1979
XXI   *Compromise in Ethics, Law, and Politics* 1979
XXII   *Property* 1980
XXIII   *Human Rights* 1981
XXIV   *Ethics, Economics, and the Law* 1982
XXV   *Liberal Democracy* 1983
XXVI   *Marxism* 1983

NOMOS LIV

Yearbook of the American Society for Political and Legal Philosophy

LOYALTY

Edited by

**Sanford Levinson, Joel Parker,
and Paul Woodruff**

NEW YORK UNIVERSITY PRESS • *New York and London*

NEW YORK UNIVERSITY PRESS
New York and London
www.nyupress.org

References to Internet websites (URLs) were accurate at the time of writing.
Neither the author nor New York University Press is responsible for URLs that may
have expired or changed since the manuscript was prepared.

Library of Congress Cataloging-in-Publication Data
Loyalty / edited by Sanford Levinson, Joel Parker, and Paul Woodruff.
pages cm.   (Nomos ; 54)
Includes bibliographical references and index.
ISBN 978–0–8147–8593–5 (alk. paper)   ISBN 978–0–8147–6091–8 (ebook)
ISBN 978–0–8147–3789–7 (ebook)
1. Loyalty. I. Levinson, Sanford, 1941–, editor of compilation.
BJ1533.L8L69   2013
179'.9—dc23   2012045599

New York University Press books are printed on acid-free paper, and their binding
materials are chosen for strength and durability. We strive to use environmentally
responsible suppliers and materials to the greatest extent possible in publishing
our books.

Manufactured in the United States of America
10 9 8 7 6 5 4 3 2 1

CONTENTS

PREFACE

SANFORD LEVINSON

The American Society for Political and Legal Philosophy selects its annual topic by a vote of the membership. "Loyalty" was the topic chosen for the gathering that took place at the Eastern Division of the American Philosophical Association in December 2007. To put it mildly, "loyalty" is a broad topic, beginning with the most basic question of whether one should ever be "loyal" to anything other than a universal good. This is the question especially addressed by Bernard Gert who, sadly, died while this volume was in press, in the first of three essays that examine general "conceptions of loyalty." Kathleen Higgins and Paul Woodruff go on to examine notions of loyalty in classical Confucian and ancient Greek traditions, respectively.

Rousseau, always suspicious of "partial" commitments less encompassing than the "general will" and its presumptive identity with the "common good," powerfully declaimed that "[w]e are justly punished for those exclusive attachments which make us blind and unjust, and limit our universe to the persons we love. All the preferences of friendship are thefts committed against the human race and fatherland. Men are all our brothers, they should all be our friends."[1] One can only imagine Rousseau's reaction to the novelist E. M. Forster's (in)famous declaration that "if I had to choose between betraying my country and betraying my friend I hope I should have the guts to betray my country."[2] Note, though, that even Rousseau is less than universalistic inasmuch as he includes the "fatherland" as an aggrieved party should citizens adopt more partial notions of loyalty evoked by Forster. Is it self-evident, though, that national loyalties necessarily trump more universalistic commitments to what he called "the human race"? Consider in this context the historian Istvan Deak's portrayal of Roman Catholicism as "represent[ing] a beautiful anachronism in our age of crazed nationalism; virtually every devout Catholic preserves in his heart some remains of his denomination's transnational loyalty and the duty of Catholics to defy immoral laws."[3] Deak's comment evokes not only "transnational" or universal loyalties but also the more specific conflict between the commands of a presumptively secular state and the ostensible demands placed on religious believers by a Divine Sovereign.

Still, for a two-day conference on such a broad topic, choices invariably had to be made by the co-editors of the anticipated volume collecting the presentations. This volume is most certainly not a "comprehensive" treatment of "loyalty," even if we can imagine such in anything less than a full shelf, if not an entire library, of books. Thus, temptations to explore more fully the important issues raised by both Deak and Forster were rejected, as were many other plausible candidates. Most of this book therefore focuses on three particular issues relevant not only to political theorists, lawyers, and philosophers but also to ordinary citizens trying to make sense of contemporary political orders. All three involve significant institutions—attorneys at law, the military, and political parties—that can raise sometimes troubling problems in determining where one's ultimate loyalties actually lie. Two of them, additionally, involve professionals; a classic index of "professionalism" is precisely the development of internal "codes of ethics" designed to "discipline" the trained professional, adherence to which can appear problematic to outsiders (and even some insiders).

From ancient times and in both secular and sectarian traditions, lawyers have been objects of suspicion precisely because they are seen as willing to place loyalty to their clients above the interests of the polity or the commands of divine justice. The critique can certainly be traced back to Socrates' attack on "sophists" and their commitment to making "lesser arguments" appear "the greater," in Plato's *Gorgias* dialogue; Sanford Levinson, one of the co-editors, assigned that dialogue when he used to teach law school courses on "professional responsibility." Daniel Markovits, a philosopher and lawyer who teaches at the Yale Law School, has written a full-scale volume, *A Modern Legal Ethics: Adversary Advocacy in a Democratic Age,* and his contribution here offers further reflections on the notion of a particular "lawyerly fidelity." Lynn Mather, a political scientist who has devoted much of her career to the empirical study of lawyers' behavior, assesses Markovits's arguments in the light of what she has learned from interviews and observation of lawyers who specialize in family law, a too often ignored field within law that can present especially exquisite dilemmas of loyalty and professional responsibility.

The Weberian state may possess a monopoly over the legitimate use of the means of violence, but it is the military as an institution that has the practical knowledge of how actually to use those means in their most deadly forms. As with lawyers, there is a literature going back centuries about the extent to which civilian officials, whether princes, kings, or democratically elected leaders, can necessarily count on the loyalty of military personnel, especially if there is perhaps justified doubt about the wisdom of decisions taken by those with ostensible authority over the military. Nancy Sherman, a philosopher whose books include *Stoic Warriors: The Ancient Philosophy behind the Military Mind* and, more recently, *The Untold War: Inside the Hearts, Minds, and Souls of Our Soldiers*, looks at what she calls the "fractured fidelity to cause" in examining the ever-important and intriguing question of exactly what impels especially soldiers on the ground to risk their lives in behalf of what are presented to the public as abstract and often highly controversial causes. A comment on Sherman by Ryan Balot, the author of a forthcoming monograph on courage, citizenship, and democracy in ancient Athens, follows. Paul Carrese, who brings to the volume his experience teaching political theory at the U.S. Air Force Academy, offers an essay, "For Constitution and Profession: Paradoxes of Military Service in a Liberal Democracy"; it concludes with a timely discussion of recent controversies about the degree to which high-level military leaders should feel free—or even feel a duty—to enter into public dissent from what they believe to be the unwise policies chosen by civilian leaders (including, of course, the president/commander in chief).

Finally, two essays address another topic of much concern to analysts especially of contemporary American politics: political partisanship and its limits. One can well believe that the vision of American politics presented by James Madison at the time the Constitution was drafted (and defended) in 1787–88 exhibited the hope that the dangers of "faction" could be significantly mitigated, even if not entirely avoided, by the intricate institutional structures of the new national government, coupled with what Madison hoped would be the civic republican commitment to the common good possessed by the elites who would be at the helm of the national government. There was, in that vision, no room for political parties, which are defined, among other ways, by the loyalties that members of a given party develop to the interests of the party itself. Russell Muirhead's essay draws from a full-length manuscript he is preparing, tentatively titled *A Defense of Party Spirit.* Like Nancy Rosenblum, who published *On the Side of the Angels: An Appreciation of Parties and Partisanship* (2008), Muirhead rejects the neorepublican critique of parties and, therefore, defends the virtues of what many, especially in recent years, often dismiss as "partisanship." Yasmin Dawood, who has written on the political theory instantiated in various election systems, points to some dangers for democracy of accepting not only the reality but also the legitimacy of what she terms "the Partisan State" generated by excessive loyalty to the interests of one's political party.

There is, of course, much more that could be said about the specific issues raised by all of these essays, not to mention many other facets of "loyalty." We are confident, however, that these essays all provide their own illumination and further the discussion of an important and often perplexing topic that will continue to be of both theoretical and practical importance.

NOTES

1. Jean-Jacques Rousseau, *Correspondance Générale de Jean-Jacques Rousseau,* vol. 4, ed. Théophile Dufour and Pierre Paul Plan (Paris: A. Colin, 1925), 82, quoted in Sanford Levinson, "Testimonial Privileges and the Preferences of Friendship," *Duke Law Journal* 1984 (September 1984): 631.

2. E. M. Forster, *Two Cheers for Democracy* (London: Edward Arnold, 1972), 66.

3. István Deák, "The Incomprehensible Holocaust," *New York Review of Books* 36 (28 September 1989): 66, quoted in Sanford Levinson, "The Confrontation of Religious Faith and Civil Religion," in *Wrestling with Diversity,* ed. Levinson (Durham, NC: Duke University Press, 2003), 192.

CONTRIBUTORS

RYAN K. BALOT
Professor of Political Science and Classics at the University of Toronto.

PAUL O. CARRESE
Professor of Political Science at the U.S. Air Force Academy.

YASMIN DAWOOD
Assistant Professor of Law and Political Science at the University of Toronto.

BERNARD GERT
Died in 2011, was Stone Professor of Intellectual and Moral Philosophy, Emeritus at Dartmouth College, and Professor of Social Medicine at the University of North Carolina, Chapel Hill.

KATHLEEN M. HIGGINS
Professor of Philosophy at The University of Texas at Austin.

SANFORD LEVINSON
Professor of Government and W. St. John and W. St. John Jr. Centennial Chair of Law at The University of Texas School of Law.

DANIEL MARKOVITS
Guido Calabresi Professor of Law at the Yale Law School.

LYNN MATHER
Professor of Law and Political Science at SUNY Buffalo Law School.

RUSSELL MUIRHEAD
Robert Clements Associate Professor of Democracy and Politics at Dartmouth College.

NANCY SHERMAN
   *University Professor of Philosophy and a Fellow of the Kennedy
   Institute of Ethics at Georgetown University.*

PAUL WOODRUFF
   *Darrell K. Royal Professor in Ethics and American Society at The
   University of Texas at Austin.*

PART I

CONCEPTIONS OF LOYALTY

1

LOYALTY AND MORALITY

BERNARD GERT

I am interested in exploring the relationship between "loyalty" and "morality" in what I take to be the most common senses of these terms. If I am correct that these are the most common senses of these terms, then my exploration may have important results, but even if I am not correct about this, the senses that I take to be the most common are still ordinary senses, and so the results should be of some interest. In order to present a clear account of the relationship between loyalty and morality, it is necessary to provide a clear account not only of loyalty but also of morality. Given the very different views about the relationship between loyalty and morality, it might be thought that there must be significant disagreements about the nature of loyalty; however, these different views about the relationship might be due to significant disagreements about the nature of morality. Regardless of the source of the disagreements, the views about the relationship between loyalty and morality can be put into three categories: (1) loyalty and morality are always incompatible, (2) loyalty and morality are never incompatible, and (3) loyalty and morality are sometimes incompatible.

LOYALTY

The *Oxford English Dictionary* provides two definitions for the term "loyalty": (1) "Faithful adherence to one's promise, oath, word of honour, etc." and (2) "Faithful adherence to the sovereign or lawful government." Thomas Hobbes would claim that the first definition entails the second, for he holds that everyone has promised to obey the sovereign. However, the dictionary does not provide an account of the most common use of the term "loyalty," which does not limit faithful adherence to the lawful government but includes faithful adherence to any group of which one is a member. Of course, this includes faithful adherence to one's country, but it also includes faithful adherence to much smaller groups, such as one's colleagues, fellow doctors, lawyers, or policemen. It also includes faithful adherence to a company for which one works. People even talk of brand loyalty, but this is clearly a marginal and parasitic sense of "loyalty," and I shall not be concerned with it at all.

A serious problem with this more common and inclusive account is the unclarity of the phrase "faithful adherence." While it is clear what "faithful adherence to one's promise" means, namely keeping one's promises, and "faithful adherence to the lawful government" can simply mean obeying the law, it is not clear what "faithful adherence" means when talking about loyalty to a group that consists of one's colleagues. Rather than talking about faithful adherence to a group, I think it clearer to regard loyalty to a group as involving acting in a way that shows that one regards its members as warranting more consideration than people not in the group. Particularly important is that someone who is loyal to a group regards avoiding or preventing harm to members of the group as more important than avoiding or preventing similar harm to people not in the group. Loyalty to a group does not seem to require acting to further the interests of the group or its members. Such action seems to go beyond what most hold that loyalty requires, although it would certainly show loyalty to a group to promote its interests.

Loyalty requires an individual to be willing to make some significant personal sacrifices to avoid causing harm to the group or to prevent or relieve harm suffered by members of the group. However, it is a matter of controversy whether loyalty to a group requires a refusal to harm the group or a willingness to prevent or relieve harm to members of the group when this involves causing greater harm to others not in the group. People sometimes cite as examples of disloyalty actions that involve doing something, such as snitching or whistle-blowing, that harms the group or some of its members, even though failure to take the action in question would result in greater harm for those not in the group. Members of a group may even be urged to show loyalty by acting to prevent harm to the group or its members, for example, not only by refusing to testify but also by lying, when this not only involves breaking a moral rule, but also involves a significant risk of greater harm to those not in the group. Although loyalty requires one to act as if harm suffered by members of one's group is more important than harm suffered by people who are not members of one's group, it is controversial whether loyalty requires harming others or violating commonly accepted moral rules.

There is another significant kind of loyalty that might be called "professional loyalty." This is the kind of loyalty that lawyers owe to their clients and is the kind of loyalty that was the primary focus of one of the essays presented at the *NOMOS* meeting on loyalty.[1] Lawyers have a duty of loyalty to their clients; the code of ethics for lawyers requires that they be zealous advocates for their clients. Accountants, engineers, and physicians also have duties of loyalty to their clients or patients; however, lawyers' duties of loyalty to their clients have attracted far more attention than the duties of loyalty of other professions. This may be due to the fact that the duties of loyalty of lawyers seem not only to allow but also sometimes even to require that they violate moral rules prohibiting deception and harming others. However, this moral controversy concerning the limits of professional loyalty is best thought of as a conflict between what is required by one's professional duty, regardless of whether it is a duty of loyalty, and what is prohibited by other moral rules. Professional loyalty may be an instance of the first definition of "loyalty," "faithful adherence to one's promise, oath, word of honour, etc.," consistent with definition quoted on page 3, but it is not an example of the kind of loyalty that I take to be what is most commonly meant by "loyalty." I shall not be concerned with it when I investigate the relationship between loyalty and morality.

Insofar as loyalty requires only personal sacrifice in order to avoid harming the group or to prevent harm to the group, no one takes loyalty to conflict with morality, and I shall not be concerned with this aspect of loyalty. In this chapter, I shall be concerned only with that aspect of loyalty to a group that involves acting as if harms suffered by members of the group to which one is loyal are more important than harms suffered by those not in the group. It is because loyalty involves taking the harm suffered by members of the group to which one is loyal as more important than the harm suffered by those not in the group that loyalty seems to conflict with the impartiality required by morality. Loyalty to a person's group may involve her spending time and effort aiding members of her group when, with that same investment of time and effort, she could prevent and relieve far more harm for people not in her group. Loyalty to a fellow doctor may involve failing to report his problems to the appropriate authorities even though one knows that several patients will die or suffer serious injuries they would not suffer if this physician were no longer allowed to practice. It is because loyalty seems to require these kinds of behavior that some hold that loyalty and morality are incompatible.

Acting as if harm suffered by one's group or its members is more important than harm suffered by those not in one's group is not acting out of loyalty if one acts in this way because one is motivated by fear or greed. A person who acts as if harm suffered by his group or its members is more important than harm suffered by those not in his group, but only because he fears retaliation from his group or its members if he does not, is not acting out of loyalty to that group. Also, someone who acts as if harm suffered by his group or its members is more important than harm suffered by those not in the group only because he is paid to act in that way is not acting out of loyalty to that group. A gang member may act as if he is loyal to his gang, but, if he acts loyally only because he fears retaliation from the gang, he is not acting out of loyalty. A hired killer may act as if he is loyal to those who hired him, but, if he acts in that way only because they are paying him more than others would, he is not loyal to that group. A test of loyalty is whether, when one refuses to harm the group or its members or acts to prevent harm to the group, one would still act in that way if one believed that no one knew or would find out how one was acting. Another test of loyalty is whether one would refuse to harm or act to prevent harm to a group even if so refusing or acting would carry significant personal costs.

Although fear and greed may result in behavior toward the group that is indistinguishable from genuine loyalty, they do not count as motives for loyalty. Motives for loyalty must not depend upon beliefs about the consequences for oneself of showing loyalty. However, gratitude, that is, a belief or feeling that one has benefited in significant ways from being a member of that group, is a proper motive. A person who is loyal can believe that he will continue to benefit from being a member of the group, but, if it is only this latter belief that motivates him, he is not loyal. In order for his loyalty to count as genuine, his primary motive for loyalty must be gratitude for past benefits; his belief about future benefits cannot be the primary motive for his actions. But gratitude is not the only motive for being loyal. A person may also be loyal because he has come to bond with other members of the group, to regard them as similar to family members. This kind of bonding often occurs when people face significant and recurring dangers together, as with members of the same gang. As indicated earlier, members of a biological family often develop the kinds of bonds that result in their being loyal to the family and its members.

Loyalty can also result from sharing common religious beliefs, from being citizens of the same country, or from belonging to the same race or ethnic group. People can even feel loyalty to the company for which they work. Although this may involve gratitude for the benefits of working for that company, it may simply come from a feeling of belonging to something like a family that works together to achieve common goals and results. Similar reasons may prompt loyalty to people involved in some task, especially when this involves cooperating in facing serious risks of death or injury, as with firefighters, police, and soldiers. People can also feel loyalty to members of the same profession, for example, doctors to other doctors and lawyers to other lawyers, simply because they identify with others in their profession. People may identify so deeply with their profession that they want to protect it and all members of it from anything that might damage the profession. However, it may simply be that one feels a bond to other members of the same profession in the same way that firefighters, police, and soldiers do.

The motives for genuine loyalty to a group must be motives that are sufficient for the person to be loyal in situations where they believe that no one will know how they are behaving. A person need not consciously believe that harms to the group or members of his group are more important than similar harms to people not in the group; he need only act as if he believes this when people in his group are at risk of harm. It is not surprising that many people value loyalty and regard it as a virtue, for everyone is a member of some group toward which loyalty is appropriate and so benefits from the loyalty of other members of the group. Loyalty is similar to morality in that both often give rise to hypocrisy. Even if one does not act morally oneself, one is likely to encourage moral behavior in others; likewise, even if one is not loyal oneself, one is likely to encourage loyalty in other members of one's group. The aspect of loyalty that I shall be concerned with in this chapter is that aspect of loyalty that involves acting in ways that seem to involve regarding harm suffered by members of the group to which one is loyal as more important than harm suffered by those not in that group.

Loyalty to one group to which one belongs is compatible with lack of loyalty to another group to which one also belongs, so, in order to understand what it means to say that a person is loyal, it is necessary to specify the group to which the person is loyal. Loyalty in this sense has some similarity to impartiality. One does not understand what it means to say that a person is impartial unless one knows with regard to what group that person is impartial, but for impartiality one must also specify in what respect that person is impartial with regard to that group.[2] However, with regard to loyalty, the necessary specification concerns only the group to which one is loyal. Nonetheless, loyalty, like impartiality is properly regarded as a trait of character. Insofar as one is loyal to a group, one is expected to act in the appropriate way with regard to this group even when one believes that no one will ever know how one is acting and even when it is counter to one's self-interest to act in that way.

MISTAKEN ACCOUNTS OF MORALITY

Anthropologists, philosophers, psychologists, and sociologists have presented many different accounts of morality. Whether loyalty to a group is always incompatible, never incompatible, or sometimes incompatible with morality depends in part on what account of morality one accepts. It also depends on an essential feature of loyalty that might be taken by some as at least sometimes incompatible with morality. That feature of loyalty involves acting as if one regards harm suffered by members of the group to which one is loyal as more important than harm suffered by those not in that group.[3] Just as my concern with loyalty is with what I take to be the most common sense of "loyalty," so my concern with morality is with what I take to be the most common sense of "morality."

Before I present what I take to be an account of the most common sense of "morality," or what I shall call "common morality," I shall present briefly some other accounts of morality. On an account of morality favored by act consequentialists morality requires, as John Stuart Mill said in the first chapter of *Utilitarianism*, complete impartiality, that is, impartiality with regard to everyone with respect to all of one's actions and inactions.[4] For act consequentialism, loyalty is not a moral virtue; rather, it is a moral vice. It is not a trait of character that might be of moral value if appropriately limited; rather, it is one that ought to be, as much as possible, eradicated.

Some act consequentialists would hold that it is not appropriate to talk about loyalty to the group of all sentient beings. They would claim that it is impossible to take harm suffered by members of the group of all sentient beings as more important than harm suffered by those who are not in that group, for they hold that beings that are not sentient cannot suffer any harm. However, for these act consequentialists, even loyalty to that subgroup of sentient beings that consists of members of one's own species leads to immoral behavior such as factory farming. Even on less expansive versions of act consequentialism, any action (or inaction) that results in the harms suffered by some moral agents being treated as more important than the harms suffered by other moral agents violates the impartiality that is required by morality.

If, as some act consequentialists maintain, morality does indeed demand this kind of complete impartiality with regard to all people, morality is always incompatible with loyalty. For loyalty involves acting as if the harm suffered by some people or by people in some group is more important than harm suffered by other people or by people not in that group. Although this kind of extreme act consequentialism seems to command an unswerving devotion from those who hold it, the act consequentialist view that morality requires such complete impartiality is not in accord with any standard account of morality, for it regards as immoral being more concerned with the harm suffered by one's children than with the harm suffered by other children. Thus, I shall consider it to be unimportant that, on the act consequentialist view of morality, loyalty is always incompatible with morality.

On the other hand, according to some anthropologists and evolutionary psychologists, acting morally is almost equivalent to showing loyalty to those in one's society. One version of this contemporary ethical relativism holds that morality is that code of conduct put forward by a society for the benefit of those in that society.[5] On this ethical relativist account of morality, both loyalty and morality require avoiding doing harm to those in one's society, and both encourage preventing harm to them, as well, even if this involves greater harm to those who are not members of one's society. No matter how many innocent people not in one's society one harms, it is morally acceptable for a person to avoid harming or to prevent harm to people in her society. This is a view that gains wide acceptance in most societies during a war. Some hold that killing or harming many innocent civilians of another society is morally acceptable if that is necessary to win the war, even when one is not thereby saving the lives of or preventing comparable harm to anything close to that number of members of one's own society.

Some take this relativistic account of morality even further, restricting morality to any group toward which a person feels loyalty, so that acting to avoid or prevent harm to those in whatever group toward which one feels loyalty is what morality requires. On this account, members of the Soprano crime family are considered to be acting morally if they are loyal to other members of the Soprano family, no matter what they do to those who are not members of their crime family. On this account of morality, loyalty is always a moral virtue. Not only does it not need to be limited in any way, but also it should not be limited. Disloyalty is always a moral vice. It is morally wrong to cause any harm to people in the group to whom loyalty is owed in order to avoid causing harm to innocent persons not in that group, even if the harm to people not in one's group is far greater than the harm that would be suffered by people in one's own group. It is also morally good to prevent any harm to people in the group to whom loyalty is owed, even if this involves causing greater harm to people not in one's group. This account of morality does not seem to be widely accepted, so the fact that, on this extreme ethical relativist view of morality, loyalty is always compatible with morality also does not seem important.

Even if act consequentialists and ethical relativists accept the account of loyalty put forward in the previous section—that it involves acting as if the harms suffered by some people are more important than the harms suffered by other people—they would still hold the relationship between loyalty and morality to be completely different. This makes it clear that accepting the common sense of "loyalty" that I have presented is not sufficient to determine the important relationship between loyalty and morality; it is also necessary to accept the common sense of "morality." Even though act consequentialists and ethical relativists both agree that loyalty involves acting as if the harms suffered by those in the group to which one is loyal are more important than the same harms suffered by those not in that group, they will still disagree about the relationship between loyalty and morality. Moreover, many universalistic accounts of morality seem to require that one always act as if the harms suffered by any moral agent are as important as the harms suffered by any other moral agent, regardless of whether that moral agent belongs to a group to which one is loyal.

IMPARTIALITY AND MORALITY

As indicated earlier, the disagreement about whether loyalty is compatible with morality involves a disagreement about the kind of impartiality required by morality. On most accounts of the impartiality required by morality, impartiality is thought to be incompatible with loyalty. However, although this is a plausible view, it presupposes a concept of impartiality that is far too simple. Many observers do not realize that a correct account of what it means to say that a person is impartial requires specifying both the group with regard to which that person is impartial and the respect in which that person is impartial with regard to this group. The basic concept of impartiality is the following: *A is impartial in respect R with regard to group G if and only if A's actions in respect R are not influenced at all by which member(s) of G are benefited or harmed by these actions.*[6] A teacher can be impartial with regard to a group G, for example, the students in her class, in respect R, for example, grading their exams, but not impartial with regard to the same group in a different respect, such as calling on them in class, for she may favor boys over girls in this respect.

Two umpires can both be impartial with regard to two teams in a given respect and yet not be impartial in the same respect with regard to pitchers and batters. If one umpire prefers a higher-scoring game and the other a lower-scoring one, they may, within the accepted interpretations of the rules, call some pitches differently. Even if, in the respect of calling balls and strikes, one umpire shows partiality toward pitchers and the other toward batters, both can still be impartial with regard to the two teams in that very same respect. The fact that two baseball umpires can both be impartial with regard to the two teams and yet differ in the way that they call balls and strikes shows that it is a mistake to think that impartiality requires unanimity. Even if they are also impartial with regard to pitchers and batters, they can still sometimes disagree, and neither one will be making any mistake or doing anything wrong. This is one of many situations in which two impartial persons can differ in their decisions and judgments.[7]

Some philosophers, for example, act consequentialists such as Peter Singer, assume that all impartial persons must always agree about moral matters. However, they have provided no reasons to accept that claim. The mistaken claim that all equally informed, impartial, rational persons must always agree has some undesirable implications. If it were correct, then every split decision made by the U.S. Supreme Court or any other court must be regarded as the result of at least one judge not being equally informed, not being rational, or not being impartial. Nonetheless, many, if not most, philosophers accept the mistaken claim that, if how one acts is not morally indifferent, there is a unique morally correct way to act in all situations, even the most controversial or problematic.[8] This mistaken claim is implied by the view that all equally informed, impartial, rational persons must always agree on their answers to every moral question.[9]

Realizing that impartiality must be specified with regard to both group and respect explains how there can be disagreements about whether the impartiality required by morality is always, never, or sometimes incompatible with loyalty. Just as loyalty requires further specification with regard to the group to which one is loyal, saying that a person is impartial similarly requires specifying the group to which he is impartial. If the group with regard to which one is supposed to be impartial were the same group to which one is loyal, then impartiality would never be incompatible with loyalty. However, it is only on an extreme ethical relativist conception of morality that the group with regard to which morality requires impartiality is limited to the group to which a person is loyal. On most universal accounts of morality, such as consequentialist, deontological, and natural law accounts, morality requires impartiality with regard to a much larger group. This group includes at least all moral agents, that is, those who understand what kinds of behavior morality forbids, requires, discourages, encourages, and allows and who can guide their conduct accordingly. Thus, these views may seem to result in loyalty always being incompatible with morality.

However, our common morality, unlike act consequentialist accounts of morality or some interpretations of Kantian and natural law views concerning morality, does not require impartiality with respect to all of one's actions. It requires impartiality only when one is violating a moral rule, such as when one is killing or breaking a promise. Morality does not require impartiality when no violation of a moral rule is involved. Morality does not even require impartiality when following some moral ideal, such as preventing pain or relieving suffering, unless a violation of a moral rule is involved.[10] People do nothing morally wrong when they give to the charity of their choice, for example, a heart fund or a cancer fund, because some friend or family member was helped by that charity, or when they concentrate their time and effort in order to help members of their own country, ethnic group, race, or religion.

For an extreme ethical relativist, there is no conflict between morality and loyalty because there is no conflict between the group with regard toward which one is supposed to be impartial and the group to which one is loyal. For many universal accounts of morality, the conflict between loyalty and morality arises because they hold that morality always requires impartiality with regard to at least all moral agents, and loyalty involves acting as if the harms suffered by those in the group to which one is loyal count for more than the harms suffered by those not in that group. Common morality, which accepts morality as universal, differs from many universal philosophical accounts of morality because, although it agrees that impartiality is required with regard to a group that includes at least all moral agents, it denies that morality requires impartiality with regard to all of one's actions. According to common morality, morality requires impartiality with respect to a very limited range of one's actions, only those that involve the violation of a moral rule. Impartiality, like loyalty, requires specification with regard to the group that is involved. However, impartiality also requires specification with respect to the kinds of actions that impartiality requires with regard to that group, and this is very significant.

Even the impartiality required by morality must be specified with regard to a group and in a respect with regard to that group. The group with regard to which morality requires impartiality includes at least all moral agents, and the respect in which morality requires impartiality with regard to this group is with respect to violations of a moral rule, for example, killing or breaking a promise. Morality does not require impartiality when one is following a moral ideal, for example, preventing pain. The correct result about the relationship between loyalty and morality results from recognition that morality requires impartiality only when a violation of a moral rule is involved. This recognition leads to the view that loyalty is a trait of character that when appropriately limited can be considered a virtue but that when not so limited is likely to be a moral vice. Morality allows acting as if the harms suffered by those in the group to which one is loyal count for more than the harms suffered by those not in that group, as long as one is not causing harm to those not in one's group or violating other moral rules with regard to them. When only the moral ideals are involved, one may act as if the harms suffered by those in the group to which one is loyal count for more than the harms suffered by those not in that group. This distinction between moral rules and moral ideals, with impartiality being required only when the former is involved, is included in what I understand to be the most commonly accepted account of morality.

Moral Rules and Impartiality

Morality is not merely that code of conduct that a person happens to regard as most important; it has a definite content. Moral rules prohibit, for example, killing and cheating; moral ideals encourage preventing and relieving pain and suffering. Morality contains moral virtues such as honesty and kindness and moral vices such as cruelty. Morality also contains a procedure for determining whether a violation of a moral rule is strongly justified, weakly justified, or unjustified. Moral rules are that part of the moral system the violation of which is prohibited unless an impartial moral agent can publicly allow it, that is, unless that moral agent is willing to allow everyone to know that the rule may be violated in circumstances with the same morally relevant features. The following is one common formulation of the moral rules.

1. Do not kill.
2. Do not cause pain.
3. Do not disable (deprive of ability).
4. Do not deprive of freedom.
5. Do not deprive of pleasure.
6. Do not deceive.
7. Keep your promises.
8. Do not cheat.
9. Obey the law.
10. Do your duty (what is required by your job, social role, or special circumstances).

A morally relevant feature of a situation where a violation of a moral rule is being considered is a feature that, if changed, may change whether some impartial, rational person would publicly allow that violation. If all of the morally relevant features are the same for two violations, then they are the same kind of violation, and, if an impartial, rational person publicly allows one of them, then she must also publicly allow the other. An impartial, rational person who publicly allows a particular violation but does not publicly allow another that seems the same must show how the two violations differ with regard to at least one of their morally relevant features. However, two different impartial, rational persons who regard a violation as of the same kind need not agree about whether to publicly allow that violation. For impartial, rational persons may differ in their beliefs about the consequences of that kind of violation being publicly allowed and not allowed or in their ranking of those consequences.

The morally relevant features determine the kind of violation under consideration. This is the crucial first step in moral reasoning about the justification of particular violations, for it determines how to describe the kind of violation. After the violation has been described using only the morally relevant features, the next step is deciding whether an impartial, rational person could publicly allow this kind of violation. This decision is made by answering the morally decisive question: "Are the consequences that would result if everyone knows that this kind of violation is allowed better or worse than the consequences that would result if everyone knows that this kind of violation is not allowed?" If all impartial, rational persons would estimate that the consequences of everyone knowing that this kind of violation is allowed are better than the consequences that would result if everyone knows that this kind of violation is not allowed, the violation is strongly justified. If all impartial, rational persons would estimate the opposite, the violation is unjustified. If impartial, rational persons disagree in their estimates about whether the consequences of everyone knowing that this kind of violation is allowed are better or worse than the consequences that would result if everyone knows that this kind of violation is not allowed, the violation is weakly justified.

The answer to the morally decisive question is not part of determining what counts as the same kind of act. Rather, it presupposes that the kind of act has already been determined. It is impossible to answer the morally decisive question "Are the consequences that would result if everyone knows that this kind of violation is allowed better or worse than the consequences that would result if everyone knows that this kind of violation is not allowed?" without first having a clear answer to what counts as the same kind of violation. Moral reasoning involving the violation of a moral rule always requires this two-step procedure: first, specifying the kind of violation; second, estimating the consequences of everyone knowing that this kind of violation is allowed and is not allowed. There are not two levels of moral thinking as R. M. Hare maintains, to be used in different situations, one for simple problems, the other for settling conflicts between general moral rules and ideals; rather, both steps of this two-step procedure are required whenever a violation of a moral rule is being considered. In some situations, the answer is often immediately apparent.

A violation of a moral rule requires not merely the basic sense of "impartiality" but also an extended sense involved in the two-step procedure. That is, a violation of a moral rule requires not only that one not be influenced by which moral agents are benefited or harmed by the violation but also that one be willing for all people to know that they can violate the rule in the same circumstances. This extended sense of impartiality required by morality is the kind of impartiality required whenever one is a member of the group with regard to which impartiality is required. Impartiality is required not only with regard to who in the group is harmed or benefited by a violation of a moral rule but also with regard to who in the group is allowed to violate a moral rule. The basic sense of impartiality, that required of judges and umpires, is that which Mill and consequentialists regard as the sense that is important for morality, while the extended sense is that which Kant thought most important and tried, unsuccessfully, to capture by means of the Categorical Imperative. Morality requires impartiality in both the basic and the extended senses, but only when one is considering whether a violation of a moral rule is justified.

Moral Ideals and Impartiality

Moral ideals are that part of the moral system that encourages acting in order to lessen the suffering of harm by anyone protected by the moral system—that is, to relieve pain. General moral ideals, like general moral rules, make no mention of person, place, group, or time. This may lead some to the mistaken view that, when one is following general moral ideals, impartiality is required just as strictly as when one is obeying moral rules and that favoring some persons over others must be excluded as rigorously as when one is obeying moral rules. The moral rules require obedience with regard to all moral agents impartially. It is not morally permissible to violate a moral rule with regard to a person not in a group to which one is loyal in order to follow a moral ideal with regard to a person in a group to which one is loyal, unless one would allow all group members to know that they can violate the rule in the same circumstances, including where there is no knowledge of who will be benefited or harmed. For example, that a person is a member of your family or of some other group to which you are loyal does not justify your killing someone not in that group in order to obtain an organ necessary to save the life of someone in the group. But, when no violation of a moral rule is involved, moral ideals do not require that one act impartially with regard to all moral agents; if two children are in danger of drowning, morality does not require flipping a coin to decide whether to rescue one's own child first. When no violation of a moral rule is involved, there is no moral requirement to act impartially.

It is not immoral to choose to follow a moral ideal with regard to some group of persons with whom one has some special relationship. African American members of the NAACP have no need to justify concentrating their efforts in following moral ideals toward aiding African Americans. Jews who contribute to the United Jewish Appeal need not justify concentrating their efforts toward aiding other Jews. Nor do citizens of the United States need to justify being primarily concerned with aiding the deprived citizens of America. It is impossible and therefore pointless to try to follow moral ideals with regard to all persons impartially. It is a mistake to think that morality requires people to justify choosing the persons or groups with regard to whom they will concentrate their efforts at helping to reduce suffering. Saying that morality requires impartiality without specifying the respect in which it does, namely when violating a moral rule, is a mistake. This mistake can be avoided only by distinguishing between moral rules and moral ideals and pointing out that it is only with respect to violations of the moral rules that impartiality is required.

LOYALTY AS A MORAL VIRTUE

Loyalty involves giving special consideration to a person or group of persons, avoiding or preventing harm to them that you would not avoid or prevent with regard to others not in that group. Loyalty to a person or group of persons involves avoiding or preventing harms to those in the group regardless of whether they are suffering more harm than those not in the group. Loyalty to your friends who have committed some crime may be incompatible with moral impartiality, for it may require you to lie to prevent their being found guilty and punished. Impartial, rational persons would not accept loyalty being used to justify violating a moral rule when that violation cannot be publicly allowed. Loyalty must be limited for it to be regarded favorably by impartial, rational persons. Loyalty is morally acceptable only when acting loyally does not involve unjustifiably violating a moral rule; impartiality is required when one is violating a moral rule.

Loyalty has a close relationship to gratitude, for often the group or individual to whom a person is loyal has provided benefits to her. Indeed, when an individual or a group is calling for loyalty by a person to a group, it is sometimes explicitly pointed out that the group has provided benefits to that person. Not surprisingly, some also regard gratitude as a moral virtue. Although there is no doubt that gratitude is a virtue—a character trait that impartial, rational persons would favor in people in their society—I prefer to call it a social virtue because it differs from the paradigmatic moral virtues, such as honesty, kindness, and trustworthiness, in a significant way. All of the paradigmatic moral virtues are closely related to a moral rule or a moral ideal. Because of this relationship, it is sometimes justifiable to violate a moral rule by exemplifying a moral virtue because one is thereby obeying another moral rule or following a moral ideal. In all of these cases, exemplifying a moral virtue may make it possible for an impartial, rational person to publicly allow an otherwise unjustified violation of a moral rule. This is because exemplifying the moral virtue provides the kind of justification that impartial, rational persons can accept. However, exemplifying gratitude cannot make it possible for an impartial, rational person to publicly allow an otherwise unjustified violation of a moral rule, because violating a moral rule out of gratitude involves harming or risking harm to one person in order to benefit another person when one would not allow that action if the people were reversed or different people were involved.

When a person has no duty to be impartial and is not violating a moral rule, then loyalty is sometimes more appropriate than impartiality.[11] Loyalty to family, friends, country, or colleagues is often admirable as long as it does not involve a violation of a moral rule, including the rule that requires one to do one's duty. Some may claim that morality should encourage loyalty, but loyalty does not need much encouragement. On the contrary, loyalty sometimes provides the most powerful motive for immoral behavior. Loyalty to family, friends, country, or colleagues provides such a powerful motive that many people who would not act immorally for reasons of self-interest are prepared to act immorally out of loyalty. How powerful loyalty is can be seen by the overwhelmingly negative attitude toward whistle-blowers held by members of the affected group even when it is absolutely clear that blowing the whistle on the immoral actions of others in that group was the morally right thing to do. Learning the limits of loyalty is one of the most important lessons that otherwise moral people can gain from a clear, precise, and explicit account of loyalty and morality and of the relationship between them.[12]

NOTES

1. Indeed, the title of Daniel Markovits's chapter is "Lawyerly Fidelity." Nancy Sherman's chapter is "A Fractured Fidelity to Cause" and is more closely related to the kind of loyalty with which I am concerned. But she is exploring a special case that involves whether one is fighting for a cause or for one's comrades in arms. To be sure, appealing to patriotism, that is, loyalty to country, is an appeal to the kind of loyalty with which I am concerned, but, as she points out, the appeal to go to war does not generally call only upon patriotism but also evokes the just and honorable cause for which the country is fighting. I am concerned with the appeal to loyalty when the appeal is primarily to patriotism with little or no concern for the cause of the war. The discussion of loyalty in the chapter by Russell Muirhead, "The Case for Party Loyalty," is closest to the sense of loyalty with which I am concerned, but he is concerned with the value of partisan loyalty to a democracy. He distinguishes between different forms of partisan loyalty—expressive loyalty versus cognitive loyalty—and favors the former because the latter is more likely to lead to immoral behavior, but he is concerned only with loyalty as it relates to the political system.

2. See Bernard Gert, "Impartiality," ch. 6 in Gert, *Morality: Its Nature and Justification*, rev. ed. (Oxford: Oxford University Press, 2005), 131–55.

3. In the remainder of this essay, whenever I talk about loyalty, I am talking about this aspect of loyalty.

4. "As between his own happiness and that of others, utilitarianism requires him to be as strictly impartial as a disinterested and benevolent spectator." John Stuart Mill, *Utilitarianism*, ed. George Sher (Indianapolis: Hackett, 1979), 16. To be fair to Mill, he provides a much better account of impartiality in ch. 5: "Impartiality . . . does not seem to be regarded as

a duty in itself, but rather as instrumental to some other duty." *Utilitarian-ism*, 44.

5. See Bernard Gert, "Definition of Morality," *Stanford Encyclopedia of Philosophy* (17 April, 2002, revised 11 February, 2008 and 14 March, 2011), http://plato.stanford.edu/entries/morality-definition.

6. The basic concept of impartiality applies to referees, umpires, and judges, where the person who is supposed to be impartial is not a member of the group with regard to which he is supposed to be impartial.

7. When I use "impartial," I mean "impartial with regard to the same group in the same respect."

8. When all fully informed, impartial, rational persons agree that it is morally indifferent which way one acts, there is not a unique, morally correct way to act.

9. See Bernard Gert, "Moral Arrogance and Moral Theories," *Philosophical Issues* 15 (*Normativity*) (October 2005): 366–85, for a fuller critique of this view.

10. The distinction between moral rules and moral ideals with regard to impartiality is discussed in the following sections: "Moral Rules and Impartiality" and "Moral Ideals and Impartiality." Kant and Mill make a related distinction when they distinguish between duties of perfect obligation and duties of imperfect obligation. Following moral ideals is often described as "morally supererogatory," that is, going beyond what is morally required.

11. This is also John Stuart Mill's position. "Impartiality, however, does not seem to be regarded as a duty in itself, but rather as instrumental to some other duty; for it is admitted that favor and preference are not always censurable, and, indeed, the cases in which they are condemned are rather the exception than the rule. A person would be more likely to be blamed than applauded for giving his family and friends no superiority in good offices over strangers when he could do so without violating some other duty; and no one thinks it unjust to seek one person in preference to another as a friend, connection or companion." Mill, *Utilitarianism*, 44.

12. I want to thank Joel Parker for many suggestions that improved this essay and John Moskop for pointing out a significant ambiguity that I have now eliminated.

2

LOYALTY FROM A
CONFUCIAN PERSPECTIVE

KATHLEEN M. HIGGINS

Confucius (551–479 b.c.e.) was one of the world's most influential ethical thinkers. His vision still provides the moral compass for populations throughout East Asia and beyond. Although striking parallels have been drawn between some of the concerns of Confucius and those of the ancient Greek philosophers, particularly in their emphasis on achieving harmony within the state, the Confucian tradition is distinctive.[1] While Western approaches to ethics have traditionally emphasized individual ethical agents and their actions, Confucian thought aims instead at nurturing human relationships. Loyalty, accordingly, figures centrally in the Confucian worldview, for it is an indispensable ingredient in the achievement of this goal.

Confucius emphasized self-cultivation with the aim of developing traits that would facilitate the development of a harmonious network of relationships. One learns through practice, and this applies to learning to live in harmony with other people as much as it does to any other kind of learning. The Confucian ethical program prescribes developing a number of relational virtues, several of which touch on matters of loyalty. *Xiao* (孝), filial piety, involves loyalty toward members of the family, particularly one's parents. *Zhong* (忠), often translated as loyalty, and *shu* (恕), deference, are reciprocal virtues, connoting the ideals of different kinds of commitment that characterize subordinates and their superiors (or equals).[2] Even the virtue of *li* (禮), ritual propriety, involves loyalty; a person who exhibits *li* maintains allegiance to the tradition, and loyalty to particular persons requires treating them in accordance with ritual. Some elaboration is necessary to convey the texture of each of these notions.

Xiao (孝)

According to Confucius, loyalty begins at home. The family is the first society that a child encounters, and relating to other members of the family is the initial political life. Accordingly, the Confucians consider family loyalty to be the basis for learning how to interact with other people generally. Learning to responsibly engage with other family members is the basis for all further moral development. Karyn L. Lai itemizes some of the moral skills that emerge from early interactions with one's family:

> Within this environment, one learns to be loyal, to empathise, negotiate, love, care, gain sympathy, express regret, balance competing loyalties and prioritise obligations. . . . The skills learnt in the family environment are vital for a person's interactions with others in later life.[3]

Confucians do not believe that their emphasis on family loyalty slights the larger social order. Filial piety, for them, is essentially political, for it is the prelude to good citizenship generally. As reported in the Confucian classic *The Analects*, Confucius makes this clear when replying to a detractor who rubs in the fact that Confucius is not currently holding an appointed public office.

> Someone asked Confucius, "Why are you not employed in governing?" The Master replied, "The *Book of Documents* says: `It is all in filial conduct (*xiao* 孝)! Just being filial to your parents and befriending your brothers is carrying out the work of government.' In doing this I am employed in governing. Why must I be `employed in governing'?"[4]

One of Confucius's disciples elaborates on this Confucian reasoning.

> Master You said: "It is a rare thing for someone who has a sense of
> filial and fraternal responsibility (*xiaodi* 孝弟) to have a taste for de-
> fying authority. And it is unheard of for those who have no taste for
> defying authority to be keen on initiating rebellion. Exemplary per-
> sons (*junzi* 君子) concentrate their efforts on the root, for the root
> having taken hold, the way (*dao* 德) will grow therefrom. As for filial
> and fraternal responsibility, it is, I suspect, the root of authoritative
> conduct (*ren* 仁)."[5]

"Authoritative conduct" is Ames and Rosemont's translation of *ren*,
the most central and encompassing of Confucian virtues. *Ren* has
been alternatively translated as "humaneness," "benevolence," and
"compassion." The character for *ren* is composed of radicals for
"human being" and for the number two. The implication is that
ren is the fundamental virtue of human beings relating to each
other.

The obligations that members of the family have to each other
are not identical. The family is an inegalitarian institution, as
are all institutions according to the Confucian worldview. The
Confucians identify five basic human relationships—father/son,
ruler/subject, husband/wife, elder brother/younger brother,
friend/friend; only that between friends might involve persons of
the same status. And, given that friends are rarely exactly the same
age, even friends typically occupy different roles in that one is senior to the other.

Xiao most straightforwardly involves obligations toward one's el-
ders. This includes not only attending to one's parents (and elder
brother) but also developing the right feelings toward the members of one's family. Confucius emphasizes that it is not simply providing for one's parents' needs; a respectful attitude is crucial.

> Ziyou asked about filial conduct (*xiao* 孝). The Master replied:
> "Those today who are filial are considered so because they are able
> to provide for their parents. But even dogs and horses are given
> that much care. If you do not respect your parents, what is the dif-
> ference?"[6]

One's filial attitude, in fact, should be evident in one's whole
comportment.

> Zixia asked about filial conduct (*xiao* 孝). The Master replied: "It all lies in showing the proper countenance. As for the young contributing their energies when there is work to be done, and deferring to their elders when there is wine and food to be had—how can merely doing this be considered being filial?"[7]

One's demeanor should express one's eagerness to tend to the needs of older family members.

Despite the emphasis on caring for one's older family members, we should not conclude that family loyalty operates only in one direction, with the younger people serving the older. Reciprocal obligations characterize the Confucian world. Parents have obligations to children, for example, just as children have obligations to parents. Confucius describes himself as aspiring to "love and protect the young," a suggestion that is taken to be exemplary by his followers.[8]

> The master said, "The young should be held in high esteem. After all, how do we know that those yet to come will not surpass our contemporaries? It is only when one reaches forty or fifty years of age and yet has done nothing of note that we should withhold our esteem."[9]

The obligations of parents to children are also implied in the following passage from the *Analects*:

> Meng Wubo asked about filial conduct (*xiao* 孝). The Master replied: "Give your mother and father nothing to worry about beyond your physical well-being."[10]

One should give one's parents no grounds for disturbance, but parental anxiety over one's health is excepted. Part of the parent's role is to be concerned about the child's well-being, even when the child is an adult.

We should also recognize that *xiao* does not require unquestioning obedience or acquiescence. Confucius urges the son to remonstrate with his father when the father does wrong. It is, however, important not to expose the father to humiliation by remonstrating in public; to air one's disapproval publicly *would* offend against filial piety.

> The Master said, "In serving your father and mother, remonstrate
> with them gently. On seeing that they do not heed your suggestions,
> remain respectful and do not act contrary. Although concerned,
> voice no resentment."[11]

The compatibility of remonstrating with those to whom one
owes loyalty is also evident in the Confucian view that rulers who
are not living up to their roles should be urged to rectify their
behavior. The ruler/subject relation is to be modeled on that of
parent and child. Confucius at times disapproves of something a
ruler has done and makes this clear from his behavior. Mencius, a
Confucian who lived about a century after the Master, is more
blunt in his objections to irresponsible rulers. Mencius was asked
how he, a Confucian, could countenance the regicide that killed
T'chou, the tyrannical last emperor of the Shang (or Yin) dynasty.
The questions insinuate that Confucius is inconsistent. The ouster
of T'chou resulted in the founding of the Zhou dynasty, the dynasty that Confucius holds up as a model for emulation, and yet
regicide is at odds with his views about legitimate succession and
obligations to the ruler as the "father" of the state. Mencius replies,

> A man who mutilates benevolence is a mutilator, while one who
> cripples rightness is a crippler. He who is both a mutilator and a
> crippler is an "outcast." I have indeed heard of the punishment of
> the "outcast T'chou," but I have not heard of any regicide.[12]

In other words, the last monarch in the previous dynasty was not
fulfilling the role of a real ruler, so his overthrow did not amount
to the killing of a king; it was simply the punishment such a criminal deserved. Mencius implicitly claims that loyalty to a ruler is
obligatory only so long as the person who allegedly rules is really
living up to his role.

Western thought has long recognized that loyalty to the family
and loyalty to the state can come into conflict. Hegel sees this conflict as evident already in Sophocles' *Antigone*, which he interprets
as resolving the conflict by giving civil law priority over the law of
the family. This resolution, according to Hegel, was an important
development in the evolution of the human spirit.[13] By contrast,
Confucian thought is loathe to represent the obligations stemming
from these two kinds of loyalty as conflicting. Instead, Confucians

take loyalty to the family to be the precondition for loyalty to the state.

Nevertheless, cases do arise in which these loyalties appear to conflict. In such cases, the Confucian insists that loyalty to the family trumps any other obligation. Confucius makes this clear in his response to a visitor who thinks that the conflict should be resolved the other way.

> The Governor of She in conversation with Confucius said, "In our village there is someone called `True Person.' When his father took a sheep on the sly, he reported him to the authorities."
>
> Confucius replied, "Those who are true in my village conduct themselves differently. A father covers for his son, and a son covers for his father. And being true lies in this."[14]

Mencius similarly defends protecting a father from the law. He is asked what the Emperor Shun, one of the legendary Sage Kings, would have done had his father killed a man when the judge whom Shun himself had appointed, Kao Yao, prepared to administer justice. Mencius responds,

> "The only thing to do was to apprehend him."
>
> "In that case, would Shun not try to stop it?"
>
> "How could Shun stop it? Kao Yao had his authority from which he received the law."
>
> "Then what would Shun have done?"
>
> "Shun looked upon casting aside the Empire as no more than discarding a worn shoe. He would have secretly carried the old man on his back and fled to the edge of the Sea and lived there happily, never giving a thought to the Empire."[15]

This story is all the more remarkable given the background of the relationship between Shun and his father. Shun's dysfunctional family background was legendary. Shun, though a commoner, was given the empire by his predecessor, Yao, who had passed over his own unworthy son. Rather than rejoicing at Shun's good fortune, his family saw it as an opportunity to enrich themselves. His parents and his younger brother, Hsiang, conspired to kill him and to take his property, attendants, and wives. At one point, his parents sent Shun to repair the barn, removed the ladder while he was working up high, and set fire to the barn to kill him. On another occasion, they sent Shun to clean out a well and then blocked his exit. In both cases, Shun managed to escape.

In spite of all this, Shun continued throughout his life to try to please his parents. Despite being handed the empire and gaining the support of his population, Shun, according to Mencius, saw this "as of no more consequence than trash." The reason was that "When one does not please one's parents, one cannot be a man; when one is not obedient to one's parents, one cannot be a son." When Shun eventually succeeded in pleasing his father, referred to in texts as "the Blind Man," he could finally enjoy his position. Even more, he had succeeded in being a model for his state. "Once the Blind Man was pleased, the pattern for the relationship between father and son in the Empire was set. This is the supreme achievement of a dutiful son."[16]

Shun similarly continued to love his brother. Asked if Shun was unaware of his brother's efforts against his life, Mencius scoffs, "How could he be unaware?"[17] Yet, instead of punishing his brother, like others who had sought to undermine his government, Shun enfeoffed him. Mencius explains:

> A benevolent man never harbours anger or nurses a grudge against a brother. All he does is to love him. Because he loves him, he wishes him to enjoy rank; because he loves him, he wishes him to enjoy wealth. To enfeoff him in Yu Pi was to let him enjoy wealth and rank.

Nevertheless, Mencius says that some people considered Shun's enfeoffing his brother a kind of banishment, since Hsiang "was not allowed to take any action in his fief." Other people administered it, and Hsiang "was certainly not permitted to ill-use the people."[18] Shun is all the more admirable for being able to fulfill his obligations as a brother at the same time that he prevented his brother from doing damage within his state.

The Confucian admiration of Shun seems to indicate that, even though obligations of loyalty within the family are reciprocal, a child should go to great extremes to protect and defend his or her parent no matter how the parent treats the child. Indeed, the Confucian worldview holds that everyone should live up to his or her role vis-à-vis other persons, even when he or she is treated

callously. Confucian heroes are admirable because they fulfill their
roles no matter what. The Duke of Zhou, Confucius's own hero
and role model, is a case in point. The Duke was appointed as re-
gent when his brother, the emperor, died and his young nephew
was too young to rule. Although many in his position would use
this opportunity as a means of gaining power for themselves, the
Duke of Zhou fulfilled his role and turned control of the empire
over to his nephew when the latter reached majority.

Confucians present their heroes as unfailing in their efforts to
fulfill the appropriate obligations of their roles, whatever the circumstances, and this is particularly true with respect to filial piety.
Shun again serves as a case in point. He married without telling his
parents, although the Confucian Classics clearly insist that sharing
the news with one's parents is obligatory. Mencius explains that
Shun did not tell his parents,

> because he would not have been allowed to marry if he had told
> them. A man and woman living together is the most important of
> human relationships. If he had told his parents, he would have
> to put aside the most important of human relationships and this
> would result in bitterness against his parents.[19]

In another passage, Mencius explains, "There are three ways of
being a bad son. The most serious is to have no heir. Shun married without telling his father for fear of not having an heir. To
the gentleman, this was as good as having told his father."[20] Shun
is justified in his apparent breach of filial piety only because, by his
actions, he fulfilled a more important duty required by his role as
son.

Similarly, against the charge that Yao failed in family loyalty because he passed over his son in making Shun heir to the throne,
Mencius observes that it was not Yao that gave the empire to Shun
but Heaven itself. The mandate of Heaven, the basis for legitimate
succession, dictates who should rule. This concept enables the
Confucians to claim that changes of dynasty can occur legitimately.
In the case of Shun, "Yao recommended Shun to Heaven and
Heaven accepted him; he presented him to the people and the
people accepted him."[21] The latter point is important. One of the
key indications that the mandate of Heaven has passed to a new

dynasty or a surprising heir to the throne is that the people accept the new ruler. Mencius also insists, "A common man who comes to possess the Empire must not only have the virtue of a Shun . . . but also the recommendation of an Emperor. . . . On the other hand, he who inherits the Empire is only put aside by Heaven if he is like Chieh or T'chou," Chieh and T'chou being the tyrannical final rulers of the Xia and Yin dynasties, respectively.[22] Yao's breach of family loyalty is ultimately acceptable only because Heaven's will overrides the obligation.

SHU (恕) AND ZHONG (忠)

Despite the emphasis on loyalty within the family, the Confucians deny that loyalty should be restricted to family relations. Mencius explicitly argues that, although concern for others develops within the family, it should be extended to a widening circle of other people. When talking candidly with the king about his methods of ruling, Mencius admonishes, "Treat the aged of your own family in a manner befitting their venerable age and extend this treatment to the aged of other families; treat your own young in a manner befitting their tender age and extend this to the young of other families, and you can roll the Empire on your palm."[23] Not only is this the appropriate direction for moral development to go; it is also good leadership.

Confucius also suggests through example that privileging one's own family members is not appropriate in every context. The *Analects* reports that Confucius's son, Boyu, was asked if he had received had special instruction from his father. He said that he had not and that his father had told him to study the classic works the *Songs* and the *Rites*. Boyu's interlocutor summarized the interaction and said, "I learned the importance of the *Songs* and of the *Rites*, and I also learned that exemplary persons do not treat their own sons as a special case."[24]

The virtues that most directly pertain to loyalty in relationships outside the family are *shu* (恕) and *zhong* (忠). *Shu* has been defined as "deference,"[25] "reciprocity,"[26] "altruism,"[27] "likening to oneself,"[28] and "consideration."[29] It involves imaginatively putting oneself in the place of the other person and acting accordingly. Confucius directly characterizes *shu* in the *Analects*.

> Zigong asked, "Is there one expression that can be acted upon until the end of one's days?"
>
> The Master replied, "There is *shu* (恕): do not impose on others what you yourself do not want."[30]

Shu, in other words, involves abiding by what appears to be a version of the Golden Rule. Confucius's negative formulation here is, however, important. It does not presuppose that others have the same agenda as oneself. It extrapolates only with respect to what one would find to be an unwanted imposition, suggesting that others would find it onerous, as well. David Hall and Roger Ames observe that a merit of the negative formulation is that it provides room for the person applying the principle to be creative in responding to the other person.[31]

Given that inequality is assumed in virtually all relationships, Confucians expect loyalty to other parties to take different forms depending on whether one occupies the dominant or the subordinate position. David Nivison contends that *shu* is most relevant to relationships with subordinates. This accords with the Confucian thinker Xunzi's elaboration on *shu*, with the term translated as "likening to oneself" in the following translation:

> For the gentleman there are three sorts of likening-to-oneself.
>   Being unable to serve your lord
>   Yet expecting obedience from a servant
> Is failure to liken-to-oneself.
>   Being unable to give parents their due
>   Yet expecting sons to be filial
> Is failure to liken-to-oneself.
>   Being unable to be respectful to an elder brother
>   Yet expecting a younger to take orders from you
> Is failure to liken-to-oneself.
>   If a knight is clear about these three sorts of likening-to-oneself
> it will be possible for him to correct his person.[32]

Zhong, by contrast, refers in particular to the steadfast support of someone in a superior position. *Zhong*, often translated as "loyalty," has also been rendered as "doing one's utmost,"[33] "doing one's best,"[34] and "giving oneself fully to the task."[35] The subordinate spares no effort to facilitate the attainment of the superior's aims.

The similarity but distinctness of the two virtues is indicated in the following passage from the *Analects*:

> The Master said, "Zeng, my friend! My way (*dao* 德) is bound together with one continuous strand."
>
> Master Zeng replied, "Indeed."
>
> When the Master had left, the disciples asked, "What was he referring to?"
>
> Master Zeng said, "The way of the Master is doing one's utmost (*zhong* 忠) and putting oneself in the other's place (*shu* 恕), nothing more."[36]

The "continuous strand" image refers to the fact that the characters for *zhong* and *shu* are related in that both contain the heart radical.

Hall and Ames give another reading of the continuity of *shu* and *zhong*. They see the difference between the two words less in terms of distinctions in social rank and more in terms of particular circumstances. In given contexts, different persons will have abilities or "excellences" that have the most bearing on the matter at hand. *Shu*, accordingly, is a methodology of deferring and being deferred to, depending on who is perceived as having some excellence that has the most to contribute to the situation. *Zhong* comes along with *shu*, according to this view. *Shu* "requires that in any given situation one either display excellence in oneself (and thus anticipate deference from others) or defer to excellence in another." *Zhong*, on this reading, is the virtue of always "doing one's best as one's authentic self."[37]

Hall and Ames's reading lends itself to using Confucianism as a resource in the contemporary world, which in many societies is not characterized by rigid social ranks of the sort found in ancient China. They describe both virtues as relevant to everyone in all cases, with *shu* amounting to appropriate deference in various contexts and *zhong* being one's devoted support of the aims of the relevant interpersonal group. Neither virtue calls for self-abnegation, as the outside caricature of Confucianism might suggest. One's own excellences will be part of the situation, and sometimes bringing them to the fore is what is called for. This interpretation also suggests the spirit of collective effort that characterizes the Confucian ideal for a harmonious social world. One conceives of oneself as defined by one's interpersonal relationships, and one's loyalty extends throughout that network.

L_I (禮)

If loyalty is understood as always a matter of allegiance to persons, the notion of *li*, ritual propriety, only indirectly obliges one to loyalty. But *li* is the means of communicating one's commitment to relationships; thus, it is not tangential but is vital to loyalty as Confucians understand it. *Li* includes formal elaborate rituals that mark important events, whether large-scale communal occasions or more personal rites of passage. It also includes the routines of etiquette and other matters of social decorum.

From an outsider's point of view, it might seem odd that Confucius held ritual propriety to be such an important virtue. Herbert Fingarette interprets Confucius as seeing in ritual a means for rebuilding a sense of community in an era in which war had become routine and trust was in short supply. Ritual, according to Confucius, enabled all involved to feel themselves fellow participants in common activity. Ritual beautifies human interaction and conveys mutual respect. In it, various individuals contribute their own energies in harmony with similar contributions from others. Because one is active in engaging in a ritual—be it as simple as the ritual of shaking the hand of someone who has extended it—one communicates respectful intentions to the others involved in that ritual. Participants in ritual are literally building community and making it their own.[38]

Accordingly, rulers should encourage ritual behavior, not coercive methods, as the best way to unify society.

> The Master said, "Lead the people with administrative injunctions (*zheng* 政) and keep them orderly with penal law (*xing* 刑), and they will avoid punishments but will be without a sense of shame. Lead them with excellence (*de* 德) and keep them orderly through observing ritual propriety (*li* 禮) and they will develop a sense of shame, and moreover, will order themselves."[39]

In a society that is structured around ritual, people do not feel social interaction as an imposition. Instead, they become self-regulating, rising to the occasion when it is appropriate, because that is how they play their own role in society: "The Master said, ` . . . someone who does not understand the observance of ritual propriety (*li* 禮) has no way of knowing where to stand.'"[40] Community is forged and also reinforced through ritual participation. By continuing to participate in established rituals, one asserts one's loyalty to the community and to one's fellow participants.

Just as loyalty begins at home, in the Confucian worldview, so the communication of loyalty through *li* is particularly important in connection with family members. Confucians emphasize, in particular, the loyalty owed to deceased parents, which is communicated through appropriate funeral rites and ancestor worship. We should note that the level of display in funeral ceremonial behavior is dictated by the social rank of the deceased. Confucius and Mencius both criticize those who arrange more elaborate rites for their parents than they are entitled to. Thus, loyalty to parents in this respect does not usurp propriety toward society at large. Of *xiao* toward parents, Confucius says, "While they are living, serve them according to the observances of ritual propriety (*li* 禮); when they are dead, bury them and sacrifice to them according to the observances of ritual propriety."[41] Ritual propriety specifies how lavish a funeral should be for someone of one's parent's specific rank.

In addition to proper funeral rituals, children owe their deceased parents extended mourning. A three-year period of mourning is specified, and Confucius takes this very seriously. Confucius suggests that for those three years, a son should take his deceased father's will as his own, doing things just as the father would have wanted: "The Master said, `A person who for three years refrains from reforming the ways (*dao* 德) of his late father can be called a filial son (*xiao* 孝).'"[42] Confucius is appalled when a person named Zaiwo suggests to him that one year of mourning one's parents is enough.

> When Zaiwo had left, the Master remarked, "Zaiwo is really perverse (*bu ren* 不仁)! It is only after being tended by his parents for three years that an infant can finally leave their bosom. The ritual of a three-year mourning period for one's parents is practiced through-

out the empire. Certainly Zaiwo received this three years of loving care from his parents!"[43]

Zaiwo is not the only one to criticize the Confucian advocacy of long periods of mourning. Mozi, the founder of the Mohist school, complained that long periods of mourning were contrary to the best interest of society, taking people out of productive roles for extended periods of time. Mozi opposes the Confucian conception of loyalty, particularly its family-first orientation. He calls for "universal benevolence" or "impartial care," treating everyone equally, as opposed to behaving preferentially toward one's family members.[44] The Confucian response, articulated by Mencius, is that Mozi's approach would lead to a lowest common denominator of concern, reducing care for one's parents but not enhancing care more generally. The Mohists do not recognize a natural tendency to care especially for those who are close to one. "'Does Yi Tzu truly believe,' said Mencius, 'that a man loves his brother's son no more than his neighbour's new-born babe?'"[45] The strong attachment one feels to members of one's family serves as a secure basis for extending care beyond the family. Mozi's approach does not reflect the realities of human motivation, Mencius argues. In fact, Mozi apparently recognized that people would not necessarily feel disposed to adopt his policies. He defended a strict system of rewards and punishments, encouraged widespread belief in vindictive spirits that threatened their own sanctions, and led a crack military organization to enforce order, all of which suggests that he recognized the need to impose his policies from without.

We might see the Communist opposition to Confucianism in China until recently as following some of the same lines of reasoning as those articulated by Mozi. Like the Mohists, the Communists interpreted particular loyalty toward the family as contrary to loyalty to the larger society. In addition, the Communists objected to the Confucian insistence on rigid hierarchical distinctions, reflected in ways that loyalty is shown and in the ritual behaviors that are appropriate.

The hierarchical structure that Confucianism defends is also rather shocking from the liberal democratic point of view. However, even if is skeptical of certain features of their worldview, the Confucians make a persuasive case that loyalty is prerequisite to the flourishing family and the well-functioning state. Although explicitly referring to the consequence of living up to one's roles, Confucius underscores the importance of loyalty toward others to whom one is related in the following exchange:

> Duke Jing of Qi asked Confucius about governing effectively (*zheng* 政). Confucius replied, "The ruler must rule, the minister minister, the father father, and the son son."
> "Excellent!" exclaimed the Duke. "Indeed, if the ruler does not rule, the minister not minister, the father not father, and the son not son, even if there were grain, would I get to eat of it?"[46]

The urgency of loyally fulfilling the commitments implied by one's roles in relation to others is even more obvious in Arthur Waley's translation of the final line: "For indeed when the prince is not a prince, the minister not a minister, the father not a father, and the son not a son, one may have a dish of millet in front of one and yet not know if one will live to eat it."[47]

The Confucian message is that human beings cannot live fully human lives without being able to depend on one another. Indeed, without the network of relationships that define him or her, a human individual is less than a person. Loyalty, from the Confucian perspective, amounts to vigilant effort to sustain the relationships in which one is embedded. Loyalty is central to the ethical aim of supporting the human world and enabling it to flourish, and yet it is neither abstract nor general in practice. At every point, it is a personal matter, one that calls for specific responses to particular other persons. Loyalty preserves humanity as a living whole, but it does this one relationship and one interaction at a time.

NOTES

1. For considerations of some of the parallels and differences between the ancient Greek and the ancient Chinese thinkers, see Steven Shankman and Stephen W. Durrant, eds., *Early China/Ancient Greece: Thinking through Comparisons* (Albany: SUNY Press, 2002).

2. David S. Nivison, *The Ways of Confucianism: Investigations in Chinese Philosophy* (Chicago: Open Court, 1996), 65.

3. Compare Karyn L. Lai, *An Introduction to Chinese Philosophy* (Cambridge: Cambridge University Press, 2008), 24.

4. Roger T. Ames and Henry Rosemont Jr., *The Analects of Confucius* (New York: Ballantine, 1998), 2.21, 80–81.

5. Ibid., 1.2, 71.

6. Ibid., 2.7, 77.

7. Ibid., 2.8, 78.

8. See ibid., 5.26, 102.

9. Ibid., 9.23, 131.

10. Ibid., 2.6, 77.

11. Ibid., 4.18, 93.

12. D. C. Lau, trans., *Mencius* (London: Penguin, 1970), 1b8, 68.

13. See G. W. F. Hegel, *Philosophy of Right*, trans. T. M. Knox (Oxford: Clarendon, 1952), 114–15.

14. Ames and Rosemont, *Analects*, 13.18, 167.

15. *Mencius*, 7a35, 190.

16. Ibid., 4a28, 127. See also ibid., 5a1, 138–39.

17. Ibid., 5a2, 140.

18. Ibid., 5a3, 140–41.

19. Ibid., 5a2, 139.

20. Ibid., 4a26, 127.

21. Ibid., 5a5, 143.

22. Ibid., 5a6, 145.

23. Ibid., 1a7, 56.

24. Ames and Rosemont, *Analects*, 16.13, 200–1.

25. David L. Hall and Roger T. Ames, *Thinking through Confucius* (Albany: SUNY Press, 1987), 283–90.

26. By Tu Wei-Ming. See ibid., 285.

27. By Wing-Tsit Chan. See ibid., 285.

28. A. C. Graham, *Disputers of the Tao: Philosophical Argument in Ancient China* (Chicago: Open Court, 1989), 20.

29. Arthur Waley, trans. and ed., *The Analects of Confucius* (New York: Random House, 1989), 15.23, 198. See Hall and Ames, *Thinking through Confucius*, 285.

30. Ames and Rosemont, *Analects*, 15.24, 189.

31. Hall and Ames, *Thinking through Confucius*, 289.

32. *Xunzi* 30/14–16, as translated and cited by Graham in *Disputers of the Tao*, 20.

33. Rosemont and Ames, "Chinese Lexicon," in *Analects*, 59.

34. D. C. Lau, *Confucius: The Analects* (Hong Kong: Chinese University Press, 1983), xiii–xiv.

35. Hall and Ames, *Thinking through Confucius*, 285.

36. Ames and Rosemont, *Analects*, 4.15, 92.

37. Hall and Ames, *Thinking through Confucius*, 287.

38. See Herbert Fingarette, *Confucius: The Secular as Sacred* (New York: Harper & Row, 1972), 6–13, 57–70.

39. Ames and Rosemont, *Analects*, 2.3, 76.

40. Ibid., 20.3, 229.

41. Ibid., 2.5, 77.

42. Ibid., 4.20, 93.

43. Ibid., 17.21, 209–10.

44. See Philip J. Ivanhoe and Bryan W. Van Norden, *Readings in Classical Chinese Philosophy* (New York: Seven Bridges, 2001), 55–102. See also Burton Watson, trans., *Mo Tzu: Basic Writings* (New York: Columbia University Press, 1963).

45. *Mencius* 3a5, 105.

46. Ames and Rosemont, *Analects*, 12.11, 156. For an analysis of the Confucian ethical outlook as an ethics of roles, see Henry Rosemont Jr. and Roger T. Ames, "Introduction," in *The Chinese Classic of Family Reverence*, trans. Henry Rosemont Jr. and Roger T. Ames (Honolulu: University of Hawaii Press, 2009), 38–64.

47. Waley, *The Analects of Confucius*, 12.11, 166.

3

IN PLACE OF LOYALTY:
FRIENDSHIP AND ADVERSARY POLITICS
IN CLASSICAL GREECE

PAUL WOODRUFF

The ancient Greeks who invented democracy had no concept that matches our concept of loyalty. No word in their language can be reliably translated by the English word. Nothing like loyalty occurs on any list of virtues that has come down to us from classical Greece; the nearest virtue is reverence (*to hosion*), which requires, among many other things, the keeping of oaths but does not bind a political community together. By contrast, loyalty figures so prominently among the virtues in the classical Chinese tradition that one famous *Analect* of Confucius (4.15) entwines it in the single thread of ethics.[1] In our own modern popular tradition, "loyal" is the second virtuous quality listed in the Boy Scout Law, after "trustworthy" but in front of "kind" and "brave."[2] "Trustworthy" does not name a quality much admired in ancient Greece, either. In the defining myths of ancient Greece, two contrasting heroes are models: Achilles, who repudiates his commander, and Odysseus, who can hardly tell the truth. Neither would succeed in the Boy Scouts.

Friendship (*philia*) has the place in ancient Greek culture that loyalty has in ours.[3] As the ancient Greeks understood it, *philia* entails a willingness to stand by family and friends, which often trumps other obligations. Classical Greek culture was ambivalent about *philia*, because of the conflicts that arise from competing personal ties. Steadfastness in personal relationships, by itself, does not support the stability of a state and may weaken it. We shall see that *philia* is a poor substitute for loyalty.

LOYALTY

Our usage of the word "loyalty" is broad and includes steadfastness in personal relationships. Let us call that sort of loyalty "personal loyalty." Personal loyalty is entailed by *philia,* although Greek has no distinct expression for this. Personal loyalty is a small part of the concept of loyalty and is irrelevant to the loyalty that calls a military unit, for example, to obey its commander. In general, we must distinguish personal loyalty from the loyalty that can trump personal connections in favor of obligations legitimized by law or religion. By "loyalty" in these pages I mean the virtue consisting in willingness to support legitimate authority steadfastly, at risk to life and limb—a virtue that may be held to prevail over duties to family and friends. This concept of loyalty is tied to that of legitimacy, and that, too, seems absent from classical Greek ethical thinking. Legitimacy means different things in different cultures. In American subcultures that treat loyalty as a virtue (such as the military), legitimacy mainly derives from the special, almost scriptural, status of the U.S. Constitution. Officers are on oath to defend the Constitution, rather than to obey anyone in particular, and therefore bear the burden of deciding, in hard cases, whether or not an order they have received represents legitimate authority. Loyalty of this kind I will call "constitutional loyalty," which is usually thought to trump the personal loyalty one might have to friends, or to a political party, or even to an admired commander. Loyalty to the U.S. Constitution is supposed to trump any of those.

The ancient Athenians had a body of law they revered; jurors and legislators swore to obey it, but this body of law was vaguely defined, and they swore also to vote in agreement with their personal sense of justice in those cases not covered by the law.[4] Such an oath did not have the disciplined effect of loyalty when measured against the oath military officers take to preserve the U.S. Constitution, an oath that has the same content as the presidential oath of office.[5]

Some traditions take legitimacy to be conferred by the divine. According to the theory of the divine right of kings, a Christian monarch was thought to represent God within that monarch's sphere of authority. The monarch's legitimacy derived from God; loyalty to a monarch so conceived could be called "religious loyalty." In classical Chinese thought, legitimacy was thought to be conferred as a mandate from Heaven to an emperor with appropriate virtues. Loyalty on these grounds was owed to a ruler whose authority was analogous to that of Heaven over Earth. Such authority emanated from the emperor insofar as he was seen as the Son of Heaven and was felt as far down the hierarchy as the family. Disloyalty to one's parents was as unthinkable as a rebellion of Earth against Heaven.

The ancient Greeks did not believe in gods who could support religious loyalty. Zeus was the patron of kings, true enough, but Zeus had rebelled (with good reason) against his father, just as many Greeks in the archaic period rebelled with good reason against their kings. By the classical period, virtually no kings ruled anywhere in Greece, and those who survived, like the military leaders of Sparta, had limited authority. Some shreds of concepts similar to loyalty came down from more ancient times, wrapped in the aura of religion, but these were buried in the momentous development of democracy in Athens and elsewhere. Democracy meant debate, and debate challenged all the old verities.

COMMITMENT TO DEBATE

The paradox of classical Greek politics arises from its adversary system, which tends to tear communities into civil war despite the strong commitment of their citizens to life in communities. The adversary system itself arises from a commitment to debate as a rational way of making decisions in the absence of perfect knowledge. The adversary system was a formal structure that gave equal time to speakers on both sides of an issue.

The classical Greeks delighted in set-piece debates. Teachers of rhetoric constructed pairs of speeches for entertainment and education, and poets composed debates for tragic plays. Historians, starting with Herodotus, composed debates to bring out what they believed to be critical issues. Thucydides loaded his history with accounts of formal debates. Debate was common on deliberative matters in any Greek assembly, and in Athenian law courts debate was formalized and kept to strict time limits.

Protagoras, one of the older teachers known as sophists, claimed to teach good judgment by means of teaching debate. I conclude, somewhat speculatively, that he and his students believed that they could cultivate good judgment by learning to consider the best arguments on both sides of an issue.[6]

A number of conservative thinkers opposed the adversary system. Plato showed his opposition in a number of ways. Unlike his contemporaries, he never published balanced set-piece debates, preferring one-on-one question-and-answer sessions controlled by Socrates. In his political writings such as the *Republic* he makes no plans for public debate. Instead, he seems committed to a model in which moral and political knowledge are like technical knowledge, which does not allow for a debate. We trust our ship to an expert navigator and do not think of staging a formal debate as to whether to tack or to gibe; so it is with Plato's ship of state.[7] Not surprisingly, ancient Greek conservatives who opposed adversary debate were able to call for a higher level of solidarity in politics than their contemporaries had been able to achieve through democracy.

The contentiousness of politics in the fifth century b.c.e. also was a result of the rise of democracy in many Greek cities and islands. Changing social conditions and military conventions gave more power to the people, while the rich and wellborn tried to hold on to their privileges. Civil wars were frequent. Oligarchs exiled democrats when they could, or else democrats exiled oligarchs. The resulting flood of exiles ran against the strong tide of civic commitment. Exile was feared because most people did not feel that they could live adequate lives outside their home cities.

COMMITMENT TO THE *POLIS*

The ancient Greeks' commitment to life in communities is related to their concept of citizenship. Citizenship gave one a place in every aspect of the life of the *polis* or city-state. Although only men had a political role, women had roles in religion and for this reason alone prized their status as citizens. Citizenship was by birth in most cases. It was rarely granted to anyone with even one noncitizen parent. Once citizens left their cities, they could expect only diminished lives, traveling from city to city, truly belonging nowhere. That is why exile was so serious a penalty and why Socrates refused to consider it.[8]

Moreover, some Greeks of the classical period held that human beings could not even survive in isolation from one another. Plato has Protagoras tell this story of the origins of political life among human beings:

> Thus equipped, then, human beings originally had scattered dwellings rather than cities; they were therefore weaker in every way than the wild beasts, who were killing them off. Although their practical knowledge was sufficient to provide nourishment, it was no help in fighting off the beasts—for human beings did not yet have political knowledge [*politikê technê*], and military knowledge is a part of that. They tried to band together and save themselves by founding cities. But when they were banded together, they would treat each other unjustly because they did not have political knowledge, and the result was that they would scatter again and be destroyed.[9]

Even if they could survive in isolation, they would not thrive, as Pericles is said to have explained in his final speech to the Athenians:

> It does not matter whether a man prospers as an individual: If his country is destroyed, he is lost along with it; but if he meets with misfortune, he is far safer in a fortunate city than he would be otherwise. Since, therefore, a city is able to sustain its private citizens in whatever befalls them, while no one individual is strong enough to carry his city, are we not all obliged to defend it and not, as you are doing now, sacrifice our common safety?[10]

Alternatively, if there were those who could thrive in isolation, they would be either sub- or superhuman, as Aristotle famously claimed:

> A person who is without a *polis* by nature and not by chance is either inferior or superior to a human being.[11]

PHILIA AS THE BASIS OF THE POLIS

Greeks of the classical period agreed that life was best for those who belonged to a *polis*—a city-state—and yet they had no concept of loyalty to their *polis*. The concept that governs citizens' duties to their *polis* is *philia,* usually but inaccurately translated as "friendship." *Philia* is a bond that does not entail affection. It is a fairly loose notion and can be articulated in ways that make sense of the paradox of classical Greek politics. *Philia* is the basis for *harmonia,* the adjustment of the competing elements of a *polis* into a working whole.

Philia has one of two foundations: family connection, or an exchange of services. Any two family members are together in a relation of *philia,* and any two people from different lands who help each other out are united in a special form of friendship called *xenia* ("guest-friendship"). Myths of common origin are nurtured in most *poleis* to allow citizens to feel that they are united by family ties. Athenians believed that their ancestors had been born out of the earth on which they now lived. To maintain the sense of family bonds, they insisted that citizenship belonged only to the children of citizens.

At the same time, shared religious rituals brought citizens together, male with male and female with female, in common tasks that cemented their *philia.* That is why classical Greek cities could tolerate new religions only when they did not threaten traditional practices that were held to be essential to the harmony of the *polis.* Shared military service also brought men together in *philia* through an exchange of services; soldiers saved each other's lives, they picked up the bodies of fellow citizens, and they made sure that their dead had proper burial rites.

The weakness of *philia* as any kind of bond is that its double foundation makes it fundamentally unstable. Family ties can undermine action-based ties of mutual service, and actions can undermine family ties. In Sophocles' *Ajax,* the hero famously says:

> I have recently come to learn
> To hate my enemy while knowing
> That one day he may be my friend—
> And that I should help my friend but know

That he may one day be my enemy.
For us, friendship is a treacherous harbor.[12]

ENMITY AND CIVIL WAR

Enmity shatters friendship. Enmity arises simply when anyone does a disservice to another person. So the adversary system of Greek politics makes citizens enemies of one another. Alcibiades won the vote to launch war against Syracuse in 415 b.c.e., but then he left Athens for the campaign with many of his supporters in his train. At that point, his political enemies arranged for him to be condemned on charges that were probably at least partially trumped up. He escaped arrest and went to Sparta, where he gave the military enemies of Athens advice that helped them eventually win the war. We are told that he felt the need to explain to the Spartans his enmity toward his fellow citizens, and these are the words that the historian Thucydides put into his mouth:

> Now in my judgment no one should think worse of me because I, who was once thought a lover of my own city, am now of my own power going against her with her greatest enemies; and I do not think you should distrust my word as coming from the zeal of a fugitive. For though I am fleeing from the malice of those who drove me out, I shall not, if you take my advice, flee from helping you. Those who have merely harmed their enemies, as you have, are not so much enemies as are those who have compelled their friends to become enemies. I do love my city, but as a place where I could safely engage in public life, not as the site of injustice to me. I do not think the city I am going against is my own; it is much more a matter of my recovering a city that is not mine. A true lover of his city is not the man who refuses to invade the city he has lost through injustice, but the man who desires so much to be in it that he will attempt to recover it by any means he can.[13]

Apparently, Alcibiades feels that, in harming the democrats (his true enemy), the Spartans have not played the part of an enemy to Athens; the democrats, on the other hand, in making Alcibiades their enemy, have thereby made themselves the enemies of Athens. A frequent theme in Greek history from this period is the readiness of exiles to ally themselves with the enemies of their home cities, in return for which the enemies support the political causes of the exiles. "My country right or wrong" is a sentiment that would have meant little to Thucydides or his contemporaries.

"Help your friends and harm your enemies" is a slogan that the classical Greeks understood very well.[14] They did recognize, however, that friends easily become enemies and vice versa, as we have seen from the lines Ajax speaks. The paradox of Greek politics is built into the double foundation of *philia,* which is brought out clearly in plays such as Sophocles' *Electra.* Those who are united in *philia* by birth—like Electra and her mother—can become enemies as a result of actions—in Electra's case, by her mother's killing of her father. Just so, in the city, citizens united by a sense of family ties can become enemies as a result of political altercations. When that happens, they tend to lack a concept of loyalty that would prevent them from harming their cities.

All the more strange in its context, then, is the attitude of Socrates in Plato's *Crito.* Socrates says he has an obligation to obey the city that has—wrongly, in his view—condemned him. Contrast the case of Themistocles, who saved Athens from the Persians at the time of the battle of Salamis but went over to the Persians when the Athenians exiled him. Thucydides finds nothing to censure in this and indeed praises him for the high quality of the advice he gave to the Persians in their continuing war against the Greeks.[15]

Thucydides was writing his history while in exile from Athens, beginning after his loss of the Athenian stronghold at Amphipolis in 424 b.c.e. He had been in command of a force that had been assigned to protect the place along with a large stretch of seacoast, but his force was too small and his theater of operations too great. So he should not have been blamed. Like Alcibiades, he also spent some of his exile in the Peloponnesus and visited Sparta. It is tempting to believe that the speech he gives here to Alcibiades reflects some of his own sentiments toward the city that had rejected him on such slender grounds as a defeat that was not his fault.

The horrors of civil war are nevertheless clear to all concerned. Thucydides brings them out in one case, saying that this is typical of all Greece at the time:

So cruel was the course of this civil war [*stasis*], and it seemed all the more so because it was among the first of these. Afterwards, virtually all Greece was in upheaval, and quarrels arose everywhere between the democratic leaders, who sought to bring in the Athenians, and the oligarchs, who wanted to bring in the Spartans. Now in time of peace they could have had no pretext and would not have been so eager to call them in, but because it was war, and allies were to be had for either party to hurt their enemies and strengthen themselves at the same time, invitations to intervene came readily from those who wanted a new government. Civil war brought many atrocities to the cities, such as happen and will always happen as long as human nature is the same, although they may be more or less violent or take different forms, depending on the circumstances in each case. In peace and prosperity, cities and private individuals alike have better judgment because they are not plunged into the necessity of doing anything against their will; but war is a violent teacher: It gives most people impulses that are as bad as their situation when it takes away the easy supply of what they need for daily life.[16]

Thus was every kind of wickedness afoot throughout all Greece by the occasion of civil wars. Simplicity, which is the chief cause of a generous spirit,[17] was laughed down and disappeared. Citizens were sharply divided into opposing camps, and, without trust, their thoughts were in battle array. No speech was so powerful, no oath so terrible, as to overcome this mutual hostility. The more they reckoned up their chances, the less hope they had for a firm peace, and so they were all looking to avoid harm from each other and were unable to rely on trust.[18]

The last great civil war in classical Athens occurred in 404–403 b.c.e. After Sparta defeated Athens in the great war between the cities (431–404 b.c.e.), their general installed a group of thirty oligarchs, later known as the Thirty Tyrants. The Thirty eventually launched a reign of terror, driving many democrats and their friends into exile. Eight months after that, a democratic army defeated the oligarchs in battle at the port of Athens, the Piraeus, but the oligarchs continued to hold Athens for the time being. The historian Xenophon reports that one of the democrats, Cleocritus, made this moving appeal to the oligarchs while the two sides were collecting the bodies of the dead after the battle:

Citizens, why are you keeping us out of Athens? Why do you want to
kill us? We never did anything bad to you. Not at all. We have joined
with you in the holiest rituals, in the most beautiful sacrifices and festivals. We have been fellow dancers with you, fellow students, and fellow soldiers. We have undergone many dangers with you on land and
sea for the sake of our common freedom and safety. For gods' sake—
for the sake of the gods of our fathers and mothers—for the sake of
our kinship, our marriage ties, and our fellowship—because many of
us share in all these—show reverence to gods and men. Put a stop to
this crime against our city, and cease to obey those Thirty, those hor-
ribly irreverent men, who, in eight months have killed almost more
Athenians than the Peloponnesians did in ten years of war.[19]

Harmony

Plato explained justice as a harmonious adjustment of the parts
of a community for the good of the whole. The aim of this justice, according to Plato, is to prevent civil strife so that the community and its members may flourish freely and happily. Most classical Greeks would have agreed with Plato about the importance of
harmony,[20] although, as we shall see, many would not have agreed
with Plato's conception of it. No one appeals to loyalty or fidelity
to maintain harmony.

The central problem of ancient Greek democracy was how to
maintain harmony in a culture that insisted on adversary debate.
Plato, like other conservatives, saw no value in adversary debate; the
one who knows should be allowed to speak; others, who are ignorant,
should keep silence. Those who know will not disagree. The result
is the harmony of perfect agreement. Plato writes of the harmony
that brings every element in the city together so that they "sing one
song."[21] This harmony Plato further explains as an agreement that
the city should be ruled by its best people—the philosopher kings.

More common than music was weaving as an image for what
should hold the state together. This at least requires difference:
the warp runs one way and the woof, another. In the *Statesman*,
Plato considers a weaving together of different characters:

Then let us say that this straight-grained fabric, made of brave and
sound-minded characters, reaches the goal of political action when-

ever the art of ruling brings these characters together in harmony and friendship. When it is complete, this is the most magnificent weaving and the best, for it embraces everyone in the city, including free people and slaves, in a single fabric. And so far as happiness is possible for a city, it has absolutely everything that governance or royal power can supply.[22]

In a play by Aristophanes, *Lysistrata*, the lead character proposes weaving (a womanly art in Greece) as the best way to unify the state:

Start out as you would with wool from a shearing:
Put it in a tub and scrub the gobs of sheep shit off the city.
Then spread it out and flog it to get rid of the bad guys—
The sticker-burrs and those that organize themselves
Into a tangle to get elected. Comb them out
And pluck off their heads. After that, comb
Good common will into a basket, mixing everyone
Together. Resident aliens, foreigners (if you like them),
And anyone who owes the city money—mix them all in.
And for the gods' sake, these cities that are colonies of ours,
Understand them as separate balls of wool, off
By themselves. Take all of these and bring them together
And join them into one, then spin them onto a huge
Bobbin and weave from that a cloak for the people.[23]

The value of the weaving image becomes especially clear in a famous fable attributed to Aesop:

A farmer's sons used to quarrel, and though he tried many times, he could not persuade them to change by means of arguments [*logoi*]; so he realized that he would have to do this through action, and he asked them to bring him a bundle of sticks. When they had done as they were told, he first gave them the sticks all together and ordered them to break the bundle. When they could not do this, no matter how much force they used, he then untied the bundle and gave sticks to them one at a time. These they broke easily, and he said, "So it is with you, my sons. If you are in harmony, you will be unconquerable by your enemies; but if you quarrel, you will be easily taken."[24]

The Greeks of the fifth century understood this fable very well, but they had not developed a culture of loyalty or the political institutions that would have woven them together. Disunited even within the scattered and warring states, with few qualms about betraying their own people after political losses, they were easy prey for the rising power of Macedon. When a democracy sustains its power, it appears to do so because its citizens feel a sense of loyalty to the whole. They go hammer and tongs at adversary politics, but they do not come apart. Loyalty saves them.

NOTES

1. On *Analect* 4.15, see Edward Slingerland, *Confucius Analects with a Selection from Traditional Commentaries* (Indianapolis: Hackett, 2003), 34–35, 238; the virtue word *zhong* (*chung* in some transliterations) is usually rendered by the English "loyalty," but he argues for "dutifulness." *Zhong* is a kind of loyalty that is sensitive to ethical considerations. On the issues, see Kathleen Higgins's chapter in the present volume of *NOMOS*.

2. The text of the Boy Scout Law may be found online at http://usscouts.org/advance/boyscout/bslaw.asp.

3. I am indebted for a conversation on this subject to R. J. Hankinson.

4. This is known as the Heliastic Oath, sworn by adult males empaneled to be selected as jurors or as *thesmothetai*. The latter determined whether proposed legislation accorded with law before a proposal was put to a vote. On the oath, see Mogens Herman Hansen, *The Athenian Democracy in the Age of Demosthenes: Structure, Principles, and Ideology*, trans. J. A. Crook (Oxford: Blackwell, 1991), 182, 70.

5. "I do solemnly swear (or affirm) that I will faithfully execute the office of President of the United States, and will to the best of my ability, preserve, protect and defend the Constitution of the United States." Article 2, Section 1, U.S. Constitution.

6. Paul Woodruff, "Euboulia: How Might Good Judgement Be Taught," *Lampas: Tijdschrift voor Classici* 41 (2008): 252–62.

7. On the ship of state see Plato's *Republic*, 6.488bc, and my comment in Paul Woodruff, *First Democracy: The Challenge of an Ancient Idea* (New York: Oxford University Press, 2005), 152–53.

8. Plato, *Apology*, 37d.

9. Protagoras in Plato's *Protagoras*, 322ab, my translation, from *Early Greek Political Thought from Homer to the Sophists*, ed. Michael Gagarin and Paul Woodruff (Cambridge: Cambridge University Press, 1995), 178.

10. Pericles' last speech, as reported by Thucydides (2.60). Such speeches are probably historical fiction, but they represent accurately the atti-

tudes of Greeks at the time Thucydides wrote. All Thucydides translations are mine, though heavily influenced by Thomas Hobbes. Paul Woodruff, *Thucydides on Justice, Power, and Human Nature* (Indianapolis: Hackett, 1995), 52–53.

11. Aristotle, *Politics*, 1.1.9 (my translation).

12. Sophocles' *Ajax*, 678–83, translated by Peter Meineck. Peter Meineck and Paul Woodruff, *Sophocles: Four Tragedies* (Indianapolis: Hackett, 2007), 31.

13. Thucydides, 6.92.1–4. Woodruff, *Thucydides*, 128–29.

14. For a famous statement of the theory, see Plato's *Republic*, 1.332d. On the complex theme in Sophoclean tragedy, see Mary Whitlock Blondell, *Helping Friends and Harming Enemies: A Study in Sophocles and Greek Ethics* (Cambridge: Cambridge University Press, 1989).

15. Thucydides, 1.138.

16. From Thucydides, 3.82. Woodruff, *Thucydides*, 90, revised in the light of C. D. C. Reeve, "Thucydides on Human Nature," *Political Theory* 27 (August 1999): 440.

17. "Simplicity, which is the chief cause of a generous spirit": literally, "simplicity [*to euêthês*], of which a generous spirit most takes part." This probably means that simplicity (or openness) is what best explains generosity. See Woodruff, *Thucydides*, 27 (footnote to 1.84.3).

18. From Thucydides, 3.83. Woodruff, *Thucydides*, 92–93.

19. Xenophon, *Hellenica*, 3.4.20–21: Translation from Paul Woodruff, *First Democracy*, 83. The terror lasted eight months, although the Thirty reigned for eighteen.

20. On this topic see the chapter on harmony in Woodruff, *First Democracy*, 81–107.

21. Plato, *Republic*, 432a.

22. Plato, *Statesman*, 311bc: Translation in Woodruff, *First Democracy*, 88.

23. Lysistrata in Aristophanes, *Lysistrata*, 574–86. Woodruff, *First Democracy*, 86–87. The play was written in 411 b.c.e., at a time when Athenians were eager for peace and some (at least) were giving up on democracy.

24. Aesop on the Farmer's Quarreling Sons: Gagarin and Woodruff, *Early Greek Political Thought*, 149.

PART II

LOYALTY AND THE LAW

4

LAWYERLY FIDELITY

DANIEL MARKOVITS

Adversary lawyers practice as partisans in the shadow of a structural division of labor between advocate and tribunal in which they are charged zealously to represent particular clients, rather than justice writ large.[1] Thus, although lawyering may be intimately connected to the deep and enduring ethical ideals of respect for persons that justice involves, it also has an ethically troubling aspect. Adversary advocates commonly do and, indeed, are often required to do things in their professional capacities that, if done by ordinary people in ordinary circumstances, would be straightforwardly immoral.

To begin with, lawyers' professional obligations impose what the leading treatise on the law governing lawyers calls "a clear and mandatory favoritism when a lawyer must choose between the interests of clients and non-clients."[2] The foundational principles of adversary advocacy require lawyers to promote the causes and to assert the claims that their clients choose, even when they doubt (or indeed, reject) the claims' merits. Indeed, lawyers must act in these ways even when their private doubts about their clients' positions are correct and even when their clients' positions are (within limits) unreasonable.

Moreover, this thin, generic idea of partisan preference operates through thicker and more structured professional duties to embrace forms of conduct that would ordinarily be classed as vices. Unlike juries and judges, adversary lawyers should not pursue a true account of the facts of a case and promote a dispassionate application of the law to these facts. Instead, they should try aggressively to manipulate both the facts and the law to suit their clients' purposes. This requires lawyers to promote beliefs in others that they themselves (properly) reject as false. Lawyers might, for example, bluff in settlement negotiations, undermine the truthful testimony of vulnerable witnesses, or make legal arguments that they would reject as judges. Furthermore, lawyers should strive to exploit strategic advantages on their clients' behalves even when they themselves (correctly) believe that the clients are not entitled to these advantages. Lawyers might, for example, employ delaying tactics, file strategically motivated claims, or exploit a law's form to thwart its substantive purposes.

To be sure, this ethically troubling regime of professional obligation does not apply equally to all lawyers in all legal systems. In every legal system, lawyers inhabit many roles and perform many tasks, which bear at most a family resemblance to one another, and not all these roles require the same measure of partisanship. And even lawyers who loyally serve particular clients often work in contexts that involve little or no advocacy—counseling clients concerning the legal, economic, and even moral consequences of some project, for example, or preparing opinions that characterize a client's legal situation for others.[3] Furthermore, some legal systems—especially those outside the United States and, in particular, those on the European continent—have been thought to de-emphasize partisanship quite generally. Thoughts such as these have even led some observers to suggest that the ethical tensions just mentioned between lawyers' professional obligations and ordinary morality are creatures not of lawyering in general but rather of the peculiar and perverse forms of lawyering practiced by American litigators.

But the ethically troubling character of lawyering cannot be dismissed so easily. To begin with, although not everything that lawyers do involves advocating for clients and against others with whom they stand in direct competition, partisanship surely does penetrate deep into the legal profession. Even lawyers who act principally as counselors and negotiators rather than directly as advocates advise and bargain in the shadow of the law,[4] that is, against the backdrop of what they can achieve for their clients through more direct advocacy. Indeed, the regulatory regimes that govern lawyers' conduct in these roles are often designed in express contemplation of endgames that involve such direct advocacy.[5] Additionally, some of the professional duties that lie at the foundation of lawyers' partisanship unquestionably arise even outside the orbit of open advocacy. Thus, the duty to preserve client confidences applies quite generally to all forms of lawyering,[6] and it may even apply more strictly outside litigation, where it is less likely to run up against competing duties requiring candor before tribunals.[7] Certainly, many more lawyers than the small minority who regularly engage in litigation count as adversary advocates, so the ethical doubts about lawyering apply well beyond this narrow group.

Moreover, non-American legal systems' retreat from adversary lawyering is often exaggerated, and lawyerly partisanship survives even in the European legal systems that are commonly called "inquisitorial" rather than "adversarial." This contrast principally refers to whether, as a matter of procedure, the legal and factual record in a dispute is developed primarily by the disputants or by the tribunal, and the structural separation between advocate and tribunal may endure however this choice is made. Even lawyers who practice under inquisitorial procedures generally retain some measure of the partisan loyalties that cast them as adversaries in the sense at issue here. As a prominent comparativist has observed, "the familiar contrast between our adversarial procedure and the supposedly non-adversarial tradition has been grossly overdrawn."[8] German legal practice, which may be taken as representative of the broader inquisitorial tradition (at least on the European continent), illustrates this point nicely. Although German lawyers play only a very limited role in developing the facts, they "advance partisan positions from first pleadings to final arguments,"[9] so that "outside the realm of fact-gathering, German civil procedure is about as adversarial as our own."[10]

In the end, lawyers' partisanship, rather than being confined to idiosyncratically aggressive forms of lawyering, is instead a deeply ingrained feature of the legal profession quite generally, which appears in all legal systems that separate advocates from tribunals, recognizing the right of disputants to engage the state's institutions through advisers who do not themselves stand in for the state. This structural separation of legal roles, in which advocates *serve* rather than *judge* their clients' causes, makes partisanship (at least in some measure) immanent in lawyering. And the ethics of lawyerly partisanship should therefore not be dismissed as the misbegotten product of a perversion of lawyering but should rather be studied carefully and with respect. It is not just that the obligations of partisanship apply broadly, across most segments of the legal profession and in most legal systems. They are also connected to legal structures—associated with the distinction between advocates and tribunals—that are uniformly accepted in open, free societies (on both sides of the divide between so-called adversarial and inquisitorial procedure) and that indeed seem, intuitively, to be a natural expression of the very idea of the rule of law.

It is therefore not surprising that a careful analysis of lawyerly partisanship illuminates not just lawyers' ethics but also the ethical nature of partiality more generally, because the way in which the ethics of partiality is developed in lawyers reveals that partiality possesses forms and purposes that are otherwise hidden from view. The partisan loyalty that lawyers show their clients involves not just a generic preference for the clients over others but also a distinctive capacity to give voice to the clients—to represent them—in high fidelity (and in particular without distortion caused by the lawyers' own judgments of what their clients deserve or ought to prefer). Moreover, lawyerly fidelity, understood in this way, enables lawyers to serve a mediating function between individual and state that is essential to the state's impartial authority, at least under conditions of deep and pervasive partisan disagreement about how the state ought to resolve disputes. The fidelity of lawyers therefore illustrates that partisan loyalty and impartiality are not simply opposite ideas but instead stand, at least under conditions of pluralism and conflict, in a more complex, nested, and even symbiotic relationship.

These pages will seek to elaborate the peculiar structure of lawyerly fidelity and to render fidelity, so understood, an appealing virtue. I shall try to identify and characterize the generic conception of fidelity that is immanent in adversary advocacy quite generally, that is, in the practice of law under any legal system that accepts the structural separation between advocate and tribunal. And I shall hope to show how this conception fits into the broader system of ideals associated with the legal systems in which it arises, including, ultimately, the ideal of the authority of law.

I. The Building Blocks of Adversary Advocacy

The foundations of adversary advocacy, being creatures of the structural division of labor between advocate and tribunal, remain constant across all forms of adversary legal practice and therefore do not depend on any particular formulation of positive law. But they are nevertheless inscribed in positive law, including in the ABA's Model Rules and their several predecessors. The basic structure of adversary advocacy may therefore be discerned from the study of the law governing lawyers. This structure involves three foundational principles, which I call *lawyer loyalty, client control,* and *legal assertiveness.*

Lawyer Loyalty

Perhaps the adversary advocate's most familiar duty is to represent her client loyally. This duty of loyalty, which is familiarly expressed in the language of zealous advocacy, has in one form or another maintained a constant presence in all major codes of legal ethics adopted over the past century. The 1908 ABA Canons of Professional Ethics stated that the lawyer should represent her clients with "warm zeal."[11] The ideal was carried forward in the 1969 ABA Model Code of Professional Responsibility; the Canons (announcing the broad norms underlying the Model Code) include the principle that "a lawyer should represent a client zealously within the bounds of the law";[12] and the more specific Disciplinary Rules state that "a lawyer shall not intentionally fail to seek the lawful objectives of his client through reasonably available means permitted by law and the Disciplinary Rules."[13] Much the same duty appears in the Model Rules; Model Rule 1.3 requires lawyers to display "diligence" in serving clients;[14] the Official Comments to this Rule, which "provide guidance for practicing in compliance with the Rule[],"[15] add that lawyers should "take whatever lawful and ethical measures are required to vindicate a client's cause or endeavor" and must therefore "act with commitment and dedication to the interest of the client and with zeal in advocacy upon the client's behalf";[16] and the Preamble to the Model Rules mentions zeal three times.[17]

These commands are not controversial. The Restatement of the Law Governing Lawyers summarizes the substance of loyalty, saying that a lawyer must "proceed in a manner reasonably calculated to advance a client's lawful objectives."[18] And the leading treatise on the law governing lawyers, which places loyalty at the very center of adversary lawyers' professional ethics, observes that "the single most fundamental principle of the law of lawyering is that so long as lawyers stay within the bounds of law, they serve society best by zealously serving their clients, one at a time."[19]

The loyalty that the law requires lawyers to show their clients is not unbounded, of course. Even as the organic structure of adversary advocacy presses lawyers toward partisanship, the more technical provisions of the various ethics codes certainly do cabin such professional duties, in any number of ways. Lawyers, put simply, may neither subvert the adversary process nor transgress its bounds.

Critics of the legal profession often ignore these limits, and the profession's defenders complain that the critics invent an extreme adversarialism that is not required by the lawyer's role and probably has never existed in law and therefore attack a straw man. There is much to this complaint, and the parade of horribles often charged against the legal profession involves substantial exaggeration. I have discussed the constraints on lawyers' loyalty in detail elsewhere and will not repeat that discussion here.[20] The crucial point, for present purposes, is that, even as the law does indeed impose substantial constraints on lawyers' partisanship, the primary principles of lawyer loyalty maintain a persistent presence beneath the law's facial emphasis on constraints, and these primary ideals inevitably bleed through the gaps in the technical rules by which the positive law limits lawyers' partisanship, so that adversary advocates remain obligated to exploit others on behalf of their clients. Indeed, this could not be otherwise. The provisions through which the law limits lawyers' partisan loyalty and zeal remain technical and self-consciously narrow and certainly fall short of an organic injunction impartially to promote truth or justice. And such technical and particularistic limits cannot possibly eliminate the organic ideal of loyalty from which the law of lawyering begins.

Nor is this really controversial. Even those who defend the legal profession by emphasizing the constraints that the positive law imposes on partisan loyalty accept that the law "does at least tolerate many litigation techniques that . . . [place loyalty to clients over concern for justice]. . . . Examples include discrediting a truthful witness on cross-examination; counseling a client not to retain certain records because they could be damaging in future litigation; cultivating an expert witness by feeding her only favorable information until she is locked into supporting the client's position; and using pre-trial motions, refusals to stipulate, and discovery requests to exploit a client's greater staying power."[21]

The enduring loyalty of lawyers is, in the end, a direct entailment of the structural separation between advocate and tribunal that frames lawyers' ethics in their entirety. If this separation means anything, it means that, whereas tribunals are to be impartial, lawyers are to be partisans whose basic professional obligations (however they are constrained by secondary rules) insistently include a duty loyally to serve their clients.

Client Control

In spite of its central importance to legal ethics, lawyer loyalty cannot stand alone. Loyalty carries no content apart from the end to which it refers—loyalty, even zealous loyalty, requires an object. And the loyalty and zeal provisions in the ethics codes, even when supplemented by the conflicts rules, do not adequately fix their own objects, because identifying "the client" as the object of the lawyer's loyalty and the end of her zeal is not enough to fix the lawyer's professional duties in a meaningful way.

Saying simply that the lawyer should be loyal to the client does not determine to what about the client the lawyer's loyalty should attach, and this choice will dramatically affect the nature of the lawyer's ethical life. Indeed, in the extreme case, if the lawyer's loyalty were tied to the client's interest in moral or legal rectitude—to the client's justice, as one might say—then the lawyer would cease to be meaningfully an adversary advocate at all. In order to represent her client loyally, she would be required first to judge her client's cause to determine what protecting his rectitude required. (The ends of the representation, which would depend upon the right outcome of the case, simply could not be identified apart from this judgment.) Lawyer loyalty underwrites a distinctively adversary legal practice only if it is owed more narrowly and immediately to the client than the suggestion about moral or legal rectitude allows. Adversary advocacy—indeed, the structural separation between advocate and tribunal—requires not just loyalty but also a client- rather than a justice-centered approach to loyalty.

The ethics codes must therefore supplement the lawyer's duty of loyalty by specifying loyalty's ends, and they must (if they are to retain their adversary character) set ends that look more or less narrowly to the client. The codes fulfill both requirements, specifically through provisions that allocate decision-making authority between lawyers and clients in ways that give clients control over the basic purposes of a legal representation—control to fix the objectives that lawyers must loyally pursue. Moreover, the ethics codes establish just how the lawyer's loyalty will be client-centered, specifically by directing lawyers to pursue clients' instructions and not just clients' interests—that is, to defer to clients' beliefs about what ends they should pursue. The ethics codes allocate authority between lawyer and client in a way that supplements lawyer loyalty with client control and requires lawyers (within limits, of course) to be the servants of their clients' points of view.

The Model Rules announce the basic principle of client control in Rule 1.2, which gives clients broad power to determine "the objectives of representation."[22] The Model Code similarly directs the lawyer to "seek the lawful objectives of his client."[23] And the Restatement elaborates on this basic structure of client control, stating that "[a] client may instruct the lawyer during the representation" and that lawyers should act "to advance a client's objectives as defined by the client."[24] The convergence concerning client control is not absolute,[25] but the basic idea is the same in all three regimes. That is not surprising: "The attorney-client relationship," as one court has observed, "is one of agent to principal, and as an agent the attorney must act in conformity with his . . . instructions and is responsible to his principal if he violates this duty";[26] and the ethics codes borrow their ideas about lawyer loyalty and especially client control from the general law of agency. The law governing lawyers proceeds, against this background, to elaborate the agency relation between lawyer and client in ways that emphasize client control.

While lawyers are permitted to offer clients independent counsel even within the sphere of client authority,[27] lawyers may advise but must never command, and they should take care, in offering advice, to avoid unduly influencing their clients. Most important, the ethics codes protect client control over ends from encroachment by the lawyer's superior knowledge and technical expertise, which often pose the gravest threats to client autonomy. Thus, although the ethics codes recognize lawyers' technical expertise by giving them limited control over the means through which to pursue the ends that clients set,[28] the line between "means" and "ends" is given a flexible rather than a rigid interpretation, one that emphasizes client control. In particular, choices that would ordinarily be classed as involving mere means and therefore allocated to the lawyer—for example, respecting the aggressiveness of a cross-examination—are treated as involving ends and are allocated to the client as soon as they impinge on the client's broader values. As the comment to Model Rule 1.2 says, when disputes about what would ordinarily be classed as means arise, "lawyers usually defer to the client regarding such questions as the expense to be incurred and concern for third persons who might be adversely affected."[29] In this way, the ethics codes restrict lawyers' control over means to areas in which lawyers have "special knowledge and skill"—in effect, to "technical, legal and tactical matters."[30] Indeed, the lawyer's control over means is best understood not as an independent value at all but rather as an instrument to serve the client's control over ends: the client's power to set and pursue ends is made more valuable by giving the client access to a lawyer with discretion to devote her expertise to pursuing the client's ends more skillfully than the client could do on her own.

Although lawyers should advise their clients broadly, they may not use their positions as advisers to subvert clients' autonomy. The strong principle of lawyer loyalty is supplemented, in the ethics codes, by an equally strong principle of client control.

Legal Assertiveness

Even taken together, lawyer loyalty and client control do not fix the nature of lawyers' professional obligations. The duties that lawyer loyalty and client control actually impose on lawyers depend on the range of objectives that clients and their lawyers may jointly pursue and the range of means that clients and their lawyers may use to pursue these objectives. And the questions therefore remain just what clients may command their lawyers to do and just what client commands lawyers may follow.

Lawyer loyalty and client control are therefore not the exclusive possessions of the law governing lawyers but instead arise against a broader background framework that allows clients to press their claims and makes room for the lawyer-client relationship to arise. For lawyer loyalty and client control to be meaningful in lawyers' professional lives, this larger framework must give lawyers substantial latitude in assisting clients who themselves enjoy substantial latitude in pressing their legal claims.

The legal structures that arise in and around adversary advocacy do just this, through a set of legal rules that allow lawyers wide latitude in assisting disputants who may press colorable but losing claims. Most narrowly, these rules give lawyers a literal privilege—which is expressly inscribed in legal doctrine—with respect to certain specific forms of conduct. For example, lawyers are in most jurisdictions absolutely immune from tort liability for defamatory statements that they make in court.[31] Similarly, although a little more broadly, lawyers are expressly protected against certain forms of legal liability that might otherwise attach to persons who do what lawyers do for their clients: thus, a lawyer who encourages a client to breach a contract is not liable to the client's promisee for tortious interference with contract;[32] a lawyer who gives legal advice to a corrupt business is not guilty of racketeering;[33] and, more broadly still, a lawyer who gives good-faith legal advice cannot be held liable as an accessory to tortious actions that her client takes on the basis of this advice.[34] In these ways, lawyers enjoy express protection against liability for the burdens that the assistance they give their clients imposes on others.[35]

These express protections, moreover, stand atop a much larger zone of protection that both clients and lawyers enjoy against liability for asserting and assisting legal claims. This zone of protection receives expression not just directly, in doctrines that narrowly cabin liability for bringing or defending lawsuits, but also indirectly, in the law's decision not to extend generally applicable standards of liability to conduct that involves asserting legal claims or defenses. Indeed, the express immunities that lawyers enjoy are made explicit precisely because they help to define the outside edge of these broader implied immunities.

To begin with, both the law governing lawyers and the broader law of procedure protect lawyers and their clients from liability for the full harms that they cause by asserting mistaken or even unreasonable legal claims (for example, claims that are dismissed or that lose on summary judgment), unless these claims are in some way frivolous or malicious. Model Rule 3.1, for example, requires only that lawyers have a "basis in law and fact" for the claims they make "that is not frivolous, which includes a good faith argument for an extension, modification or reversal of existing law."[36] And the Federal Rules of Civil Procedure similarly require only that filings not be made for an improper purpose, be nonfrivolous, and have or be likely to have evidentiary support.[37]

The precise limits on the adversary assertiveness that these rules allow are, of course, a subject of substantial dispute. But it is unquestioned that these rules do not impose strict liability or even negligence standards on lawyers and disputants. Strict liability would hold disputants liable whenever they asserted claims or defenses that eventually lost. And even negligence would (following a prominent interpretation of reasonableness) hold disputants liable whenever their arguments failed to minimize the total costs—including both error costs of inaccurate dispute resolution and transaction costs of litigation—that they, their opponents, and third parties had jointly to bear. Although the rules prohibiting frivolous litigation sometimes use the word "reasonable," they have never been seriously thought to require disputants and their lawyers to bring only claims that are reasonable in the tort-law-like sense that their expected social benefits exceed their expected social costs. Certainly, the prohibition that they establish is not violated every time a party brings a claim that loses on summary judgment. Indeed, these rules do not require even that the exclusive motive for bringing a dubious claim be the (small) chance that the claim might succeed. Instead, a partially strategic motive for bringing a claim does not render the claim frivolous or unreasonable for purposes of Model Rule 3.1 and Rule 11, not even when the strategic advantages that the claim secures are inefficient and undeserved. Accordingly, regardless of how the interpretive

controversies that surround the rules against frivolous litigation
are resolved, these rules clearly give disputants and lawyers substantially greater leeway than ordinary standards of liability would
allow.[38]

Moreover, this retreat from ordinary standards of liability for
harming others is carried over in the often unnoticed but important fact that tort law also declines to apply the ordinary law of
negligence to harms caused when one person asserts legal claims,
including losing legal claims, against another. Thus, although
there do exist torts of malicious prosecution and abuse of process,
they are subject to narrow limits and certainly do not apply generally to impose liability in connection with unreasonable lawsuits or
legal arguments that burden others, even when it was predictable
that the lawsuits would fail.[39] Once again, the law clearly does not
require clients or their lawyers to proceed only with claims that are
reasonable (for example, in the sense of joint cost minimizing).

These rules (and, indeed, the narrower immunities discussed
a moment ago) do not, of course, protect clients or even lawyers
from liability for all actions taken in connection with asserting
legal claims. But the adversary system writ large does unambiguously insulate parties and their lawyers from liability for the harms
that they impose simply by asserting losing (including predictably
losing) claims. This is a subtle but enormously important point.
The legal system entitles clients, with the help of their advocates,
aggressively to pursue their legal claims by denying legal recognition to many of the harms that persons' assertions of their legal
rights cause others.

Indeed, the protection that lawyers enjoy against liability for
pressing losing claims is a mark—perhaps even the characteristic
sign—of the distinction between advocate and judge, and the protection that losing clients enjoy is similarly a mark of the parallel
distinction between party and judge. Both give an unfamiliar but
important gloss on the common idea that the rule of law forbids
a person from being a judge in her own case. This idea is ordinarily understood to say that judges ought not be partisans. But the
arguments just rehearsed reveal that it has a second meaning also,
namely that disputants and their advocates *may* be partisan and
should not be required to bear responsibility for accurately (and
impartially) judging their own causes.

The discussion of legal assertiveness provides the background needed to complete a basic characterization of the lawyer's professional role. When set against a backdrop of legal assertiveness, the principles of lawyer loyalty and client control together give substance to the adversary system's core commitment to placing lawyers at their clients' disposal. The principle of legal assertiveness entitles clients to press even losing (and even unreasonable) legal claims and entitles lawyers to assist them. And, with this license in place, the principle of client control allows clients to choose the legal claims that they assert and to set the ends that they and their lawyers pursue, while the principle of lawyer loyalty requires lawyers to advance legal and factual arguments designed effectively to promote the ends that their clients have set.

II. An Organizing Ideal

In order loyally to serve their controlling and legally assertive clients, adversary advocates must take a particular attitude toward their work, an attitude that I shall call "professional detachment." This usage is unconventional but not, I think, abusive. It takes an idea that is familiar in legal ethics and emphasizes its less noticed but not less important implications.

The familiar idea of professional detachment is straightforwardly stated and receives doctrinal expression on the face of the ethics codes. The most prominent (but far from the only) contemporary statement of the doctrine appears in Model Rule 1.2, which declares that "[a] lawyer's representation of a client . . . does not constitute an endorsement of the client's political, economic, social or moral views or activities."[40] (One might add that a lawyer's representation of a client does not constitute an endorsement of the client's factual or legal claims, either.) Put simply, lawyers should not ordinarily be taken to endorse either the claims that their professional activities assert or the causes that these activities promote.

Now the principle of professional detachment's most practical purpose and the reason for which it is insisted on by the bar is to support lawyers' various immunities from the *legal* responsibility that they might otherwise bear for actions that they take in representing their clients. Moreover, lawyers (commonly) add that their professional role insulates them not just from legal but also from *moral* responsibility for the things that they do for their clients. Indeed, the principle that "lawyers should not be held accountable for their clients" has been called "the most basic proposition about [adversary] advocacy."[41] This moral application of professional detachment is more surprising than the legal one and is certainly less secure. The argument for moral nonaccountability must translate the role understandings and subjective attitudes that directly constitute lawyers' professional detachment into propositions of generally applicable morality, and this movement of thought, although much attempted, has proved difficult to achieve.

Although both the legal and moral nonaccountability associated with lawyers' professional detachment belong among the mainstays of legal ethics, I shall not for the moment pursue either. I have instead introduced professional detachment with a different, although complementary, purpose in mind and with an eye more to the antecedents of professional detachment than to its consequences. This aspect of lawyers' professional detachment is much less remarked on than the alleged connection between detachment and nonaccountability, but it is no less important for going unnoticed.

In order for lawyers' professional detachment to have any hope of underwriting their moral nonaccountability—indeed, in order for detachment to be possible at all—professional detachment must be *required* of lawyers. If lawyers have a choice about how to stand with respect to their clients' claims and causes, then detachment will be foreclosed in every case. Lawyers who may choose whether or not to adopt a detached approach to particular representations cannot prevent decisions that are ostensibly about detachment from becoming, in effect, expressions of personal approval or disapproval of their client's claims and causes. A lawyer who purports to exercise her right to detach from a client will unavoidably express her personal disapproval of the client's case, and a lawyer who fails to exercise this right will unavoidably express her personal approval. Lawyers for whom professional detachment is a choice cannot avoid becoming personally implicated, in one way or another, in every representation they take on.

The mandatory aspect of professional detachment—and its connection to the complex of principles that makes lawyers' professional lives ethically troubling—is not generally made explicit in the ethics codes.[42] This is probably because professional detachment runs so deep in the self-understandings of an adversary legal profession that it is simply assumed. But a lawyer's obligation to remain professionally detached from her clients is insistently reasserted in the rare cases in which lawyers betray it. In these cases, lawyers who are overwhelmed by their disapproval of their clients become unable to restrain their private views and, abandoning their professional obligations to advocate even for clients whose claims they regard as unjustified, instead repudiate their clients' causes.[43] The lawyers abandon lawyer loyalty and client control and reject professional detachment in favor of its opposite. Far from setting aside their private views, these lawyers aggressively promote the outcomes that they privately regard as accurate and just.

Courts that confront this style of lawyering uniformly reject it and reassert the ideal of professional detachment against lawyers who deviate from it. Indeed, the courts reach this result through an argument that insistently places professional detachment at the very center of adversary advocacy, so that the path to this conclusion is as important as the result itself. Thus, the courts all agree, for example, that a criminal defendant has a right to a lawyer devoted "solely to the interests of his client,"[44] who "set[s] forth all arguable issues"[45] and certainly does not "argue the case against his client."[46] They insist that this right requires lawyers to serve rather than judge their clients—that the lawyer's role does not "countenance disclosure to the Court of counsel's private conjectures about the guilt or innocence of his client" because "[i]t is the role of the judge or jury to determine the facts, not that of the attorney."[47]

Moreover, the courts insist that a lawyer who abandons professional detachment and judges rather than serves her client commits more than an ordinary dereliction of duty. She not only fails to work for her client as effectively as she ought but instead, by "adopt[ing] and act[ing] upon a belief that [her] client should be convicted";[48] she also "essentially joins the prosecution's efforts in obtaining a conviction"[49] and therefore "suffers from an obvious conflict of interest."[50] Indeed, it is so profoundly improper for a lawyer to compromise a client's case because her conscience

demands it that this motive *in itself* renders otherwise unobjection-
able conduct impermissible: in the words of one court, "the failure
to argue [a] case before the jury, while ordinarily only a trial tactic
not subject to review, manifestly enters the field of incompetency
when the reason assigned is the attorney's conscience."[51] And, finally, the lawyer who abandons professional detachment and argues her conscience against her client thereby "`fail[s] to function
in any meaningful sense as the Government's adversary,'"[52] so her
breach of professional detachment not only contravenes the law
governing lawyers[53] but also renders her performance constitutionally defective, even without the showing of prejudice that is usually
required,[54] by bringing her conduct within the narrow range of
cases in which a defendant suffers an "actual or constructive denial
of assistance of counsel altogether."[55] Thus, the courts have gone
so far as to say that a loyal counsel (a counsel who remains professionally detached) is a "jurisdictional prerequisite" for a criminal
trial.[56] In other words, the courts in these cases treat a lawyer who
abandons professional detachment and judges rather than advocate for her client as being *no lawyer at all.*

The constitutional dimension of these cases and, in particular,
the insistence that defendants have an individual right to effective and therefore detached counsel obviously invokes the criminal context. But, although the consequences of finding an individual lawyer ineffective—in particular, the client's (that is, the
defendant's) entitlement to a new trial—depend on principles of
criminal procedure and constitutional law, the account of lawyers'
professional obligations that constitutes the core argument of the
cases does not depend on any idiosyncratic features of criminal
law but instead applies quite generally to all areas of legal practice.
And, although lapses of professional detachment are rarer in civil
than in criminal cases—perhaps because lawyers generally respect
their civil clients more than their criminal ones and therefore find
the deference associated with professional detachment easier to
sustain—such lapses do occur and receive fundamentally the same
criticism from the courts as arises in the criminal context. For example, courts, drawing a direct analogy to criminal cases in which
lawyers attempt to force clients to accept plea agreements, have
held that lawyers who doubt the merits of their clients' civil cases
may not impose their views by forcing resistant clients to accept

settlements that the lawyers regard as reasonable.[57] Indeed, courts have even carried the internal workings of the argument for professional detachment into civil cases, suggesting that a lawyer who promotes her private view of a client's case too aggressively develops a conflict of interest with the client.[58] Like criminal lawyers, civil lawyers who allow their private beliefs about their clients' causes to have too great an influence on their representations of their clients abandon the principles of lawyer loyalty and client control that their professional ethics require. And professional detachment is as essential to adversary advocacy in the civil context as it is to such advocacy in the criminal context.

When it is seen in this light—operating not as a shield but as a sword—professional detachment is revealed to reprise at a structural level the commitments of adversary advocacy that the argument has been elaborating in more particular detail. The principle of professional detachment reveals that lawyerly loyalty, client control, and legal assertiveness together impose on lawyers the basic requirement that they *serve* rather than *judge* their clients.

III. A Lawyerly Virtue

The earlier accounts of lawyer loyalty, client control, and legal assertiveness make plain that lawyers' core professional obligations inevitably "impose substantial constraints on [their] ethical autonomy."[59] Moreover, professional detachment, understood as an organizing ideal for lawyers' ethics, reveals the ethical costs for lawyers of working subject to these constraints. Ordinary good people facing a choice aspire accurately to judge for themselves what ought to be done and then to do their best to promote the all-things-considered judgments that they have reached. But the good lawyer, acting in her professional capacity, aspires to suppress her personal judgments and to promote her clients' judgments instead, including when she would not (if she were to pursue the matter) share her client's purposes. As even the Model Rules admit, the adversary lawyer faces a tension between her professional obligations and her "interest in remaining an upright person."[60]

But, even as the turn to professional detachment reaffirms (and entrenches) the tensions between adversary advocacy and ordinary morality, it also initiates a more hopeful development in lawyers' professional ethics. Perhaps surprisingly, the principle of professional detachment—the requirement that adversary advocates withdraw from their own judgments of their clients' cases—may *itself* be recast as a characteristically lawyerly virtue, which I call "fidelity." Fidelity is a complex virtue, quite different from loyalty *simpliciter* and its cognates and much more difficult to achieve. Certainly, fidelity differs importantly from the virtues in whose terms lawyers' ethics are more commonly characterized, namely fraternity[61] or even friendship[62] toward their clients. Indeed, the contrast to these alternative accounts of lawyerly virtue helps to illuminate the nature of fidelity.[63]

The compatriot or friend characteristically serves the object of her affection engagedly, that is, at least partly on her own terms; she promotes his good as she sees it, and, although she may respect his contrary views and even adjust her behavior in light of this respect, she never completely *defers* to him.[64] In this way, the compatriot or friend throws her entire self, including all her judgments and ambitions, into her relations. The lawyer, by contrast, must display precisely the deference to her client's purposes and objectives that the compatriot and friend reject.[65] Indeed, lawyers must *repress* their private views of what is right for their clients in just the ways in which compatriots and friends should not. Lawyers are therefore in an important respect the polar opposites of compatriots or friends. Rather than throwing themselves into the lawyer-client relation, lawyers *withdraw* important parts of themselves from it.

The root of the difficulty with the idea that lawyers are like compatriots or friends may be identified by returning to the basic structure of lawyers' professional ethics. These metaphors treat lawyer loyalty as an application of ordinary ideas of loyalty. But the basic principles of legal ethics are, as I have said repeatedly, lawyer loyalty *plus* client control *conditioned on* legal assertiveness, and the version of loyalty that lawyers display must be understood in light of the principle of client control and against this backdrop. Moreover, the discussion of professional detachment elaborates just how these other principles intervene to give the lawyer's loyalty to her client a distinctive character that the ordinary loyalty associated with fraternity or friendship does not share. In particular, lawyers must not just prefer their clients' interests over the interests of others but also must prefer their clients' points of view—that is, beliefs about what is true and fair, applied, recall, against the backdrop of the free-play established by the principle of legal assertiveness—over other points of view, including especially their own. I call this attitude "fidelity" in order to capture that it involves not just a concern for clients' ends but also, and indeed predominantly, a concern for deference and accuracy in identifying and representing clients' conceptions of what these ends are. As the arguments to come will reveal, the features that make fidelity distinctive account for a substantial part of fidelity's appeal, which makes the distinctiveness of fidelity essential to the more hopeful strands of lawyers' professional ethics.

The difficulty of fidelity, and also its virtue, may be appreciated by taking the argument in an unexpected direction, to develop an unlikely analogy between lawyers on the one hand and poets on the other. Although this comparison between lawyers and poets may seem strange and even misplaced, it is in fact a species of the familiar analogy, most famously developed by Plato in Book IV of *The Republic*, between the state and the soul.[66] The analogy attempts to cast the lawyer's role in political life in the same mold as the poet's role in spiritual life.

John Keats's ideas about the nature of poetic sensibility, specifically his idea of "negative capability,"[67] provide the starting point for this discussion of lawyerly fidelity. Keats proposed that the poet's negative capability provides a distinctive service to both the poet's subject and his audience. Each of these two elements of poetic negative capability has an analog in the professional life of the adversary advocate, and these analogs together elaborate characteristically lawyerly fidelity.

Keats argued that the negatively capable poet is unusually able to efface himself, maintaining "no identity" of his own, and (through this self-effacement) to work continually as a medium "filling some other body—The Sun, the Moon, the Sea . . ."[68] and rendering this ordinarily mute body articulate. The lawyer is similarly required, by the sword-like component of professional detachment, to efface herself or at least her personal beliefs about the claims and causes that she argues. And, through this self-effacement, the lawyer becomes able to work continually as a mouthpiece for her client. Just as the self-effacing poet enables his otherwise insensible subjects to come alive through him, so also the lawyer enables her other-wise inarticulate clients to speak through her.

The analogy to poets therefore casts the deference that lawyers show their clients as an unusually selfless (in the literal sense) kind of empathy.[69] Ordinary good people acting in ordinary circum-stances adopt a first-personal moral ambition of authenticity; they seek to form their own opinions about the world they confront and to express themselves in the service of these opinions. But the good lawyer, acting in her professional capacity, adopts the first-personal moral ambition to take her client's part and, steadfastly suppressing her own ego, to speak her client's mind. The good lawyer aims to address the world, negatively capably, through her client's eyes.

Moreover, the good lawyer—again like the poet, at least on Keats's view—must make his negative capability into a second na-ture, which comes even to supplant his natural, pre-professional ambitions to authenticity. The totality of the required conceal-ment—and hence the extent of the suppression of the lawyer's personal judgments of her clients—is hard to overstate. It is illus-trated by an extraordinary story Charles Curtis tells about Arthur Hill, the lawyer who represented Sacco and Vanzetti (taking a case, Curtis says, and not adopting a cause) and who, twenty years later, still refused to express his own opinion about their guilt, telling Curtis, "I have never said, and I cannot say, what I think on the subject because, you see, Charlie, I was their counsel."[70] In the limit, even the lawyer herself will cease to know her own mind. Keats, discussing himself as a poet, once said that "It is a wretched thing to confess; but it is a very fact that not one word that I ever utter can be taken for granted as an opinion growing out of my identical nature—how can it be when I have no nature?"[71] And, as Macmillan similarly observed, "No advocate can be a *sincere* . . . man in the performance of his daily business."[72]

These thoughts cast fidelity as a dubious starting point for a reno-vation of the lawyer's ethical life; they suggest that lawyerly fidelity is less a virtue than a form of professional disfigurement. And, indeed, it has often been observed that the lawyer's capacity to argue all sides and his allegiance to procedures rather than outcomes makes him unsuited to moral leadership. The lawyer will, as Bacon says, "desire rather commendation of wit, in being able to hold all arguments, than of judgment in discerning what is true; as if it were a praise to know what might be said and not what should be thought."[73] These two shortcomings, moreover, are related. Because lawyers' experience of life is at once infinitely various and absolutely vicarious—because lawyers' "experience of human affairs is made up of an infinite number of scraps cut out of other people's lives"—lawyers (at least insofar as they pursue their negatively capable professional ethic) "see too much of life in one way, too little in another, to make them safe guides in practical matters."[74]

But, even as the lawyer's distinctive virtue renders her suspect as a leader, it places her among the indispensible supports of political life. This suggestion is invited by a return to the analogy to poets. Although the poet can see through his subject, he does not see only through his subject or become his subject's exclusive property. Instead, the negatively capable poet can occupy multiple points of view simultaneously and therefore has a capacity "of being in uncertainties, Mysteries, doubts, without any irritable reaching after fact & reason," a capacity of "remaining content with half knowledge"[75] that allows insight, however uncertain, to which the brighter but more uniform light of their more positive capabilities leaves ordinary people blind. The lawyer, once again, has similar capacities. She is, as has been said, "trained in disbelief, or at least unbelief or suspended belief, and [is] required to act in that frame of mind in many of [her] professional duties," so that she "is not supposed to `know' whether [her] client is guilty in a criminal case, or whether he is entitled to prevail in a civil case."[76] And the lawyer is therefore able to sustain all sides of an argument, to equivocate without any irritable reaching after a conclusion, to remain content with persuasion rather than proof. The good lawyer follows Keats's dictum "to make up one's mind about nothing—to let the mind be a thoroughfare for all thoughts. Not a select party."[77] This allows "the arguments of counsel to hold [a] case, as it were, in suspension between two opposing interpretations of it."[78] And, because she can do this, the lawyer sees more clearly and widely than ordinary people see and can sustain resolutions to disputes that remain closed off from those who insist passionately on substantive justice or right.[79]

The analogy to poets therefore casts lawyerly fidelity and, in particular, the suppression of lawyers' personal convictions that fidelity demands as a characteristically lawyerly version of the procedural virtues. Ordinary good people acting in ordinary circumstances aspire, once they have heard all sides to a question, to make up their minds and to promote the all-things-considered judgments that they have reached. But the good lawyer, acting in her professional capacity, employs a distinctive subtlety of mind and an unusual practical imagination to construct compatible possibilities where others see contradictory certainties, to distract attention from the deepest conflicts, to redirect energies toward shallower matters, and in this way to achieve an accommodation among otherwise incompatible positions. Negatively capable lawyers cultivate, as Anthony Kronman has observed, a distinctive blend of sympathy and detachment, which renders them distinctively capable of containing and even resolving recalcitrant disputes.[80] One might even say that lawyers, through their distinctive fidelity, give essential support to the legitimacy of the law.

IV. THE GOOD OF FIDELITY

A proper understanding of the contributions that lawyers, through their fidelity, make to political legitimacy requires more careful argument. This argument begins, in the spirit of fixing ideas, by briefly reprising the problem of political legitimacy in general. Next, it identifies two very different models of legitimation and distinguishes between two very different sites of legitimation. Once these distinctions have been drawn, the characteristic contribution that lawyers make to legitimacy under one of these models and at one of these sites can be properly appreciated.

The Problem in Brief

The problem of political legitimacy arises because people come into conflict about how their collective affairs should be arranged. They have incompatible interests, and, insofar as they each pursue these narrow self-interests, this generates discord. Moreover, even people who all display an impartial regard for one another will continue to disagree about their collective affairs and to come into conflict with one another insofar as they have inconsistent beliefs about what their several interests consist in or about what balance among these competing interests is fair. Like self-interest, morality tends not to promote harmony but in fact itself presents an independent source of conflict, which is an *expression* of persons' moral commitments and not a *retreat* from them.

These conflicts are, moreover, ineliminable. They are inevitable expressions of the competition for scarce resources and the fact that the diversity of human experience and the complexity of human reason make pluralism the natural state of ethical life.[81] Collective life (and, indeed, peaceful coexistence) therefore requires people who are naturally free and independent and who are capable of objecting and resisting against collective decisions to accept and obey collective decisions even when they remain unpersuaded of the decisions' merits. Politics takes as its central task elaborating and marshalling reasons to obey.

The most obvious reasons for obeying collective decisions, in almost every case, arise in virtue of the collective's power to coerce compliance with its directives (including, most familiarly, by threatening credibly to punish those who disobey). But collective government that is experienced by the governed as coercive at every turn or even just as principally coercive is unlikely to remain stable for long, because the opportunities for resistance tend to outstrip the means of coercion. And so there are good grounds for hoping that other reasons for obeying collective decisions also exist and, indeed, that these other reasons take the lead in persons' practical deliberations about whether or not to obey. It is therefore unsurprising that government naturally (indeed, almost universally) aspires not just to acquire the power to enforce collective decisions but also to generate voluntary compliance by sustaining an agreement about which decisions to obey, even in the face of disagreement about which decisions to adopt. Government aspires to achieve *political legitimacy*, which is to say to attain a distinctively political kind of authority over the governed.

Legitimacy in Theory and in Practice

Identifying lawyerly fidelity's distinctive contribution to political legitimacy—and hence to the project of stable collective life—requires drawing a distinction between two kinds of legitimation.

One approach to legitimacy, exemplified in the work of John Rawls,[82] seeks to articulate freestanding political (as opposed to moral) principles "which all citizens [whatever their interests and moral views] may reasonably be expected to endorse."[83] The idea here is to justify the ground rules for political life to each citizen, from that citizen's own point of view, even in the face of intractable first-order disagreement about what political policies are best and even when government pursues (within these ground rules) particular policies that some citizens find unappealing. This *theoretical* approach to legitimacy places the *understanding* at the center of politics, proposing to achieve legitimacy by generating an agreement on abstract propositions about political essentials that may be sustained solely on the basis of reason and entirely apart from any participatory engagement with the actual political process.[84]

This theoretical approach to political legitimacy has been given powerful developments, including, of course, by Rawls himself. But these several theoretical elaborations of political legitimacy, through their very appeal, emphasize a structural (and therefore ineliminable) shortcoming of theoretical approaches to legitimacy.[85] Even as each theory of legitimacy purports (credibly) to regulate political power in ways that fairly resolve disagreements among citizens about what first-order ends power should serve and therefore to justify power to every citizen from her own point of view, the theories of legitimacy themselves remain inconsistent with one another. To be sure, this lack of unanimity does not in itself undermine the universalist aspirations of the theoretical approach to legitimacy—justification is a normative concept, after all, so that a theory of legitimacy may *justify* political power to someone even though (perhaps because of cognitive errors or self-dealing) she remains, as it happens, *unpersuaded.*[86] But the enduring liveliness of the field of political philosophy directly illustrates that the disagreement among theories of political legitimacy is not disagreement *simpliciter* but rather *reasonable* disagreement. It does not reflect simple cognitive errors or failures of respect or concern for other persons but (like moral disagreement) instead arises inexorably out of the diversity of perspectives and experiences of free and equal participants in any shared political life.[87] And, even though brute disagreement does not necessarily undermine justification, reasonable disagreement does. The theoretical approach to legitimacy therefore cannot, on its own, meet the need for legitimation that the circumstances of politics present.

A second, *practical* approach to sustaining political legitimacy is therefore worth exploring, at least as a complement to the theoretical view and perhaps even as a (partial) substitute. This approach is practical because it replaces the theoretical approach's emphasis on abstract propositions about justified political power with an effort to elaborate a set of political institutions and practices through which the participants in politics might come to take *ownership* of political outcomes, including even outcomes that they find substantively unappealing and that they sought through their political participation to oppose. Whereas the theoretical approach seeks substantive principles of legitimacy that may be appreciated apart from any participation in political practice, this practical approach emphasizes the affective consequences of actual engagement with political practice—that is, the influence that political participation aspires to have on the political attitudes of the participants. One might say, as a shorthand, that the practical approach to legitimacy replaces the theoretical approach's emphasis on the understanding with an emphasis on the *will*.

Unlike theoretical principles of legitimacy, which attempt (and promise) principled resolutions to political disagreements that establish settled limits on the exercise of political power, the practical approach to legitimacy seeks to stave off rather than to resolve political disagreements. The practical approach aspires to establish a provisional—although, one hopes, renewable—holding pattern, in which disputants must actually go through the political process in order to accept the authority of the political outcomes that the process generates. Elaborating the practical account of legitimacy therefore requires identifying the political practices and institutions that sustain this holding pattern and the individual ownership of political outcomes that it sustains in turn.

Legitimacy at Wholesale and at Retail

Locating the distinctive place occupied by adversary lawyers—and their distinctive fidelity—in the overall scheme of legitimation that modern, open politics provides also requires drawing a second, basic distinction between two sites of legitimation.

Citizens may naturally object to their government's authority at two places: first, when the government decides disagreements about which general rules it should employ to structure how it will exercise its power; and, second, when the government decides disagreements about how to apply these general rules to particular facts in particular cases, including even over persons who continue to insist that the applications in question are unjust or otherwise unwarranted. A political system must therefore supply political legitimacy in each place—both at wholesale and at retail, as it were.

Democratic politics—either conducted among citizens directly or conducted indirectly, involving democratically elected representatives—is the principal supplier of wholesale political legitimacy in the modern world, and I have taken up democracy's contribution to political legitimacy (and its limits) elsewhere.[88] But democratic politics can supply legitimacy *only* at wholesale, so that, although democracy is a powerful legitimating force in politics, it cannot complete the legitimation of political power by itself. Once again, even when a political system has achieved agreement about which general principles concerning the exercise of collective power to obey, there will always arise cases in which these general principles do not straightforwardly resolve themselves into consensus outcomes.

It is therefore unsurprising that both political philosophy and political practice typically pair the democratic legitimacy through which they address the wholesale authority of governments with a second source of legitimacy designed to sustain government authority concerning the specific application of democratic laws to particular cases. The central and characteristic practice that provides this second source of legitimacy is adjudication.[89] Indeed, one might even say that what democracy is to political legitimacy at wholesale, adjudication is to political legitimacy at retail.

Lawyerly Fidelity and the Legitimacy of Adjudication

Applying these two distinctions together makes it possible to identify the good of fidelity. This distinctively lawyerly virtue serves as an essential support for adjudication's retail legitimation of political power on the practical model. That lawyerly fidelity should figure in retail rather than wholesale political legitimation is too obvious to require argument. But accounts of the (retail) legitimacy of adjudication naturally proceed in both the theoretical and the practical registers. And it is therefore worth noting briefly why the theoretical approach to the legitimacy of adjudication fails before considering in more detail how the practical approach succeeds and what contribution lawyers—through their distinctive fidelity—make to this success.

The dominant theoretical argument for the legitimacy of adjudication is the adversary system excuse: insofar as the balance between partisan lawyers that adversary adjudication establishes best secures the legal rights of all disputants, all disputants have reason to agree to be bound by the results of adversary adjudication even as they continue to disagree about what these results should be. But, in spite of its initial appeal, this approach suffers serious shortcomings. In particular, critics of the adversary system excuse propose that, in spite of its familiarity and intuitive appeal, that argument justifies only a much more limited moral division of labor than is commonly supposed. To begin with, in actual legal systems, the unequal distribution of legal services makes it simply implausible that disputing through partisan lawyers will best respect all disputants' rights, even only on balance.[90] Moreover, even in an ideal legal system, adversary advocates commonly promote their clients' interests through actions that violate the rights of others. In such cases, the aggregative conception of impartiality on which the traditional statement of the adversary system excuse relies faces challenges from rival conceptions, associated with deontological moral theories that apply impartiality separately to every relation between persons. These conceptions insist that when a lawyer's preference for her client violates a third party's rights this violation cannot be simply offset by benefits that arise elsewhere in the adversary administration of justice, and they thus cast further doubts on the adversary system excuse's legitimation of partisan lawyering.[91]

Together, such considerations inexorably erode the partisanship that lawyers might legitimately display. The theoretical approach to the legitimacy of adjudication threatens to turn adversary advocacy into a residual category. Adjudication, on this approach, reaches its highest expression when lawyers "think like judges in determining what the relevant law is"[92] and, moreover,

act like judges (and avoid ordinarily adversary advocacy) except
in cases in which adversary advocacy is anyway ineffective, because
there exist real judges who are capable of effectively imposing
this judicial sensibility largely uninfluenced by lawyers' adversary
efforts.[93] The theoretical approach to the legitimacy of adjudication therefore does not support but rather undermines lawyerly
partisanship, which is a distinctive practice precisely insofar as it
requires lawyers to think and to act very differently from judges
and to impose outcomes that reflect these differences. Indeed, the
theoretical approach to the legitimacy of adjudication threatens
to take aim at the structural separation between advocate and tribunal that forms the most basic commitment of adjudication as
it is actually practiced. This is a familiar theme of any number of
recent critical treatments of the adversary system excuse.[94]

The practice of adversary adjudication, however, remains recalcitrant even in the face of these arguments. The lived experience
of parties who subject their disputes to this practice attributes legitimacy to adversary adjudication even when lawyers display partisan fidelity to their clients that substantially exceeds what the theoretical approach to legitimacy countenances.[95] This experience
is best explained in terms of the legitimating powers of affective
engagement with the legal process, something that the theoretical
approach ignores but that provides practical accounts of the legitimacy of adjudication with a natural center of gravity.

The theoretical approach to the legitimacy of adjudication—
through the adversary system excuse—approaches the legal process as a technology for satisfying process-independent claims. The
theoretical approach treats process, to borrow a word from legal
sociology, as *transparent*, in the sense that it has "no effect on the
values, goals, and desires of those who use the system,"[96] so that
one can look back through a legal process, from its end to its beginning, and see the same claims asserted throughout in undis-
torted form. But this is, as sociology points out, a mistaken account
of legal process, associated with the formalism of classical jurisprudence and now discredited. Instead, "the relationship between
objectives [in a dispute] and mechanisms [of dispute resolution]
is reciprocal; not only do objectives influence the choice of mechanisms, but mechanisms chosen may alter objectives."[97] Indeed,
when the legal process is properly managed, its transformative

powers cause the disputants to come, through their legal engagements, to take ownership of the resolutions that the process produces, including even resolutions that they continue to dispute on
the merits. This possibility opens up the way to a practical recon-
struction of the legitimacy of adjudication, which emphasizes the
affective consequences of engagement with the legal process—the
transformations wrought by the process. Finally, this practical account places lawyerly fidelity and negative capability at the center
of the transformative power of the legal process and therefore at
the foundation of its legitimacy.

The transformations that engagements with adjudication engen-
der in disputants arise at three levels. Most shallowly, the legal process "translates [disputants' private complaints], and reconstitutes
the issues in terms of a legal discourse which has trans-situational
applicability."[98] Lawyers "objectify" their clients' arguments and
"set them apart from the particular interests they represent,"[99]
so that the clients' positions come to be seen as participating in
broader principles "in terms of which . . . binding solutions [to
disputes] can be found."[100] In this way, the lawyers who administer
the legal process serve as "culture broker[s]" for their clients,[101]
organizing and transforming their clients' claims in terms of this
discourse in order to render them more persuasive.[102] At an intermediate depth, lawyers and the legal process "test the reality of
the[ir] clien[ts'] perspective[s],"[103] piercing unreasonable hopes
and inaccurate perceptions[104] and, by contrast, legitimating the
other elements of their clients' positions that are not pierced.[105]
And, at the deepest level, an engagement with the legal process
does not just translate or test disputants' claims but fundamentally
reconstitutes them, specifically by transforming brute demands
into assertions of right, which depend on reasons and therefore
by their nature implicitly recognize the conditions of their own
failure (namely that the reasons do not support the claims in the
case at hand).[106] Indeed, the legal process can sometimes even in-
duce disputants to recognize a still deeper contingency in their demands, as they come to see a "problem as an adjustment between
competing claims and interests, rather than as one warranting a
fight for principle."[107]

These transformations, taken collectively, can have real staying power. When it is successful, the legal process, to borrow Lon

Fuller's form of words, has the "capacity to reorient the parties to-ward each other, not by imposing rules on them, but by helping them to achieve a new and shared perception of their relationship, a perception that will redirect their attitudes and dispositions to-ward one another."[108] Indeed, the transformative effect on a dis-pute of the legal process is potentially so powerful that "the trans-formed dispute can actually become *the* dispute,"[109] with the parties abandoning any of their demands that cannot be accommodated within the transformation. When this happens, the legitimacy of the legal process follows, because the reconstructed disputes and the resolutions that the legal process proposes have been tailored to suit each other, so that parties who come (through their affec-tive engagements with the legal process) to see their disputes as the legal process proposes also come to accept the resolutions that the legal process recommends.

These suggestions concerning adjudication's power to legiti-mate through transformation find support, moreover, in empiri-cal work on procedural justice (although the empirical studies do not address the precise mechanisms of transformation that I propose).[110] Thus, there exists substantial evidence that people's compliance with the law, as it is applied to them, depends signifi-cantly on their judgments concerning the legitimacy of the author-ities who apply it[111] and that judgments concerning legitimacy, in turn, depend on judgments concerning the procedures that the authorities employ in determining what the law requires and es-pecially in resolving disputes about this.[112] Furthermore, people's judgments concerning procedures are practical and affective, rather than theoretical and detached; when people make such judgments, "they focus more on their opportunities to state their case than they do on their influence" in producing decisions that they regard as accurate.[113] Finally, although people do not require direct influence, they do insist that their opportunities to be heard be genuinely participatory, rather than merely formal: "Providing structural opportunities [for disputants] to speak is not enough [to promote the legitimacy of a process of dispute resolution]";[114] instead, disputants "must also infer that what they say is being con-sidered by the decision-maker."[115] Of course, insofar as processes of adjudication possess a formal or technical character that makes a tribunal's willingness and, indeed, capacity seriously to consider disputants' views depend on their receiving a particular and (literally) extraordinary expression, lawyers (as specialists in this form of expression) will play a central role in adjudication's legitimacy, which the argument will in a moment take up in earnest.

This account follows in a long tradition that emphasizes the legal process's contribution to political cohesion. It is as old, at least, as Tocqueville's impressed assessment of the lawyerliness of Americans, who, even in "their daily controversies," tend to "borrow . . . the ideas and even the language peculiar to judicial proceedings."[116] One might say, by way of summary (and using words that would be conclusory but for what has come before), that someone who engages the legal process to resolve a dispute but denies its legitimacy when her claims fail on their legal merits commits bad faith against her opponent and against the legal process itself; she in fact retains unreconstructed and perhaps even unreasonable brute demands even as she purports to be asserting reconstructed, reasonable claims of right. And she therefore escalates the dispute from a simple disagreement into a case of deception and manipulation—one might even say fraud. Disputants (who believe, after all, that they are in the right) naturally shrink from such an escalation, and the legal process leverages this attitude—the natural good faith of disputants—in support of the legitimacy of its outcomes, including outcomes that disputants initially opposed.[117]

Of course, this practical account of retail political legitimation and the legal process depends on the effectiveness of the legal process at penetrating disputants' attitudes and at sustaining the transformations in these attitudes and the attendant sense of ownership of outcomes to which it aspires. These legitimating attitudes are not easy to sustain. Moreover, because legitimacy is a normative and political ideal, rather than just a matter of positive psychology, not every way of sustaining such attitudes and establishing the *perception* of legitimacy will *actually* legitimate. Even if the argument succeeds in demonstrating that justice is an inappropriate standard for judging the legal process, the practical approach to the legal process cannot rest on the *bare fact* that disputants accept ownership of the resolutions that the legal process proposes. Rather, the legal process can legitimate the retail application of political power only where the ownership of outcomes that follows engagements with the process is durable and secure; it must also be assumed freely, rather than because of fraud or force, and it must be authentic rather than ideological. These requirements are, to be sure, weaker than the requirement, associated with the theoretical approach to the legitimacy of the legal process, that adjudication must secure substantive justice. But they nevertheless have real bite. Thus, the practical legitimacy of the legal process requires that the sense of ownership of outcomes that the process produces survives even when disputants learn whose interests it serves, for example, or how (that is, by what methods) the legal process established this sense of ownership in them (and how the transformations that followed their engagements with the legal process fit into their broader ethical and political attitudes). In short, the practical political legitimacy of the legal process requires that the experience of ownership that the legal process engenders remain stable in the face of the rational reflection of those who experience it when they apply the critical faculties that they have or can develop.[118]

These considerations naturally return the argument to adversary advocacy (in the broad sense in which I am using the term) and, in particular, to lawyerly fidelity, which lies at the center of the legal process's retail legitimation of political power. Lawyerly fidelity is essential to the legal process's capacity to transform disputants' attitudes so that they take ownership of its outcomes even in spite of its initial strangeness and, moreover, to ensuring that this sense of ownership remains stable in the face of rational reflection among those who experience it. It is, as Karl Llewellyn said, one of the "law-jobs" to sustain authoritative resolutions of "trouble cases."[119] Lawyers "sell . . . legitimacy,"[120] not at wholesale but at retail, one client at a time. And in order to be an effective salesman—one who has (appropriately) satisfied customers—the lawyer must display fidelity and cultivate negative capability. The professional habits of adversary advocates therefore gain in stature insofar as they contribute to the retail legitimation of political power that the legal process is called on to provide.

It is not surprising that the practical approach to legitimating the legal process should, in the end, focus on lawyers and emphasize the lawyer-client relation. Lawyers, as even the harshest critics of the legal profession observe,[121] serve as experts who "mediate between the universal vision of legal order and the concrete desires of [their] clients."[122] And the lawyer-client relation is the nexus of this mediation. It is, as Talcott Parsons observed, "focused" on the "smoothing over" of "situations of actual or potential social conflict."[123]

Certainly, the connection between disputants' *perceptions* of legitimacy and their lawyers' activities has empirical support. A study of felony trials, for example, reported that defendants' attitudes toward the legitimacy of their trial courts were substantially determined by the intensity of their interactions with their lawyers, measured by factors "such as how often their attorney had consulted with them in deciding how to resolve their case."[124] Indeed, the subjective experience of legitimacy seems to have been influenced more by the intensity of defendants' interactions with their *lawyers* than by the intensity of their interactions with their *tribunals* (for example, whether their cases were resolved by plea bargain or trial).[125] Results like these probably should not surprise. After all, the transformative engagements with the legal process that generate the experience of ownership of outcomes on which practical legitimacy depends are administered directly through the lawyer-client relation.

Moreover, lawyers play a central role not only in sustaining *positive perceptions* of legitimacy but also in establishing *actual* legitimacy, understood as a *normative* ideal. The fidelity of lawyers figures particularly prominently in this context, coming into its own as a support for the transformative influence of the legal process. The lawyer, Gordon observes, "cannot deliver unless she can make plausible arguments rationalizing her client's conduct within the prevailing terms of discourse,"[126] and she can do this only insofar as she is able, negatively capably, "to understand the day-to-day world of the client's transactions and deals as somehow approximating, in however decayed or imperfect a form, the ideal fantasy world of the legal order."[127] Adversary advocacy—including lawyerly fidelity and negative capability—is therefore a necessary condition for the transformative power of the legal process, without which the legal process could not appropriately penetrate disputants' attitudes and certainly could not underwrite transformations that remain stable in the face of disputants' rational reflection.

The adversariness of lawyers is necessary for sustaining all the transformations that the legal process engenders, from the shallowest to the deepest. Even the most superficial transformations, associated with the mere translation of claims from ordinary into legal language, will be stable only if clients place a high degree of trust in lawyer-translators. Specifically, clients must trust in lawyers' capacity to *understand* their claims and, moreover, in lawyers' commitments to high fidelity in translation (even when fidelity requires lawyers to ignore their own assessments of the clients' claims).

Only negatively capable lawyers can earn and sustain such trust, because only negatively capable lawyers have the empathy necessary for understanding their clients and the open-mindedness necessary to avoid judging them. If lawyers retreat from adversary ideals of lawyer loyalty and client control and abandon the fidelity that adversariness involves, their efforts at translation will come to be experienced by clients as judgmental and thus foreign and hostile, so that they disrupt rather than enhance the clients' engagements with the legal process. Insofar as lawyers reject fidelity in favor of a more positively capable conception of their professional roles, lawyers' professional behavior "grows introverted, preoccupied with its own norms and activities,"[128] so that the "institution [of the legal profession] develops a carapace, impermeable to external information, prescription, or influence."[129] And, when this happens, lawyers' efforts at translation inevitably fail, and "the problems [the legal profession] handles are the problems defined by the institution, not the society; the solutions it generates are solutions for the institution, not the society."[130] As one bar group has warned, lawyers who judge their clients become "servants of the system rather than the bulwark between organized power and the individual."[131] Rather than serving as intermediaries whose interpretive efforts connect clients to the legal process, nonadversary lawyers confront clients as an unmediated part of the process. And, rather than bringing clients into the legal process in ways that support its legitimacy, nonadversary lawyers alienate clients in ways that undermine the legal process's authority.

Moreover, lawyers' ability to dampen disputes by encouraging clients to abandon or modify their most unreasonable positions—the intermediate of the three transformations in client attitudes that sustain the practical legitimacy of the legal process—also depends on their commitment to fidelity and on the negative capability that follows from this commitment. This is, to begin with, a matter of psychology and even of emotion. Disputants' most unreasonable positions often reflect frustration and anger, rather than considered judgments, so that the disputants are open to being talked down and may even seek out ways to back off their most extreme positions. But only a sympathetic and nonjudgmental counsel will inspire the trust needed to cool passions in this way. As Parsons says, "In order to be capable, psychologically, of 'getting things off his chest' a person must be assured that, within certain limits . . . sanctions will not operate. . . . The confidential character of the lawyer's relation to his client [and, Parsons might have added, the lawyer's loyalty and deference more generally] provides such a situation. The client can talk freely, to an understanding and knowledgeable ear, without fear of immediate repercussions."[132]

In addition, the adversary lawyer's unique capacity to deflate her clients' most extreme claims has an ethical component. Both ethical theory[133] and empirical research[134] suggest that disputants have a natural ethical inclination in favor of resolving disputes through reasonable reciprocal concessions. But most clients, being inexperienced in the disputes in which they are engaged, are uncertain which concessions are in fact reasonable. Lawyers have experience and expertise that clients do not and can therefore help to resolve this uncertainty. But lawyers will be trusted to do so only when clients are confident that they remain faithful in spite of giving deflationary advice and that the advice they give reflects a refined and sympathetic understanding of the clients' positions—only, that is, when lawyers accept the adversary obligations associated with fidelity and display the negative capability needed sensitively to discern what fidelity requires.

In these ways, adversary advocates support both the psychological and the ethical mechanisms through which engagements with the legal process persuade disputants voluntarily to abandon their most aggressive and unreasonable demands. And adversary advocates therefore transform disputants' attitudes in legitimacy-enhancing ways, whereas lawyers who abandon their adversary obligations and judge their clients, rather than serving them, undermine trust and therefore have an opposite, delegitimating effect.[135]

Finally, lawyers' adversary commitments are especially important for transforming clients' claims from brute demands into assertions of right whose implicitly defeasible character makes the deepest contribution to the legitimacy of the legal process. Once again, "a high degree of trust and confidence are usually necessary [if lawyers are] to `sell' [the] new definition of the situation" that the conversion of brute demands into claims of right involves,[136] and lawyers' adversary commitments justify their clients' trust. Furthermore, the internal logic of the legal process (and not just the willingness of clients to go along) also emphasizes the importance for legitimacy of using adversary advocates to convert disputants' brute demands into assertions of right. The legal process insists that disputants frame their demands as assertions of right because of a commitment, on which its legitimacy depends, to address every assertion of right that can be made in support of a disputant's position. Accordingly, the lawyers who help disputants to transform their brute demands into assertions of right must not fail to assert any rights that are immanent in their clients' positions. (Such unasserted rights cannot be addressed in adjudication and therefore threaten to undermine legitimacy by coming between disputants and the resolutions to disputes that the legal process proposes.) And lawyers can do this only if they keep faith with their clients and, negatively capably, amplify and refine all their clients' claims, rather than evaluating and choosing among them.

Lawyers who abandon their adversary role in favor of positively capable personal assessments of their clients' claims quite literally prejudge these claims. And, when this happens, the legitimacy of the legal process becomes dependent on the legitimacy of the lawyers' judgments. But these judgments, being creatures of the lawyers' individual minds, are virtually impossible to legitimate and certainly cannot be legitimated by reference to the transformative powers of a legal process that has not yet begun. Lawyers who abandon their adversary role merely shift the burden of legitimation forward to their own assessments, which necessarily address their clients' demands in an untransformed and hence intractable state.[137]

These arguments do not, to be sure, countenance untrammeled partisanship in lawyers. Both the adversary system and the ideals of fidelity and negative capability that govern the conduct of adversary advocates are self-limiting, in the sense of imposing boundaries on the partisanship that they countenance. Even as these ideals require lawyers to be partisan champions for their clients, they contain within them the seeds of restrictions against partisan excess. (For example, even as a negatively capable lawyer must preserve client confidences, she may not allow her own reputation to be used, positively capably, in the service of a client's fraud.) Moreover, this self-regulating tendency reappears in the present context, as well, because, just as a disputant may become alienated from adjudication if her own lawyer judges rather than serves her, so she may also become alienated if left at the mercy of an opposing lawyer whose partisanship in favor of his client is too aggressive and succeeds at subverting the legal process into a one-sided tool of his client's will.

But, although excessive partisanship undermines the legitimacy of adjudication, some partisanship—that is, legal representation by advocates who are recognizably adversary and therefore expose themselves to the lawyerly vices that render their ethics so difficult—remains essential for legitimacy. In order to legitimate its outcomes, the legal process must welcome, rather than estrange, the disputants who might engage it. If, as Lon Fuller observed, "The distinguishing characteristic of adjudication lies in the fact that it confers on the affected party a peculiar form of *participation* in the decision,"[138] then "Whatever heightens the significance of this participation lifts adjudication toward its optimum expression," which is to say that it increases the legal process's legitimacy.[139] And, because lawyers provide the principal connection between disputants and the legal process, the burden of inviting disputants to engage the legal process and of sustaining disputants' participation falls principally on them.

In order successfully to shoulder this burden, lawyers must deny the potentially alienating features of adjudication (in particular, the legal process's divided sympathies) any foothold within the lawyer-client relation itself; instead, they must structure the lawyer-client relation so that they are able, through it, to "bring . . . the client's case in a nonjudgmental way to the authoritative institutions of society."[140] Only adversary advocates, who practice the negatively capable lawyerly virtues that I have elaborated, can achieve this. And these virtues therefore carry all the ethical significance of being necessary for sustaining the transformations in disputants' attitudes on which the legitimacy of the legal process depends.

V. CONCLUSION

As Parsons observed, "The primary function of the legal system is integrative."[141] The law "serves to mitigate potential elements of conflict and to oil the machinery of social intercourse."[142] Moreover, this integrative function is essential to social coordination. "It is, indeed, only by adherence to a system of rules that systems of social interaction can function without breaking down into overt or chronic covert conflict."[143]

The law integrates through the transformative powers of the legal process, which operate through the efforts of the lawyers who administer this process and invite disputants to engage it. To be sure, lawyers, including perhaps particularly adversary ones, may encourage conflict in particular cases. But, when viewed from a more fundamental perspective—one that asks not how persons decide about incremental assertions of their legal rights but rather how persons who face intractable disagreements at every level of principle can nevertheless sustain peaceful social coordination at all—lawyers are peacemakers. And lawyers can successfully invite litigants to engage the legal process (and open themselves up to the transformations that the process engenders) only if they resist themselves judging their clients—only, that is, if they serve their clients faithfully, in a way that cultivates the fidelity that I have described.

Lawyerly fidelity is therefore not a makeshift or even a sham ideal but instead lies at the very center of the law's claim to legitimacy; indeed, it appears as a retail analog to the democratic virtues that are so notoriously celebrated throughout the civilized world.

> Viewed in this light, the role of the lawyer as a partisan advocate appears not as a regrettable necessity, but as an indispensable part of a larger ordering of affairs. The institution of advocacy is not a concession to the frailties of human nature, but an expression of human insight in the design of a social framework within which man's capacity for impartial judgment can attain its fullest realization.[144]

NOTES

This essay condenses arguments elaborated at greater length in Daniel Markovits, *A Modern Legal Ethics: Adversary Advocacy in a Democratic Age* (Princeton: Princeton University Press, 2008). I would like to thank Sandy Levinson for the invitation to participate in this volume and Joel Parker for outstanding and patient editorial work.

1. The adversary advocate's duty of zeal in support of her client appears on the face of all the major statements of the law governing lawyers in the past century. See *Canons of Professional Ethics*, Canon 15 (1908) (requiring a lawyer to represent a client with "warm zeal"); *Model Code of Professional Responsibility*, Canon 7 (1969) (requiring a lawyer to "represent a client zealously within the bounds of law"); *Model Rules of Professional Conduct*, R. 1.3 cmt. 1 (2003) (requiring a lawyer to act "with zeal in advocacy upon the client's behalf").

2. Geoffrey C. Hazard Jr. and W. William Hodes, *The Law of Lawyering: A Handbook on The Model Rules of Professional Conduct*, vol. 1, 2nd ed., Supp. § 1.3:106 (Englewood Cliffs, NJ: Prentice Hall Law & Business, 1993), 75 n.1.

3. See *Model Rules of Prof'l Conduct*, R. 2.3.

4. Cf. Robert H. Mnookin and Lewis Kornhauser, "Bargaining in the Shadow of the Law: The Case of Divorce," *Yale Law Journal* 88 (April 1979): 950–97.

5. The ethics rules governing lawyers who give tax advice present an illustrative example. These rules permit lawyers to advise their clients to take positions on tax returns as long as the positions have "a realistic possibility of success if litigated," a standard that expressly allows a lawyer to advise reporting a position "even where the lawyer believes the position probably will not prevail, there is no `substantial authority' in support of the position, and there will be no disclosure of the position on the return." *ABA Commission on Ethics and Professional Responsibility*, Formal Op. 85–352 (1985).

6. See *Model Rules of Prof'l Conduct*, R. 1.6.

7. Ibid., R. 3.3 and cmt. 14.

8. John H. Langbein, "The German Advantage in Civil Procedure," *University of Chicago Law Review* 52 (Fall 1985): 824.

9. Ibid. More specifically, they "suggest legal theories and lines of factual inquiry, they superintend and supplement judicial examination of witnesses, they urge inferences from fact, they discuss and distinguish precedent, they interpret statutes, and they formulate visions of the law that further the interests of their clients."

10. Ibid., 841.

11. See *Canons of Prof'l Ethics*, Canon 15. The phrase comes from George Sharswood's pioneering essay on legal ethics, which instructed lawyers to display "[e]ntire devotion of the interests of the client [and] warm zeal in the maintenance and defense of his rights." George Sharswood, *An Essay on Professional Ethics*, 5th ed. (Philadelphia: T. & J. W. Johnson, 1896 [photo. reprint 1993]), 78–80.

12. *Model Code of Prof'l Responsibility*, Canon 7.

13. Ibid., DR 7-101(A)(1).

14. *Model Rules of Prof'l Conduct*, R. 1.3 ("A lawyer shall act with reasonable diligence and promptness in representing a client.").

15. Ibid., Preamble ¶ 14.

16. Ibid., R. 1.3 cmt. 1.

17. See ibid., Preamble ¶¶ 2, 8, 9.

18. *Restatement (Third) of the Law Governing Lawyers*, § 16(1) (2000).

19. Hazard and Hodes, *The Law of Lawyering*, vol. 1, 2nd ed., § 1.2:103 (1990), 24. Hazard elsewhere says that "the partisanship principle remains at the core of the profession's soul." Geoffrey Hazard, "The Future of Legal Ethics," *Yale Law Journal* 100 (March 1991): 1245.

20. See Daniel Markovits, *A Modern Legal Ethics: Adversary Advocacy in a Democratic Age* (Princeton: Princeton University Press, 2008), 22–78.

21. Ted Schneyer, "Moral Philosophy's Standard Misconception of Legal Ethics," *Wisconsin Law Review* 1984 (1984): 1555.

22. *Model Rules of Prof'l Conduct*, R. 1.2.

23. *Model Code of Prof'l Responsibility*, DR 7-101(A)(1) (1980).

24. *Restatement (Third) of the Law Governing Lawyers*, § 21(2)–(3) (2000).

25. The several ethics regimes differ, for example, in how friendly they are to efforts to change the boundaries of client control by contract.

26. Olfe v. Gordon, 286 N.W.2d 573, 577 (Wis. 1980) (quotation marks and citation omitted).

27. *Model Rules of Prof'l Conduct*, R. 2.1.

28. Specifically, Rule 1.2 says that, "as required by Rule 1.4, [the lawyer] shall consult with the client as to the means by which [the client's objectives] are to be pursued." *Model Rules of Prof'l Conduct*, R. 1.2(a). Rule 1.4 addresses consultation and communication between lawyer and client. See *Model Rules of Prof'l Conduct*, R. 1.4.

29. *Model Rules of Prof'l Conduct*, R. 1.2 cmt. 2. See also *Restatement (Third) of the Law Governing Lawyers*, § 23 and cmt. c (2000) for more on the client's control of her lawyer's actions with respect to harming third parties.

30. *Model Rules of Prof'l Conduct*, R. 1.2 cmt. 2.

31. This privilege is, fundamentally, a creature of tort law. See *Restatement (Second) of Torts*, § 586 (1977). The privilege is also recognized by the law of agency, see *Restatement (Third) of Agency*, § 7.01 cmt. e (2006); and the

law governing lawyers, see *Restatement (Third) of the Law Governing Lawyers*, § 57(1) (2000); see also Hazard and Hodes, *The Law of Lawyering*, vol. 1, 2nd ed., Supp. § 1.1:205 (1998), 18.38. Cases applying the privilege are collected in Ronald E. Mallen and Jeffrey M. Smith, *Legal Malpractice*, vol. 1, 3rd ed., § 6.25 (St. Paul, MN: West, 1989), 353–54. The privilege is critically appraised in Paul Hayden, "Reconsidering the Litigator's Absolute Privilege to Defame," *Ohio State Law Journal* 54 (1993): 985–1058.

32. See, e.g., Salaymeh v. Interqual, Inc., 508 N.E.2d 1155 (Ill. 1987). An exception exists for cases in which the lawyer's advice reflects "actual malice" against the victim of the breach that is "unrelated to [her] desire to protect [her] client." Salaymeh v. Interqual, Inc., 508 N.E.2d 1155, 1160 (Ill. 1987).

33. Reves v. Ernst & Young, 507 U.S. 170 (1993) (interpreting the "conduct or participate" language of the Federal RICO statute). Similarly, a lawyer who files an application on behalf of a client seeking to seize goods on the basis of trademark violations is not an "applicant" under the Lanham Act and so not liable if the seizure turns out to be unwarranted. See, e.g., Electronic Laboratory Supply Co. v. Cullen, 977 F.2d 798 (3d Cir. 1992).

34. See *Restatement (Second) of Torts*, § 772 (1979). See also Hazard and Hodes, *The Law of Lawyering*, vol. 1, 2nd ed., Supp. § 1.1:205 (1998), 18.37. See also Mallen and Smith, *Legal Malpractice*, vol. 1., § 6.23, 348–52.

35. *Restatement (Second) of Torts*, § 10, cmt. d (1965). ("The most frequent instances of such absolute or indefeasible privileges are those given to the judiciary and to other persons such as witnesses, jurymen, and counsel who aid in the administration of the law.")

36. *Model Rules of Prof'l Conduct*, R. 3.1 (2003). Rule 1.2(d) similarly forbids lawyers to counsel clients to do something illegal but allows them to counsel clients to make good-faith efforts to determine the "validity, scope, meaning or application of the law." See *Model Rules of Prof'l Conduct*, R. 1.2(d) (2003).

37. See *Federal Rules of Civil Procedure*, R. 11; see also R. 26(g) (extending Rule 11 to the discovery process); 28 U.S.C. § 1927 (2006) (making lawyers personally liable for costs and attorney's fees that result when they "multipl[y] the proceedings in any case unreasonably and vexatiously" in federal court).

38. Courts have given this license to exploit procedure practical effect. See, e.g., Sussman v. Bank of Isr., 56 F.3d 450 (2d Cir. 1995); see also Hazard and Hodes, *The Law of Lawyering*, vol. 1, 2nd ed., Supp. § 3.1:202 (1996), 550 n. 1.01.

39. See William L. Prosser, *Handbook of the Law of Torts*, 4th ed. (St. Paul, MN: West, 1971), 851–52.

40. *Model Rules of Prof'l Conduct*, R. 1.2(b) (2003).

41. David Luban, "Selling Indulgences: The Unmistakable Parallel between Lynne Stewart and the President's Torture Lawyers," *Slate* (14 February 2005), http://www.slate.com/id/2113447/. Luban is, of course, a critic of lawyers' nonaccountability.

42. The old ABA Canons of Ethics provide the most important exception to this rule. Canon 5 expressly associated the "right of the lawyer to undertake the defense of a person accused of crime regardless of his personal opinion as to the guilt of the accused" with the duty, "having undertaken such defense," to use "all fair and honorable means . . . to present every defense that the law of the land permits." *Canons of Professional Ethics,* Canon 5 (1965). A less important, because only partial, statement of the mandatory character of professional detachment survives to this day in the rule that lawyers may not vouch for their clients in court, that they may not "assert personal knowledge of facts in issue . . . or state a personal opinion as to the justness of a cause, the credibility of a witness, the culpability of a civil litigant, or the guilt or innocence of an accused." *Model Rules of Prof'l Conduct,* R. 3.4(e) (2003). A virtually identical command appears in the Model Code and in the Restatement. See *Model Code of Prof'l Responsibility,* DR 7-106(C)(4) (1980) and *Restatement (Third) of the Law Governing Lawyers,* § 107(1) (2000). Professional detachment is more familiar in the lore of the bar. Macmillan, for example, said not just that, "[i]n pleading a case, an advocate is not stating his own opinions" but added that "it is not part of his business and he has no right to do so." See, e.g., Lord Macmillan, *Law and Other Things* (Cambridge: Cambridge University Press, 1937), 181.

43. A lawyer might refuse to ask a jury to acquit his client (see Johns v. Smyth, 176 F. Supp. 949 (E.D. Va. 1959)), tell the jury in open court that he believes his client to be guilty (see People v. Swanson, 943 F.2d 1070 (9th Cir. 1991) (citing Osborn v. Shillinger, 861 F.2d 612, 629 (10th Cir. 1988))), tell an appellate court that, although his client claims that the evidence at trial was insufficient to support a conviction, he does not agree (see People v. Lang, 11 Cal. 3d 134, 138 (1974)), or argue at sentencing that his client has a bad character and deserves a harsh punishment (see Osborn v. Shillinger, 861 F.2d 612, 628–29 (10th Cir. 1988)).

44. Von Molke v. Gillies, 332 U.S. 708, 725 (1948). The point is also made elsewhere. See, e.g., Wood v. Georgia, 450 U.S. 261, 271–72 (1981) (holding that the Sixth Amendment right to counsel contains a "correlative right to representation that is free from conflicts of interest"); State v. Christenson, 820 P.2d 1303, 1306 (Mont. 1991) (holding that the Sixth Amendment right to effective assistance of counsel includes a right to counsel's "undivided loyalty").

45. People v. Lang, 11 Cal. 3d 134, 139 (1974).

46. Ibid.

47. United States *ex rel* Wilcox v. Johnson, 555 F.2d 115, 122 (3d Cir. 1977); see also State v. Jones, 923 P.2d 560, 566 (Mont. 1996).

48. Frazer v. United States, 18 F.3d 778, 782 (9th Cir. 1994) (quoting United States v. Swanson, 943 F.2d 1070, 1074 (9th Cir. 1991)).

49. State v. Jones, 923 P.2d, 566.

50. Frazer v. United States, 18 F.3d at 782. See also Osborn v. Shillinger, 861 F.2d 612, 629 (10th Cir. 1988); United States v. Swanson, 943 F.2d, 1075; State v. Jones, 923 P.2d, 566.

51. Johns v. Smyth, 176 F. Supp. 949, 953 (E.D. Va. 1959).

52. Frazer v. United States, 18 F.3d, 782 (quoting *Swanson*, 943 F.2d, 1074 (quoting *Osborn*, 86 F.2d, 625 (quoting United States v. Cronic, 466 U.S. 648, 666 (1984)))).

53. Sanctions have been recommended against lawyers who breach their duties of professional detachment. See, e.g., United States v. Swanson, 943 F.2d, 1076.

54. See Strickland v. Washington, 466 U.S. 668 (1984).

55. United States v. Cronic, 466 U.S. 648, 659 (1984); see also Cuyler v. Sullivan, 446 U.S. 335, 349–50 (1980); Wood v. Georgia, 450 U.S. 261, 272 (1981); Burger v. Kemp, 483 U.S. 776, 783 (1986); Mickens v. Taylor, 535 U.S. 162 (2002).

56. State v. Jones, 923 P.2d 560, 566 (Mont. 1996) (quoting *Frazer*, 18 F.3d, 784). A loyal and professionally detached counsel is in this respect like an impartial and engaged fact finder (that is, a fact finder that seeks without bias to impose its view of the truth), which is also essential to the authority of the judicial process. See, e.g., United States v. Nelson, 277 F.3d 164 (2d Cir. 2002). The different requirements that apply in the two cases—the lawyer's loyalty and detachment and the fact finder's impartiality and engagement—are explained by the different contributions that lawyers and fact finders make to the overall authority of adjudication. I take up the lawyer's contribution in detail in Part III.

57. See, e.g., *In re* Harshey, 740 N.E.2d 851 (Ind. 2001). Moreover, the rule that a lawyer may not impose her private judgment of a client's claim on settlements applies even outside the immediate shadow of a tribunal. For example, "A lawyer may not ethically break off negotiations with an opposing party simply because she has doubts about the viability of her client's case." See *ABA Commission on Ethics and Professional Responsibility*, Formal Op. 94–387 (1994).

58. See, e.g., Singleton v. Foreman, 435 F.2d 962, 970 (5th Cir. 1970). The Singleton court expressly added that the conflict can arise even when the adversity between lawyer and client is not "of an economic character."

59. Geoffrey C. Hazard Jr., "Ethical Opportunity in the Practice of Law," *San Diego Law Review* 27 (January 1990): 135–38.

60. *Model Rules of Prof'l Conduct*, Preamble ¶ 8 (1983). Moreover, the tension between a lawyer's professional obligations and her personal ethics also cannot be resolved by the suggestion, which dominates legal ethics and again appears in the Model Rules, that the *adversary system* in which the lawyer participates allows her to "be a zealous advocate on behalf of a client and at the same time assume that justice is being done." Even if the adversary system defense can be established, so that the partiality that lawyers are charged with displaying is revealed to be a mere illusion, brought on by taking too narrow a view of the lawyers' activities, this will not refute the separate charge that lawyers are vicious. The adversary system defense merely casts the lawyerly vices as necessary evils. But lawyers have good reason, as the remark in the Model Rules about "remaining an upright person" implicitly acknowledges, to want to understand themselves as not evil at all.

61. Something like an ideal of lawyerly fraternity is developed in Anthony T. Kronman, *The Lost Lawyer: Failing Ideals of the Legal Profession* (Cambridge, MA: Belknap Press, 1993).

62. The canonical account of lawyerly friendship appears in Charles Fried, "The Lawyer as Friend: The Moral Foundations of the Lawyer-Client Relation," *Yale Law Journal* 85 (July 1976): 1060–89.

63. The contrasts that I emphasize in the main text are not the only ones. Another, familiar difference is that lawyers may look to their private interests in entering the lawyer-client relation in ways in which compatriots and friends may not.

64. The true patriot, for example, does not endorse her country right or wrong but instead serves her country by insisting that it improve, and the true friend insists that her wayward comrade mend his ways.

65. Recall Model Rule 1.2.

66. Note, however, that where Plato's analogy is between two harmonies—between a state governed by the wise and a soul governed by reason—the analogy that I shall develop is between two disharmonies. The lawyer and the poet both preside, as we shall see, over perpetual conflict. Plato, of course, had his own views about poets; see Plato, *The Republic*, trans. Paul Shorey, § 603a (1930), in *The Collected Dialogues of Plato, including the Letters*, ed. Edith Hamilton and Huntington Cairns (New York: Pantheon, 1961). I shall not even try to address the complicated question of the relation between Plato's account of poets and Keats's.

67. Keats introduced the term "negative capability" in John Keats, "Letter to George and Tom Keats, 21, 27 (?) Dec. 1817," in *Letters of John Keats: A New Selection*, ed. Robert Gittings (London: Oxford University Press, 1970), 43.

68. John Keats, "Letter to Richard Woodhouse, 27 Oct. 1818," in *Letters of John Keats,* 157.

69. Such empathy should not be confused with warmer self-sacrificing virtues such as generosity, which is why it is not undermined by the fact that lawyers are paid and, indeed, for hire.

70. See Charles P. Curtis, "The Ethics of Advocacy," *Stanford Law Review* 4 (December 1951): 17.

71. Keats, "Letter to Richard Woodhouse, 27 Oct. 1818," in *Letters of John Keats,* 158.

72. Macmillan, *Law and Other Things,* 1.

73. Francis Bacon, "Essay 32: Of Discourse," in *Francis Bacon, The Essays,* ed. John Pitcher (Harmondsworth, Eng.: Penguin, 1985), 160.

74. Frederick Scott Oliver, *Ordeal by Battle* (London: Macmillan, 1915), 201.

75. Keats, "Letter to George and Tom Keats, 21, 27 (?) Dec. 1817," in *Letters of John Keats,* 43.

76. Hazard and Hodes, *The Law of Lawyering,* vol. 1, 2nd ed., Supp., Introduction § 403 (1998), Intro–26.

77. Keats, "Letter to George and Tom Keats, 21, 27 (?) Dec. 1817," in *Letters of John Keats,* 43.

78. Lon L. Fuller and John D. Randall, "Professional Responsibility: Report of the Joint Conference," *ABA Journal* 44 (December 1958): 1160 (excerpted in Lon L. Fuller, "The Forms and Limits of Adjudication," *Harvard Law Review* 92 (December 1978): 383).

79. In this feature, my account of negative capability displays some similarity to certain ideas Roberto Unger has developed under the same heading. See, e.g., Roberto Mangabeira Unger, "The Critical Legal Studies Movement," *Harvard Law Review* 96 (January 1983): 650–53.

80. Kronman, *The Lost Lawyer,* 66–74.

81. John Rawls has famously called this the "fact of pluralism." See John Rawls, *Political Liberalism* (New York: Columbia University Press, 1993), 36, 64, 144.

82. Ibid.; see also John Rawls, *A Theory of Justice* (Cambridge, MA: Belknap Press, 1971).

83. Rawls, *Political Liberalism,* 217 (and on the back of the dust jacket).

84. Process plays a role in Rawls's theory, to be sure, in particular, in the Original Position and the idea of pure procedural justice. See Rawls, *A Theory of Justice,* 86. But the Original Position remains, as Rawls stresses, a "purely hypothetical" situation (ibid., 120), and the appeal of the principles of justice that arise out of the Original Position depends on the theoretical appeal of the Original Position as a device for *representing* the

problem of justice and not on any affective engagements that result from actually *inhabiting* it.

85. My emphasis on the need for political philosophy to take into account disagreement not just about the first-order uses of political power that a theory of legitimacy seeks to justify but also about legitimacy itself (disagreement, in other words, at every level of the theory) resembles Jeremy Waldron's emphasis on the importance of taking into account disagreement about justice. See Jeremy Waldron, *Law and Disagreement* (Oxford: Clarendon, 1999).

86. This is a familiar and, I take it, uncontroversial point. See, e.g., Thomas Nagel, "Moral Conflict and Political Legitimacy," *Philosophy & Public Affairs* 16 (Summer 1987): 218; Joseph Raz, "Facing Diversity: The Case of Epistemic Abstinence," *Philosophy & Public Affairs* 19 (Winter 1990): 32. In order for political philosophy even to get off the ground as a rational and critical enterprise, it must answer to standards apart from persons' actual, brute beliefs.

87. This formulation of course tracks Rawls's account of reasonable *moral* pluralism. Rawls characterizes reasonable moral pluralism as "the inevitable long-run result of the powers of human reason at work within the background of enduring free institutions" (Rawls, *Political Liberalism*, 4), and he therefore insists that it is "not an unfortunate condition of human life" (ibid., 144). By applying the same logic to reasonable pluralism about political legitimacy, I am turning the method of pluralist political philosophy in on itself. (The relation to Waldron's work is particularly close here; see Waldron, *Law and Disagreement*.)

88. See Daniel Markovits, "Democratic Disobedience," *Yale Law Journal* 114 (June 2005): 1897–1952.

89. Adjudication is not, of course, the only available method for resolving disputes about how general principles should be applied in particular cases. *Contract*, perhaps surprisingly, presents an alternative form of retail dispute resolution. I take up this possibility and also the relationship between contract and adjudication in Daniel Markovits, "Arbitration's Arbitrage: Social Solidarity at the Nexus of Adjudication and Contract," *DePaul Law Review* 59 (Clifford Symposium on Civil Justice) (Winter 2010):431–88.

90. The need to moderate adversary advocacy in the face of imperfections in the legal system is emphasized by David Luban and by William Simon. See David Luban, *Lawyers and Justice: An Ethical Study* (Princeton: Princeton University Press, 1988), 67–103; William Simon, *The Practice of Justice: A Theory of Lawyers' Ethics* (Cambridge, MA: Harvard University Press, 1998), 53–76.

91. This idea is developed in Luban, *Lawyers and Justice*, and in Arthur

Applbaum, *Ethics for Adversaries: The Morality of Roles in Public and Professional Life* (Princeton: Princeton University Press, 1999).

92. Robert W. Gordon, "The Radical Conservatism of the Practice of Justice," *Stanford Law Review* 51 (April 1999): 922 (reviewing Simon, *The Practice of Justice*).

93. Ibid.

94. Prominent examples include Luban, *Lawyers and Justice*; Simon, *The Practice of Justice*; and Applbaum, *Ethics for Adversaries*.

95. To be sure, dissatisfaction with adversary adjudication, especially among those who have just gone through it, is one of the banalities of contemporary legal culture. But the acceptance of adjudication's legitimate authority in spite of this dissatisfaction is equally entrenched in the culture. Disputants commonly satisfy verdicts without the need for separate enforcement proceedings (and often with little credible threat of sanctions should they resist). Even when voluntary compliance with adjudication breaks down—for example, in connection with the collection of child support from absentee fathers, see Drew A. Swank, "The National Child Non-Support Epidemic," *Michigan State Law Review* 2003 (Summer 2003): 358–59, although even here there is some reason to believe that delinquency is caused by inability rather than unwillingness to make payments, see Ronald K. Henry, "Child Support at a Crossroads: When the Real World Intrudes upon Academics and Advocates," *Family Law Quarterly* 33 (Spring 1999): 237—the success of resistance against judgments only emphasizes the extent to which compliance with the legal process more generally exceeds whatever compulsion legal institutions could credibly assert. And, although the dissatisfaction is more discussed, the degree of acceptance of the legitimacy of adjudication is *much* more striking, since it requires losing disputants to accept the authority of decisions that they (reasonably) believe mistaken on the merits.

96. David Trubek, "The Handmaiden's Revenge: On Reading and Using the Newer Sociology of Civil Procedure," *Law and Contemporary Problems* 51 (Autumn 1988): 115. "Transparent procedure," as Trubek says, takes the litigants as they come to the court" (ibid.). It "does not add or subject anything" to their dispute, so that it "should not make a difference to the [right] outcome of a dispute" (ibid., 114).

97. See William L. F. Felstiner, Richard L. Abel, and Austin Sarat, "The Emergence and Transformation of Disputes: Naming, Blaming, Claiming . . . " *Law & Society Review* 15 (Special Issue on Dispute Processing and Civil Litigation) (1980–81): 640.

98. Lynn Mather and Barbara Yngvesson, "Language, Audience, and the Transformation of Disputes," *Law & Society Review* 15 (Special Issue on Dispute Processing and Civil Litigation) (1980–81): 791.

99. Ronen Shamir, *Managing Legal Uncertainty: Elite Lawyers in the New Deal* (Durham, NC: Duke University Press, 1995), 38.

100. Maureen Cain, "The General Practice Lawyer and the Client: Towards a Radical Conception," *International Journal of the Sociology of Law* 7 (November 1979): 343.

101. Mather and Yngvesson, "Language, Audience, and the Transformation of Disputes," 792.

102. Stewart Macaulay, "Lawyers and Consumer Protection Laws," *Law & Society Review* 14 (Autumn 1979): 125.

103. Felstiner, Abel, and Sarat, "The Emergence and Transformation of Disputes," 646.

104. Jeffrey Fitzgerald and Richard Dickins, "Disputing in Legal and Nonlegal Contexts: Some Questions for Sociologists of Law," *Law & Society Review* 15 (Special Issue on Dispute Processing and Civil Litigation) (1980–81): 698.

105. This effect emphasizes "the impact on the client of the lawyer's *attitude,* his expression or implied approval of this as so legitimate that a lawyer is willing to help him get it, whereas other elements of the client's goals are disapproved and help in getting them is refused." Talcott Parsons, "The Law and Social Control," in *Law and Sociology: Exploratory Essays*, ed. William M. Evan (New York: Free Press of Glencoe, 1962), 70.

106. See Fuller, "The Forms and Limits of Adjudication," 368. Fuller imagines a baseball player who transforms his brute claim to play catcher into a claim of right based on his being the best catcher available and therefore implicitly acknowledges that he must abandon his claim in case a more skilled catcher appears.

107. Macaulay, "Lawyers and Consumer Protection Laws," 128.

108. Lon L. Fuller, "Mediation: Its Forms and Functions," *Southern California Law Review* 44 (Winter 1971): 325. Fuller wrote these words as part of a discussion of mediation, which he sought in certain respects to contrast with adjudication (ibid., 328), so that my appropriation of Fuller's characterization stands in some tension with his official position on adjudication. I quote Fuller nevertheless because I believe that my account is generally in sympathy with Fuller's broader emphasis on the legitimating character of adjudication. See, e.g., Fuller, "The Forms and Limits of Adjudication."

109. Felstiner, Abel, and Sarat, "The Emergence and Transformation of Disputes," 650 (emphasis added).

110. These studies do, however, suggest that the importance of process for legitimacy is not confined to trivial disputes but instead increases when the stakes are high. See Tom R. Tyler, "The Psychology of Disputant Concerns in Mediation," *Negotiation Journal* 3 (October 1987): 367–74; Tom R. Tyler, *Why People Obey the Law* (New Haven: Yale University Press, 1990), 105.

111. Tyler, *Why People Obey the Law*, 103.

112. Ibid., 102.

113. Ibid., 126.

114. Ibid., 149.

115. Ibid.

116. Alexis de Tocqueville, *Democracy in America*, ed. Francis Bowen (Boston: J. Allyn, 1876), 357.

117. This argument for the legitimacy of adjudication has its limitations, of course. Most immediately, its practical character and its focus on legitimacy entail that the forms of adjudication that it describes will fall short of producing justice, especially when measured by the more exacting standards of theoretical models. Stability is not the only value, after all, and even peace is not worth every price. There is much in this view, to be sure, and the peaceful resolutions to disputes that the transformative legal process sustains certainly can come at an unacceptable cost to justice, including perhaps in some of the cases just mentioned. But this argument should not be taken too far. Insofar as procedure is transformative, then the outcomes that disputants are prepared to accept after having engaged the legal process *necessarily* differ from the outcomes that they set out to pursue through this process or that they regarded as antecedently just, and disputants who have come through the legal process will prefer these outcomes to alternatives that they initially rated more highly. Accordingly, unless one is prepared to cast the legal process's transformative powers as absolutely and irredeemably oppressive, so that the aims parties bring to a dispute are necessarily more worthy of respect than the aims that they take from it, one must approve some portion of the inevitable departures from antecedent notions of justice that the process generates. And such an extreme skepticism of adjudication's transformative powers neglects the *political* character of legitimacy. It is unreasonable to evaluate post-process outcomes based exclusively on pre-process attitudes and standards, because legitimacy is the most that can be hoped for in the shadow of the deep and intractable disagreements that disputes involve. *Only* transformative procedures can hope to sustain a stable political life in the face of these disagreements. And it is therefore a piece of good fortune—and not a thing to be lamented—that our practical nature leaves us susceptible to the transformative effects of procedure, for if we were not so susceptible, collective life would not be possible for us.

118. The practical account of political legitimacy follows a middle path between insisting on justice on the one hand and affirming whatever people can be made to accept on the other. In this way, the practical account proposes a decentralized and also naturalized approach to political philosophy: the practical account of political legitimacy replaces elaborate

theorizing about which political arrangements are best or most just with a much sparer account of what people whose reasoning is functioning normally (but not necessarily ideally) are willing to accept. Here I borrow from critical theory. See, e.g., Raymond Geuss, *The Idea of a Critical Theory: Habermas and the Frankfurt School* (Cambridge: Cambridge University Press, 1981).

119. K. N. Llewellyn and E. Adamson Hoebel, *The Cheyenne Way: Conflict and Case Law in Primitive Jurisprudence* (Norman: University of Oklahoma Press, 1941), 293.

120. Robert Gordon, "The Ideal and the Actual in the Law: Fantasies and Practices of New York City Lawyers, 1870–1910," in *The New High Priests: Lawyers in Post-Civil War America*, ed. Gerard W. Gawalt (Westport, CT: Greenwood, 1984), 53–54.

121. Richard L. Abel, *American Lawyers* (New York: Oxford University Press, 1989), 34–35.

122. Ibid.

123. Parsons, "The Law and Social Control," 63.

124. Tyler, "The Psychology of Disputant Concerns in Mediation." See also Jonathan D. Casper, *Criminal Courts: The Defendant's Perspective* (Washington, DC: National Institute of Law Enforcement and Criminal Justice, 1970); Jonathan D. Casper, Tom Tyler, and Bonnie Fisher, "Procedural Justice in Felony Cases," *Law & Society Review* 22 (1988): 483–508.

125. Tyler, "The Psychology of Disputant Concerns in Mediation."

126. Gordon, "The Ideal and the Actual in the Law," 53–54.

127. Ibid.

128. Richard Abel, "A Comparative Theory of Dispute Institutions in Society," *Law & Society Review* 8 (Winter 1973): 265.

129. Ibid.

130. Ibid.

131. This language, quoted in Ted Schneyer, "Professionalism as Politics: The Making of a Modern Legal Ethics Code," in *Lawyers' Ideals/Lawyers' Practice: Transformations in the American Legal Profession*, ed. Robert L. Nelson, David M. Trubek, and Rayman L. Solomon (Ithaca, NY: Cornell University Press, 1992), 122, was used by the American Trial Lawyers Association to support the expansion of the duty to keep client confidences enacted by the 1983 version of the Model Rules. That version of the confidentiality principle was probably too broad, and the principle has since been narrowed. See *Model Rules of Prof'l Conduct*, R. 1.6(b)(2)–(3) (2003). But, although the trial lawyers employed the idea that lawyers must serve rather than judge their clients to support an extreme and unjustified conclusion, this conception of the adversary advocate clearly does support some duty of confidentiality, which requires lawyers to lie in some measure.

132. Parsons, "The Law and Social Control," 67. These ideas are also emphasized in the client-counseling literature. See, e.g., David A. Binder, Paul Bergman, and Susan C. Price, *Lawyers as Counselors: A Client Centered Approach* (St. Paul, MN: West, 1991); Anthony G. Amsterdam, *Trial Manual 5 for the Defense of Criminal Cases*, vol. 1, 5th ed. (Philadelphia: ALI-ABA, 1988), 106–10.

133. The capacity to understand and abide by fair terms of social cooperation is, as Rawls says, one of the basic powers of human moral personality. See, e.g., Rawls, *Political Liberalism*, 19.

134. See Dan M. Kahan, "The Logic of Reciprocity: Trust, Collective Action, and Law," *Michigan Law Review* 102 (October 2003): 71; see also Ernst Fehr and Simon Gächter, "Fairness and Retaliation: The Economics of Reciprocity," *Journal of Economic Perspectives* 14 (Summer 2000): 159.

135. This is perhaps most evident in the criminal context, where "In the eyes of many defendants, their attorney is the most despicable member of the cast of characters who have conspired to deprive them of their liberty; of all the figures in the courtroom, only defense counsel *pretends* to be on their side." Jay Sterling Silver, "Truth, Justice, and the American Way: The Case *against* the Client Perjury Rules," *Vanderbilt Law Review* 47 (March 1994): 364.

136. Fitzgerald and Dickins, "Disputing in Legal and Nonlegal Contexts," 698.

137. This is vividly illustrated by the alienation that arises between lawyer and client in totalitarian legal systems in which, as a Bulgarian lawyer once said, "'there is no division of duty between the judge, prosecutor, and defense counsel. The defense must assist the prosecution to find the objective truth in a case.'" Monroe H. Freedman, *Lawyers' Ethics in an Adversary System* (Indianapolis: Bobbs-Merrill, 1975), 2.

138. Fuller, "The Forms and Limits of Adjudication," 364 (emphasis added).

139. Ibid.

140. Stuart Scheingold, "Taking Weber Seriously: Lawyers, Politics, and the Liberal State," *Law & Social Inquiry* 24 (Fall 1999): 1063.

141. Parsons, "The Law and Social Control," 58.

142. Ibid.

143. Ibid.

144. Fuller and Randall, "Professional Responsibility," 1161 (excerpted in Fuller, "The Forms and Limits of Adjudication," 384).

5

LAWYERLY FIDELITY:
AN ETHICAL AND EMPIRICAL CRITIQUE

LYNN MATHER

How do lawyers' loyalty to clients and advocacy on their behalf contribute to political legitimacy in a democratic system? This intriguing and profoundly important question is addressed by Daniel Markovits in his essay "Lawyerly Fidelity." Markovits's answer is elegant and creative, offering fresh insights into an age-old topic. Yet, at its base, his argument rests on a flawed depiction of lawyerly fidelity in contemporary legal ethics and on inaccurate assumptions about how lawyers actually behave with their clients. As an exercise in philosophical ethics, Markovits writes that he seeks "to elaborate what is, rather than to command what should be," and he selects "the detailed body of rules that constitutes the law of lawyering"[1] to give a picture of "what is." The problem with this approach lies first in his highly selective and distorted portrayal of the law of lawyering and second in the fact that the Model Rules of Professional Conduct and judicial opinions about the ethics of lawyers' behavior present an incomplete and skewed picture of what lawyers do in actual practice. Examination of the empirical research about lawyers at work—advising clients, negotiating with opposing counsel, and advocating before courts and agencies—presents a quite different and more complex view of lawyerly fidelity. This research reveals a wide range of lawyers' conduct as they counsel, negotiate, and advocate for clients, in contrast to the one-dimensional model of fidelity put forth by Markovits.

After providing a brief sketch of Markovits's argument, I explore aspects of the law of lawyering that Markovits overlooks or rejects. The bulk of my essay is devoted to presenting some of the empirical work on lawyers' ethical conduct that bears on and challenges his conception of lawyerly fidelity to clients. Instead of the picture that Markovits paints—of a sturdy, mutually reinforcing structure of clients, lawyers, and the political order—I see a house of cards: full of holes, shaky supports, and uneven sides. His scaffolding has omitted large parts of the legal profession, and the parts that appear to support the structure are distorted in size. The entire structure rests on a set of questionable assumptions. I conclude with speculation about how a theory of lawyers and political legitimacy might look in light of what lawyers actually do when representing clients and interacting with opposing counsel and the legal system.

I. Markovits's Three Building Blocks—Loyalty, Client Control, Legal Assertiveness—and Their Relation to Political Legitimacy

I begin by presenting a reprise of Markovits's argument in this volume. Lawyerly fidelity—rather than being a vice, as some critics allege—is in fact, he writes, "an appealing virtue."[2] Adversary lawyers, according to Markovits, are partisan advocates for their clients, and this partisanship is "a deeply ingrained feature of the legal profession quite generally, which appears in all legal systems that separate advocates from tribunals."[3] The separation of advocacy from impartial adjudication involves three basic principles: lawyer loyalty, client control, and legal assertiveness. Together, these three principles constitute what he calls "adversary advocacy." The principles are defined as follows. *Lawyers' partisan loyalty* to clients is inscribed in the law of lawyering and is "not controversial," lying at "the very center" of professional ethics.[4] Instead of seeking truth or justice, lawyers are committed to their clients; they are steadfast and zealous in their loyalty to clients, regardless of whether the clients are right or wrong, innocent or guilty.

Client control, according to Markovits, refers to the principle that the client determines the objectives of the case and the lawyer is the loyal servant to those objectives. He cites a common formulation of the relation, expressed by a 1980 appellate court: "The attorney-client relationship is one of agent to principal, and as an agent the attorney must act in conformity with [the client's] . . . instructions and is responsible to his principal if he violates this duty."[5]

Legal assertiveness constitutes the third building block of adversary advocacy. In advocating for their clients, lawyers are protected through a broad legal framework that allows them to do on behalf of their clients what others may be sanctioned for. Markovits writes that lawyers are legally protected against legal liability for pressing a losing claim. And, although federal rules prohibit "frivolous" litigation, he notes that the law does not require lawyers to pursue only "reasonable" claims in the "tort-law-like sense that their expected social benefits exceed their expected social costs."[6] Lawyers are free—and, indeed, are expected and encouraged—he says, to assert whatever claims their clients have expressed and to leave to the judge the responsibility for evaluating the merits of those claims. Lawyers should not evaluate those claims themselves because to do so would undermine the principles of lawyer loyalty and client control.

In order to fulfill these basic principles, Markovits argues that lawyers take on an attitude of professional detachment toward their work.[7] This attitude separates lawyers from their clients' cases both legally and morally[8] and applies to all areas of legal practice— civil and criminal.[9] Professional detachment, which has a long history in discussions of legal ethics and the nonaccountability of the bar, is essential to adversary advocacy, in Markovits's view, in order that lawyers may meet "the basic requirement that they *serve* rather than *judge* their clients."[10]

Moreover, Markovits explains, professional detachment may be recast as the lawyerly virtue of *fidelity*.[11] Fidelity is not the same as friendship. A friend does not pay for advice and support, as William Simon eloquently noted in response to Charles Fried's conception of lawyer-as-friend.[12] A true friend might also suggest alternative courses of action and not defer completely to an act or objective that she deems to be wrong. But Markovits insists that a lawyer, acting out of fidelity to her client, is expected to withdraw personal judgment in the process of representation and adopt instead the client's point of view. Through fidelity to their clients, lawyers come to see the world through their clients' eyes and to advocate for their view of the world. A lawyer, then, is like the "self-effacing poet" who enables "otherwise insensible subjects to come alive" just as "the lawyer enables her otherwise inarticulate clients to speak through her."[13]

Having moved from the three building blocks of adversary advocacy (loyalty, client control and legal assertiveness) to the lawyerly virtue of fidelity, Markovits then explains how lawyers' fidelity to their clients contributes to political legitimacy. The fundamental problem of political order, he writes, rests on the inevitable conflicts that arise between different ideas and values about collective life. How do we get people to obey collective decisions even when they are not persuaded by the merits of those decisions? Since use of coercion by the state is costly and leads to instability, governments seek legitimacy for their decisions through other means. One practical approach to sustaining political legitimacy is to establish "a set of political institutions and practices through which the participants in politics might come to take *ownership* of political outcomes."[14] Rather than relying on general theories or abstract political principles—an alternative posited by philosophers to provide the basis for legitimacy—Markovits seeks, rightly, I think, instead to ground legitimacy in actual participation and political processes. Lawyers, through fidelity to clients and advocacy for their points of view, engage in daily practices that help to legitimize particular legal decisions and rules against which clients might otherwise rebel. Adjudication, with the crucial role of lawyers, thus provides an important source of political legitimacy.[15]

Markovits's argument, to its credit, takes seriously the work that lawyers do and examines it for its ethical and political content. That is, it subjects lawyering, including lawyer-client interactions, to detailed critical analysis with an eye toward helping lawyers better understand what they do with their clients and why, giving specific attention to the political meaning of everyday legal practices. Markovits recognizes, as many other observers do not, that lawyers are *political* actors and that their everyday work contributes directly to the formation and acceptance of legal decisions. While political scientists readily acknowledge the importance of legal arguments made in appellate cases, they too often—and mistakenly—leave to the sociologists the arena of routine lawyer-client interactions. Yet, such interactions may provide a crucial link between conflicts in society and the political order. Markovits draws in part on the law and society literature, including my own research on how lawyers transform disputes through rephrasing and expansion to construct legal cases, and he discusses the broader political consequences of such transformations.[16] Markovits also uses the psychological research on procedural justice to support his view that defendants perceive greater legitimacy in the legal process through their lawyers' fidelity.[17] Nevertheless, as I suggest in the next two sections, Markovits's argument about lawyerly fidelity and its contribution to political legitimacy falls short of his laudable and ambitious goals because of his skewed presentation of both what lawyers are expected to do (the law of lawyering) and what lawyers do in fact do.

II. THE AMBIGUOUS LAW OF LAWYERING

The first problem lies in the way Markovits crafts the building blocks of lawyerly fidelity out of legal ideals and ethical rules for lawyers: "The basic structure of adversary advocacy" he writes, may "be discerned from the study of the law governing lawyers."[18] He turns to the current Model Rules of Professional Conduct and their predecessors, various commentaries, and judicial opinions on professional misconduct and liability for the raw material needed to construct the three basic principles of adversary advocacy. But since this body of law is notoriously uncertain, vague, ambiguous, and contradictory,[19] it allows Markovits to present it selectively, focusing on interpretations that bolster his particular conception of adversary advocacy and marginalizing the alternatives. For example, even when he admits that there are "substantial" legal constraints on lawyers' partisan loyalty to clients, he argues that the "primary ideals" of loyalty "inevitably bleed through the gaps in the technical rules by which the positive law limits lawyers' partisanship."[20] How is one to know which rules are "primary" and which are "technical"? It is precisely the ambiguity of the formal rules that allows them to be interpreted so differently across the range of practitioners and scholars. Judges also interpret the rules in diverse ways, and, indeed, during its 2009-2010 term, the U.S. Supreme Court granted certiorari in an unprecedentedly high number of cases (ten) involving the law of lawyering, constituting more than 13 percent of its docket.[21]

I suggest that the rules governing professional conduct that deal with lawyers' responsibilities to clients reveal far more ambivalence toward and limitations on these three principles than are presented by Markovits. Although *lawyers' partisan loyalty* to clients is a core element of the lawyer's role, it is not the sole element. Lawyers have other core responsibilities—in particular, to the legal system and to the public. These multiple duties are expressed in the opening words of the ABA's Model Rules: "A lawyer, as a member of the legal profession, is a representative of clients, an officer of the legal system and a public citizen having special responsibility for the quality of justice."[22] Despite their obligation to faithfully represent a client's position, lawyers must also serve the law and be bound by it. Therefore, lawyers are *intermediaries* between the state and its citizens. Markovits acknowledges this general point in citing Richard Abel's depiction of lawyers as experts who "mediate between the universal vision of legal order and the concrete desires of [their] clients."[23] But Markovits glosses over the substantive and procedural legal limits on loyalty. Although Canon 7 of the 1969 Model Code states that "a lawyer should represent a client zealously within the bounds of the law,"[24] the 1983 Model Rules *de*-emphasized zeal by placing it in the Preamble, where it is clearly aspirational, not the basis for discipline. Even further, the current Rules link zeal only to advocacy and not to lawyers' other roles: adviser, negotiator, and evaluator. Moreover, a lawyer's duty of loyalty to the client co-exists with the duties of candor to the tribunal and fairness to others. Consequently, conflicts are often unavoidable in a lawyer's role because of simultaneous expectations "to be both zealous advocates for the interest of their clients *and* officers of the court."[25]

The Model Rules of Professional Conduct set specific constraints on what lawyers may do out of loyalty to clients: lawyers must not lie to the court, must not assert claims that they know to be factually untrue, must not subvert the adversary process through disruption, the presentation of false evidence, or illegal influence, and so forth. These limits on the principle of lawyer loyalty are not "technical and self-consciously narrow," as Markovits so dismissively puts it.[26] Instead, they are serious constraints, arising from the history of and texts on legal ethics and potentially leading to sanctions on lawyers if violated. It is true that these limits have shifted in relative importance across generations.[27] In fact, the very concept of lawyer loyalty to client includes *both* the broad, client-centered view articulated by Markovits—which is also found in some case law—and the much narrower, more constrained view expressed by the Rules themselves and by the *Restatement (Third) of the Law Governing Lawyers*.[28] The language of the Rules alone does not support the expansive reading of loyalty to clients.

Similarly, the ethical rules of the profession qualify the notion of *client control* far more than Markovits acknowledges. Although the Model Rules of Professional Conduct assert an ostensibly straightforward division between the client's role in setting the objectives of a case and the lawyer's role in determining the means,[29] the ABA's comment on the rule immediately blurs the distinction and provides more leeway for lawyer direction of the client's case: a "clear distinction between objectives and means sometimes cannot be drawn."[30] Since the lawyer determines the means to pursue the case and since means and ends can be difficult to distinguish in practice, the client is often not fully in control. In addition, lawyers must (not "may") provide "independent professional judgment and render candid advice," and such advice may go beyond the law to include "moral, economic, social and political factors, that may be relevant to the client's situation."[31] Moreover, the Model Rules require lawyers to cease representation if continuing "will result in violation of the rules of professional conduct or other law."[32] And the Rules permit lawyers to withdraw from representation if the client's objective is one "that the lawyer considers repugnant or with which the lawyer has a fundamental disagreement."[33] All of these qualifications on client control provide support for a more independent role for lawyers, in contrast to the hired-gun role where the lawyer is the agent and the client is the principal in control. It is clear that "the professional rules permit the lawyer to practice in accordance with the hired gun model or the independent lawyer model, as he chooses."[34]

Finally, *legal assertiveness*, the third principle of adversary advocacy, takes the first two principles one step further by putting in motion the expectations created by loyalty and client control. That is, having understood and committed themselves to the client's objectives, lawyers must press the client's case to the fullest and allow the courts to evaluate their merits. Numerous legal rules,

Markovits explains, "allow lawyers wide latitude in assisting disputants who may press colorable but losing claims."[35] Other legal rules, however, may penalize lawyers for raising frivolous or malicious claims and impose sanctions for improper delay or overzealous litigation. Markovits also ignores informal norms that reflect cultural values against unreasonably aggressive legal conduct and may override a formal requirement of assertiveness. Trial judges may apply these informal rules (or "soft law"), for example, by expressing their displeasure with attorneys who persistently "abuse" the adversary system. Thus, legal assertiveness is not the clear-cut ethical command for lawyers that Markovits presents.

In sum, in presenting the lawyerly virtues, Markovits overstates the force and clarity of the ethical rules behind adversary advocacy. For each principle, he biases his presentation of the rules in favor of the client as always right and the lawyer as humble and partisan servant—to the neglect of other virtues, such as respect for the substantive law, the lawyer's role as an officer of the court, or the advice of the lawyer about the best interest for the client and the risks of various alternatives. In addition, his lawyerly virtues are essentially the same principles of adversary advocacy that engendered much criticism among legal ethics scholars decades ago.[36] That criticism, along with scandals of lawyer misconduct and public dissatisfaction with the legal profession, led to modifications of the ethical rules and additional constraints on partisan lawyer loyalty, particularly for lawyers who handle civil—not criminal—disputes.

III. The Reality of Advocacy in Actual Legal Practice

A second and more fundamental problem with this conception of lawyerly fidelity stems from its reliance on ethical codes and appellate law over lawyers as the basis for constructing the lawyer's role. Instead, why not examine what lawyers actually do in legal practice, including what they think they should do? This section explores adversary advocacy and lawyerly fidelity using empirical sociolegal research on lawyers—their conduct and their norms. I organize my discussion according to the same three elements of advocacy—loyalty to client, client control, and legal assertiveness—but point to factors other than the indeterminate professional rules that

shape the meaning of these principles in practice. The empirical literature clearly demonstrates that lawyers vary a great deal in
how they understand advocacy and enact it with their clients. The
model lawyer for Markovits appears to be a corporate litigator, a
well-resourced lawyer representing a knowledgeable client who
has clear objectives and is engaged in litigation against a similarly
situated party. But what about other kinds of lawyers—those representing criminal defendants, husbands and wives in divorce, ordinary individuals in personal injury, immigration, or bankruptcy
cases? These areas constitute a good deal of legal practice (family
law, for example, accounts for the highest proportion of all civil
cases in the state courts) and exhibit far less adversarial advocacy
by attorneys. Moreover, as discussed later, even lawyers in many
of the specialty areas of corporate law, such as tax, securities, and
patents, operate within the constraints of federal regulations (e.g.,
Sarbanes-Oxley, Patent and Trademark Office rules) that may limit
their adversary advocacy in practice.

A. Loyalty to Client

Instead of taking the lawyer-client relation as a given, the starting
point for loyalty, we need to go back a step and consider first how
the two come together. Private lawyers in the United States are
free to accept only those clients they want to represent, and clients
in civil cases have no right to a lawyer.[37] Pressures have increased
on lawyers to select clients carefully, attending to the lawyers' own
professional and personal identities, economic considerations,
and possible conflicts of interests.[38] Lawyers evaluate possible clients according to whether the cause is worthy, the client sympathetic, or the case financially rewarding and whether the client
presents any conflict with existing clients. Cause lawyers screen clients according to the fit between the client's case and the lawyer's
political values and ideological commitments. Cause lawyering has
increased in recent years on both liberal and conservative political issues. Plaintiff lawyers, working on contingent fees, screen on
the basis of the likelihood and size of an award (considering, for
example, legal liability, the depth of the pockets of the defendant,
and the personal characteristics of the plaintiff). Divorce lawyers
in one study overwhelmingly (more than 90 percent) reported

that they screened clients, possibly rejecting those they saw as "difficult"—that is, unrealistic in expectations, vengeful, demanding, or simply too high-maintenance.[39]

Specialization of the legal profession has spurred attention to client selection as part of a successful business model for practice: concentrate only on certain kinds of cases and clients to maximize firm revenue. Some patent law firms, for example, prosecute patents only for business inventors and automatically reject all individual inventors as clients.[40] Large law firms screen out clients whose interests would be in direct conflict with those of existing clients, but they also often reject those who present "positional" or "issue" conflicts, that is, where the preferences of the new client might be inconsistent with those of an existing client, even though there is no direct relation or conflict between them. Many large-firm lawyers believe that positional conflicts threaten their economic base, and, consequently, "they will not represent or will not sue certain industries or niches within industries, whether for fear of creating `bad law' for their regular clients or simply out of concern for maintaining the appearance of loyalty."[41] In this way, lawyer loyalty works to protect certain well-established corporate interests, while rejecting clients and claims that might challenge those interests.

Once the lawyer-client relationship has begun, what is the client's goal to which the lawyer must be loyal? Clients bring messy, sprawling real-world problems to the law office, and the lawyer's job is to rephrase those problems into legal language and categories. Clients, especially those with one-shot dealings with the legal system, often do not know what they want (other than a vague notion of "winning") because they lack knowledge of the options and depend on their lawyers for guidance in defining a "win." The rephrasing process gives the lawyer considerable discretion, discretion that profoundly affects the practical meaning of loyalty to clients. In personal plight cases such as criminal defense, personal injury, immigration, or divorce—where individuals often face their first encounter with the legal system—much of the lawyer's work goes into the construction of the client's objective to make it consistent with the legal alternatives available. Divorce lawyers report that they are frequently asked by clients to provide emotional and personal counseling, conversations that many lawyers say they are not equipped for. Lawyers then steer their divorce clients away from issues of guilt, blame, hurt, and anger to get them to focus on the legal issues of property, support, and custody.[42] During this process of education and redirection, clients shift their perspective, moving from immediate emotional issues such as "why did he leave me?" or "it's all because of my mother-in-law" to the longer-term ones like "will I be able to keep the house?" or "when can I see my kids?" Most divorce lawyers try to avoid identifying too closely with a client since they believe it would compromise their effective representation.

Criminal defense attorneys similarly see their responsibility as helping their clients define "realistic" objectives. Very few defendants can expect a trial that will prove their innocence. But many defendants can hope for some kind of reduction in the possible sanctions against them. When an incarcerated drug defendant asks his defense counsel to "get me out of here," the lawyer may respond by suggesting a quick plea bargain or a transfer to drug court. While experienced defendants might understand the differences between these, it is often the lawyer—not the client—who sets the goal for the case. Legal services lawyers, like many defense attorneys, report that their clients frequently *expect* them to take charge, define the issues, and sort out their problems for them. This presents an intractable dilemma: legal services lawyers are committed to client empowerment and client autonomy as part of their legal practice, but their clients prefer to remain dependent on the lawyer for both solutions and strategies.[43]

In contrast to personal plight lawyers, lawyers who represent organizations and business tend to face clearer goals from their clients and express greater loyalty to them. Such lawyers, who typically practice in large law firms, often have lengthy relationships with clients and are extremely familiar with their legal issues. In a classic study of large Chicago law firms, lawyers rarely perceived any conflict between their personal values and what they were asked to do by their clients.[44] They also were heavily dependent on the business from a relatively small number of clients. Moreover, corporations often have in-house counsel to set their legal objectives, so attorneys in the outside law firms are given clear instructions about how to proceed. "The in-house lawyer has the ability to develop defined goals and use client resources to manage the relationship," noted a study of lawyers in Silicon Valley.[45]

In recent years, however, corporate lawyers have sometimes struggled with the concept of loyalty out of concern for "who is the client?" Although in-house counsel may give directions to outside lawyers, the lawyers must remember that their client is the organization itself, not its spokespersons. Since 2002, the federal Sarbanes-Oxley law has set constraints on lawyer loyalty to corporate clients (at least for companies that are publicly traded) by imposing requirements on lawyers to report "up the ladder" of the organization if corporate managers are not providing full disclosure or are engaged in legally questionable practices. Another illustration of ambiguity over who is the client comes from the area of transnational practice—global deal making. Instead of thinking of a dyadic lawyer-client relationship, this growing area of practice requires a new paradigm. Lawyers in global corporate law firms may find themselves representing "the deal"—a complex transaction between large and small multinational corporations and banks and other lending companies—rather than a single client.[46]

B. *Client Control*

The starkest contrast between this concept as posited by Markovits and the reality of lawyers' conduct appears in the two distinct and nearly opposite meanings of the phrase "client control." Unlike Markovits and other legal academics who use the phrase to mean "control of the case *by the client*," sociologists who have studied lawyers use it to refer to "control of the client *by the lawyer*." In a well-known 1967 study, Jerome Skolnick defined client control as the challenge criminal defense attorneys face in persuading their clients to trust them and accept their recommendations.[47] Considerable research has built on Skolnick's work on criminal case decision making and found that most criminal defense attorneys assume an independent advisory role, rather than acting as agents for their clients. Independence is typically easier for private attorneys than for public defenders, since defendants who have initially selected and are paying for private counsel are more likely to accept their advice.[48] But even public defenders report that they exert considerable direction over their clients. For instance, a 1998 survey of public defenders in five urban offices found that most of the respondents thought that the lawyer (not the client) should control both strategy and tactics "even in the face of the defendant's contrary opinion or explicit objection."[49] Case law has supported this view; for example, the U.S. Supreme Court held in *Jones v. Barnes* that a defense lawyer has no constitutional duty to raise every issue suggested by the defendant.[50] Interestingly, Justice William J. Brennan's dissent in this case cites Skolnick's article on client control: "It is no secret that indigent clients often mistrust the lawyers appointed to represent them. . . . A constitutional rule that encourages lawyers to disregard their clients' wishes without compelling need can only exacerbate the clients' suspicion of their lawyers."[51] More recently, the view of lawyer-in-charge prevailed in the Unabomber case when the court denied Ted Kaczynski's request to represent himself because he disagreed with the defense approach proposed by his counsel.[52]

Most divorce lawyers, like most criminal defense attorneys, see themselves as in charge of the case. One divorce attorney characterized lawyers as "expensive cab drivers. The passenger decides on the destination and I decide on the route."[53] Although that image evokes the familiar legal ideal from Model Rule 1.2(a) in which the "lawyer shall abide by a client's decisions concerning the objectives of representation and . . . consult with the client as to the means by which they are to be pursued," the ends and means in divorce are subject to considerable negotiation between lawyer and client. Moreover, divorce lawyers report using numerous techniques, including education, persuasion, delay, increased fees, and even threats to withdraw representation, in their efforts to influence clients to set "realistic expectations" and to aim for "reasonable settlements."[54] The media often depict divorce lawyers as hired guns for clients, but such cases typically involve celebrities—movie stars, pro sports figures, or the like—not your average spouse in a divorce. Indeed, exceptions to the general model of divorce representation—or of criminal defense, described earlier—appear more often for wealthier clients. Lawyers "follow the money" just as others do, leading to lawyer-client decision making shaped in part by client resources and fee structures.

The lawyer-client relationship in the typical personal injury (PI) case also shows the lawyer, not the client, in the controlling role—on both the plaintiff and the defense side. In a seminal study of "who's in charge?" of lawyer-client decision making, Douglas

Rosenthal found that most plaintiffs passively deferred to their law-yers.[55] More recent research also shows that PI plaintiff lawyers ex-ercise control over clients in the settlement process; in very high-volume practices, face-to-face meetings between lawyer and client are rare, and lawyers are paternalistic, not participatory.[56] Defense attorneys in PI cases have a complex relationship with their clients since it is the insurance company that pays the attorney's bill, not the insured individual. By the terms of the insurance contract, the insured has delegated responsibility for defense and settlement to the insurance company, which in turn hires the insurance defense lawyer. As a result, the insurance defense lawyer often has little contact with the insured; as one lawyer explained, "When the case settles, I will send a letter to the client notifying him that the settle-ment has occurred."[57] This is a far cry indeed from client control over decision making depicted by Markovits.

The economics of a high-volume legal practice serving indi-vidual clients who lack much information or legal experience en-courage lawyers to develop standard procedures for their client interactions. Research on legal aid lawyers based on sociolinguistic methods found that attorneys dominate conversations with clients, control their problem definitions, and routinize issues to steer them into established case categories.[58] Similarly, a small observa-tional study of lawyers handling consumer bankruptcy concluded that most followed routine patterns, exercising almost "exclusive control over the structure, sequence, content, and length of the dialogue with clients."[59] These lawyers engaged with clients as if they were selling them a product, a Chapter 7 or a Chapter 13 bankruptcy plan, rather than developing a client relationship to represent a particular individual.

But, for corporate attorneys, the reverse holds. Business clients do tend to participate actively in decisions and direct their lawyers on what actions to take. Research on large-firm lawyers cites a cor-porate attorney who compared his previous work in legal services (where he had more autonomy to define issues) with his current corporate law job, where "you are a tool of your client."[60] Lawyer as "agent," "tool," "mouthpiece," or "hired gun" is far more common in the representation of repeat player clients, those who regularly use the legal process, than in the representation of occasional one-shot litigants. Most corporate litigators in one study reported behaving according to the lawyer-as-agent model, taking directions from the client and "passing moral responsibility along to their client-as-principal."[61] A smaller group of corporate litigators saw themselves as active fiduciaries for their clients' interests, rather than as agents, but even these lawyers were sometimes hesitant about voicing their concerns and "retreated to the safe ground of ethical pragmatism" by writing a "cover-your-ass" memo.[62] Corporate litigators typically work directly with in-house counsel, and they are the most "vocal partisans of the litigator-as-agent model."[63] In-house counsel develop stories to tell in litigation and direct litigators to tell them. Litigators construct the narrative desired by their clients through discovery, speaking objections, and witness preparation.[64] Similarly, a study of litigators on intellectual property (IP) matters found that "patent clients exert a great deal of influence over how discovery is done."[65] The fierce competition for corporate clients, the dangers of losing clients by questioning their directions, and the internal controls within large law firms all lead litigators to act as faithful agents of their clients.

Nevertheless, even corporate litigators face constraints that can compete with client loyalty. Interviews with litigators in the fields of IP and securities—where federal regulations mandate candor in discovery—suggest that lawyers do worry about the risks of noncompliance and counsel clients accordingly. Lawyers in both fields described giving clients "the talk" about just what is expected under the law, explaining the risks to them, and even threatening withdrawal from the case if a client insisted on noncompliant behavior. However, when pressed on this last point, none of the IP litigators admitted to ever firing a client but noted that they instead made a record of their objections.[66] Securities lawyers expressed greater caution; in a survey conducted two years after Sarbanes-Oxley was passed, more than one-quarter of securities attorneys said that they had encountered problems of legal compliance that required them to withdraw from representation.[67] Not all of the securities attorneys surveyed were litigators, however. Corporate attorneys engaged in transactional work appear more likely to advise and collaborate with clients in decision making than to act as agents for clients. This difference in a lawyer's role makes perfect sense if you compare the adversarial nature of litigation to the task of constructing an agreement that will be acceptable to all the parties involved or drafting a document to govern future business dealings.

In sum, the picture of client control in which the client is firmly in charge of the case and the lawyer simply follows the client's directions does not apply to lawyer-client interactions in many areas. Individual clients in personal plight cases involving criminal charges, divorce, personal injury, bankruptcy, and the like are frequently represented by lawyers who see themselves as directing the case, with some or little client input. On the other hand, corporate clients do exercise considerable control over their lawyers, especially litigators.

C. Legal Assertiveness

The notion that lawyers are obliged to vigorously advocate the claims of their clients, no matter how unreasonable they may be, ignores lawyers' other responsibilities—to follow the law and to show respect for the court and their professional peers. It also ignores lawyers' obligation to provide the best representation they can for their clients; sometimes cooperation achieves better outcomes for clients than does zealous advocacy. The formal professional rules that allow attorneys the freedom to make whatever arguments their clients desire can be trumped by the disapproval of judges who dislike having their time wasted or the loss of credibility lawyers face from other lawyers. This is particularly true for certain areas of law such as criminal defense, divorce, and PI, where attorneys routinely appear against one another. Informal social pressures exert particular force in small communities and in any area of practice where lawyers work closely with/against one another. Research by Donald Landon and Joel Handler shows the difficulty of exercising zealous advocacy in small communities where attorneys have ongoing relationships.[68] Studies of lawyers in urban criminal courts have also documented the cooperative relationships that often develop between prosecuting and defense attorneys. Cooperation stems from organizational pressures to expedite cases, shared knowledge of likely case outcomes for certain defendant and case characteristics, sanctions on defendants for taking risks at trial and on attorneys for overly zealous conduct, limited resources for attorneys on both sides of the case, and the

informal social relationships of the courtroom. Most criminal defense attorneys adapt to the system, representing clients—depending on the case, the attorney, and the court culture—through
cooperation with prosecutors in plea negotiation, adversarial negotiations, advocacy at trial, and/or advocacy for treatment under
the new drug or mental health treatment plans.[69]

Lawyers' reputations are key to their success in contingency-fee
civil practices both for attracting clients and for engaging in credible negotiations with opposing counsel. This also requires some
autonomous professional judgment over their clients' often exaggerated expectations for an award. Personal injury lawyers inflate
claims in negotiations with each other, but they also must show
that they know "what a case is worth." That same crucial standard
about the valuation of case outcomes emerges whether the case
involves medical malpractice, first-degree robbery, patent infringe-
ment, or tax fraud. For an attorney to argue for something that is
completely unattainable or unreasonable is to risk failure not only
in the individual case but, more important, in future case negotiations and future appearances before the same judge or against the
same advocate. Thus, when lawyers do present unrealistic offers in
negotiations, they may do it with a wink and a nod, conveying the
client's demand while simultaneously and tacitly acknowledging to
opposing counsel their own views.

The importance of repeat play for dispute settlement has been
noted in game theory, as well as in observational studies of legal negotiations. Repeated interaction between lawyers should increase cooperation and sharing of information, which, in turn, should result
in more efficient and less costly case settlements.[70] A large empirical
study of federal court litigation supports this view. Examining more
than 2,200 civil cases in one federal district court, Jason Johnston
and Joel Waldfogel found that "cases that involve attorneys who interact repeatedly . . . are resolved more quickly and with less likelihood of trial than other cases."[71] Although these results held regardless of the type of client involved, the effect was larger in cases with
one-shot individual clients than in cases with institutional clients.
The authors suggest that the reputational incentive for cooperation
was stronger for lawyers who represent individuals; institutional clients (such as business litigants) have their own reputational interests that may prevail over the interests of their lawyers.

Divorce is another legal context in which lawyers routinely confront one another and where excessively zealous client advocacy carries risks. The top professional organization for divorce lawyers, the American Academy of Matrimonial Lawyers (AAML), specifically criticizes existing bar codes for their insistence on overly zealous advocacy and argues for a more appropriate and reasonable set of standards for dispute resolution in family law. Instead of promoting the interests only of their client—the husband or wife—divorce lawyers have an "ethical obligation" to protect the interests of the children, according to the AAML and the views of many divorce attorneys. Indeed, the recent nationwide movement for "collaborative law" involves divorce lawyers who pledge to cooperate in divorce settlements and seek to reduce the acrimony that results from excessive legal advocacy. Divorce lawyers interviewed in New England were asked whether their primary goal in negotiating a divorce was to reach a settlement fair to both parties or to get as much as possible for their own client. Although "most for client" would reflect the ideal of legal assertiveness, fewer than one-quarter of the lawyers (23 percent) chose that goal, while 35 percent selected "fair settlement" and 42 percent ignored the forced choice and sought to combine the alternatives (e.g. "reaching a settlement that is fair to my client").[72] To explain their distinctive style of advocacy, divorce lawyers referred to the legal frameworks of no-fault and equitable property distribution, a concern for the long-term health and well-being of clients (especially if children are involved), and their own professional reputations. As one attorney said, "if you overreach, even if you get an agreement from the other side . . . you might go to court and the judge might say, `I'm not going to endorse this, you've overreached.'"[73]

Corporate litigators, by contrast, exemplify legal assertiveness in action. In complex or high-stakes cases, discovery constitutes the bulk of a litigator's work, and here we see lawyers pushing the envelope on behalf of their clients. Short of advising clients to withhold legally required documents or to lie about events, which would clearly be unethical, litigators describe the "grey area" of discovery tactics: preparing witnesses in advance to "educate" them about the issues, asking leading questions in depositions, raising speaking objections designed to alert a witness to key facts or to remind them of the theory of the case, or reading document requests as narrowly as possible to withhold material. Noting that judges rarely sanction lawyers for stepping over an ethical line in complex litigation, corporate litigators nevertheless justify such ethically questionable tactics by pointing to the adversarial nature of the game.[74] Both sides know the rules and how far they can push them. And both sides seek to reconstruct facts to tell a story that will be advantageous to their clients. As one litigator said, "We are aggressive, but not over the line. It's a badge of honor to know how to push the limit but not go over the line."[75] Although litigators like this one were firmly committed to aggressive representation for their clients, they also acknowledged "the importance of not being a jerk," and they "much preferred working with opposing counsel who took reasonable positions in discovery and who could be trusted not to `play games.'"[76] Thus, within the adversary game of litigation, rules of civility operate, along with the ethical rules. A modest degree of cooperation—even between litigators— can benefit clients by reducing unproductive and costly fights over discovery.

IV. A Macro Picture of Lawyers and Clients

As shown by this brief review, lawyers vary enormously in loyalty, client control, and legal assertiveness according to client differences, the nature of legal roles (counseling or litigation), and area of practice. The ambiguous and indeterminate law of lawyering provides lawyers with great discretion to shape their conduct according to contextual features of their practice, as David Wilkins argued in 1990.[77] Understanding the nature of lawyerly fidelity to clients thus requires disaggregating the legal profession and paying attention to the micro-level patterns in different communities of legal practice.[78] But, despite the diverse lawyering styles described earlier, could it be that adversary advocacy is the most common? It is impossible to get a definitive answer to that question, but aggregate data suggests that the answer is no. The most recent (2005) statistics on lawyers in the United States show that they worked in the following settings:[79]

10 percent government
 8 percent in-house counsel

75 percent private practice (60 percent of private lawyers in firms of from one to five attorneys, 22 percent in firms of between six and one hundred attorneys, and 16 percent in firms with more than one hundred attorneys)

7 percent other (legal aid/public defender, education, inactive)

Markovits explicitly excludes government lawyers from his argument. And his model of fidelity does not really apply to in-house counsel since they are *employees* of clients and thus serve them in a fundamentally different way. That leaves lawyers in private practice. We know from lawyer surveys that solo and small-firm lawyers tend to represent individuals in personal plight cases and that large-firm lawyers are more likely to represent business and organizations. Firms with more than one hundred lawyers generally represent large corporations. Of large-firm lawyers, many (one-half or more?) work in departments focused on counseling or transactional tasks, rather than litigation. On the basis of this admittedly crude look at the numbers and generalizing from the micro-studies discussed in the previous section, it appears that only a small fraction of all lawyers work in contexts routinely characterized by adversary advocacy.

Instead of speculating about the number of lawyers, another way to assess attorney conduct is to examine the time lawyers spend serving different clienteles. Heinz and Laumann's 1975 survey of the Chicago bar revealed two hemispheres of legal work, divided roughly in half between the personal plight and the corporate sectors. Since then, demand for legal work on the corporate side has increased; in a 1995 survey of Chicago lawyers, 64 percent of legal effort was devoted to corporate clients and only 29 percent to personal and small business clients.[80] To the extent that corporate clients consume the largest share of legal work, these figures could support partisan loyalty and client control over decision making posited by Markovits, at least as measured by lawyers' time spent. However, breaking the client sectors down further, the Chicago survey found that corporate and small business *litigation* constituted only 19 percent of all legal effort, with 16 percent of legal effort devoted to personal plight matters (family, divorce, criminal defense, civil rights, PI plaintiff) and the remainder distributed across real estate, tax, securities, patents, probate, regulatory, government, and other areas of the law. Therefore, under either measure of lawyers' work, adversary advocacy characterizes only a minority of lawyers.

What does the macro-picture of lawyering look like from the client's perspective? First, a great many individuals with civil law problems do not become "clients" because they cannot obtain a lawyer. Legal services funding has sharply decreased, and an estimated 80 percent of those who qualify for legal assistance are unable to get it, even for very serious legal problems. Although pro bono services by private lawyers have increased, they do not meet current legal needs.[81] Most individuals getting a divorce do so without a lawyer. Two-thirds of parties in immigration courts lack legal representation, and many turn to websites like Legal Zoom for help in representing themselves or in drafting their own legal documents. Middle-class individuals with civil injuries face tough screening by contingency-fee lawyers to see if the case will be sufficiently rewarding. Unlike civil cases, all individuals charged with crime are constitutionally guaranteed a lawyer. But that leads to the second issue from the client's perspective: the nature of legal services.

Although all criminal defendants are entitled to lawyers, legal aid and public defender services are underfunded and short-staffed. A defendant's response to a researcher decades ago still stands: "Did you have a lawyer when you went to court? No, I had a Public Defender."[82] This view does not give credit to the dedicated, hardworking public defenders, but, unfortunately, it captures some client perceptions. Private criminal defense attorneys can provide more individualized attention to clients, but in urban areas they also often have high-volume practices, with routinized defense strategies. But, when defendants are paying for private lawyers, they have a greater incentive to listen to and follow their lawyer's advice. On the civil side, lawyers working in high-volume areas such as family law, immigration, personal injury, bankruptcy, and legal services have established ways of providing service to individual clients. Individuals with more resources may hire a specialized, high-priced lawyer with a lighter caseload who will offer more individualized representation—perhaps (though not necessarily) with greater lawyerly loyalty, client control over decision making, and more legal assertiveness. But we don't really know much about how individual clients perceive such differences in representation. Perhaps they feel empowered by the eloquent expressions of their problems by their lawyers; yet, it could also be that such clients are more attuned to legal costs and whether they are justified.

Lacking survey data to shed light on systematic differences in clients' perceptions of lawyers, we might instead extrapolate from sociological research on common understandings of legality, that is, the cultural schemas that individuals hold about law. Patricia Ewick and Susan Silbey's study of legal consciousness among a random sample of ordinary individuals identified three distinct clusters: people see themselves as suppliants *before* the law, viewing it as impartial and objective, with rules and procedures to be followed; or they are *with* the law, pursuing their self-interest by seeing the legal process as a game to be played with whatever resources, experiences, and skill they have; or they are *against* the law, seeing it as a power struggle and exercising resistance (e.g., through humor or forgetting their paperwork) or simply making do.[83] If clients bring to their lawyers this rich mosaic of expectations about law, along with their quite different legal problems and varying resources to address them, and if lawyers represent clients by a wide range of different lawyering styles, as suggested in this chapter, then it is difficult indeed to argue, as Markovits does, that one particular version of lawyerly fidelity is best for the polity. As a purely philosophical exercise, his discussion of fidelity and its relation to political legitimacy provides interesting food for thought. But, as a claim to offer insight into modern legal ethics and their implications, it should be grounded more firmly in real-world ethical rules and norms and perhaps in actual legal practice, as well. As a social scientist and legal scholar, I think we should consider how to create a politically legitimate democratic structure that incorporates the multiple professional responsibilities of lawyers and also the diversity of lawyering styles and clients. That ambitious task awaits another essay. But I conclude with a few thoughts based on what I have shown thus far.

V. Conclusion

Given what we know about lawyers' actual conduct in different practice contexts, how, if at all, does their work in representing clients contribute to political legitimacy? That is, how do lawyers' actions encourage citizens (both individuals and corporations) to accept government outcomes that they do not agree with? How does legal representation facilitate compliance with law? The disorganized masses and powerful organized interests both pose legitimacy problems for government, as we see daily in the news of the world. The costs of coercion are high.

For the many individuals without legal counsel, one message conveyed by lawyers is that the legal system is out of their reach. Law is the province of the rich and powerful—Ewick and Silbey's "against the law" cultural schema. Those who can afford a lawyer for their legal problems (or who have one appointed for them) may be dissatisfied with the high-volume processing—and they just go along with it—or they might appreciate having an advocate on their side, someone to explain what is going to happen next. Routinized representation might not bother them because that's simply the way the law is—all rules and procedures that must be followed ("before the law"). Or, clients might take satisfaction in the fact that they have an insider to navigate the legal system for them, working the angles to arrange an informal deal ("with the law"). Lawyers who regularly represent one-shot litigants implicitly know these different cultural views of law, or else they quickly learn them on the job. And they probably have a repertoire of responses to reinforce their clients' understandings of law or to reframe them more positively. Much of lawyers' efforts with personal plight clients consist of rephrasing their issues in terms of the categories and language of the legal system. This work involves legal socialization, educating people about what they can expect from law and "cooling out" their unrealistic expectations. In this way, lawyers *are* helping people to accept outcomes they disagree with, not through adversary advocacy and the voice of the self-effacing poet but, more likely, by acting as an altruistic broker doing the best she can under difficult circumstances, a self-interested legal provider who excels at selling clients cut-rate services, or a private practitioner struggling to help clients resolve their legal problems.

Through informal negotiations to promote dispute settlement for one-shot clients, lawyers who work regularly with one another also promote the acceptance of case outcomes through their mediation. That is, the process of adjudication in which a third party decides a zero-sum conflict in favor of one side or the other can be unstable over time, as Martin Shapiro points out.[84] Once the judge rules for one party, the losing party sees a two-against-one situation, aggravated especially in the criminal context, where both the judge and prosecutor work for the same side—the government. Most criminal defendants do not expect to be exonerated. The evidence is lined up against them, but uncertainty lies in the amount of punishment they will receive. When criminal defense lawyers negotiate with prosecutors to achieve sentence reductions, they not only encourage clients to accept case outcomes but also contribute to mitigating what many who work in the criminal courts see as unfair sentencing. Criminal court regulars may thus construct their own informal legal categories that reflect the social realities of their clients. Not all bargaining occurs in the shadow of the law. Since there are so few trials to set legal parameters for negotiations, lawyers working together over time in many legal fields develop their own legal norms for case settlement. These norms may bring their clients' interests into law and thus further legitimize it.

Finally, how does lawyering for organized interests contribute to their support for the legitimacy of the system? The answer lies simply in Marc Galanter's well-known argument for "why the `haves' come out ahead."[85] Repeat-player clients hire repeat-player lawyers and direct them to play the legal game to further the clients' advantage: structuring transactions, shaping legal rules, and assessing the short- and long-term risks of trial or settlement. With so much of lawyers' efforts in the United States devoted to corporate and organized interests and with lawyerly loyalty, client control over decisions, and legal assertiveness especially visible in high-stakes litigation, corporate clients and organizations can trust the law in the long run to be responsive to their interests. Lawyerly fidelity thus achieves its greatest contribution to political legitimacy through its work for corporate citizens.

NOTES

I am grateful for detailed comments from Leslie Levin on a draft of this chapter. My essay also benefited from discussion and suggestions at a Boston

Public Law seminar and at a SUNY Buffalo Law Workshop. Particular thanks to Guyora Binder, Tom Burke, David Engel, Bruce Jackson, Bob Kagan, Sandy Levinson, Linda McClain, Mark Miller, Jack Schlegel, Susan Silbey, Mark Tushnet, and Jim Wooten for their helpful comments. I also want to acknowledge Joel Parker's patient and expert editorial assistance.

1. Daniel Markovits, "Lawyerly Fidelity," this volume (this quotation is from the original version of the chapter on which I was invited to comment). The point is repeated in Daniel Markovits, *A Modern Legal Ethics: Adversary Advocacy in a Democratic Age* (Princeton: Princeton University Press, 2008), 19–20. My comments here are based solely on his chapter in this volume, not on his book. In an October 27, 2009, e-mail to me about the relation between "Lawyerly Fidelity" and his book, Markovits wrote that the essay is "a summary of one of the book's three themes. It pulls together and re-organizes, and partly revises, material from several . . . of the book's chapters."

2. Markovits, "Lawyerly Fidelity."

3. Ibid. Markovits writes that his argument holds beyond the Anglo-American legal system and cites German legal practices for support. However, I will not address that broad claim in my comments. There are enough problems with his argument as it applies to U.S. legal practices without examining the claim about its wider applicability.

4. Ibid.

5. Ibid., citing Olfe v. Gordon, 286 N.W.2d 573, 577 (Wis. 1980).

6. Markovits, "Lawyerly Fidelity."

7. Ibid.

8. Ibid.

9. Ibid.

10. Ibid.

11. Ibid.

12. See William Simon, "The Ideology of Advocacy: Procedural Justice and Professional Ethics," *Wisconsin Law Review* 1978 (1978): 29–144, arguing that Fried's conception of "lawyer as friend" is akin to prostitution, since money provides the basis of the relationship and the relationship lacks the qualities of genuine friendship. See also Charles Fried, "The Lawyer as Friend: The Moral Foundations of the Lawyer-Client Relation," *Yale Law Journal* 85 (July 1976): 1060–89.

13. Markovits, "Lawyerly Fidelity."

14. Ibid.

15. Ibid.

16. Ibid. See Lynn Mather and Barbara Yngvesson, "Language, Audience and the Transformation of Disputes," *Law & Society Review* 15 (Spe-

cial Issue on Dispute Processing and Civil Litigation) (1980–81): 775–822; William L. F. Felstiner, Richard L. Abel, and Austin Sarat, "The Emergence and Transformation of Disputes: Naming, Blaming, and Claiming," *Law & Society Review* 15 (Special Issue on Dispute Processing and Civil Litigation) (1980–81): 631–54; and Maureen Cain, "The General Practice Lawyer and the Client: Towards a Radical Conception," *International Journal of the Sociology of Law* 7 (The Legal Profession) (November 1979): 331–54.

17. Markovits, "Lawyerly Fidelity."

18. Ibid.

19. See, for example, Richard L. Abel, "Why Does the ABA Promulgate Ethical Rules?" *Texas Law Review* 59 (April 1981): 639–88; Deborah L. Rhode, "Why the ABA Bothers: A Functional Perspective on Professional Codes," *Texas Law Review* 59 (April 1981): 689–722; David B. Wilkins, "Legal Realism for Lawyers," *Harvard Law Review* 104 (December 1990): 468–524; and Paul G. Haskell, *Why Lawyers Behave as They Do* (Boulder, CO: Westview, 1998).

20. Markovits, "Lawyerly Fidelity."

21. Renee Newman Knake, "Prioritizing Professional Responsibility and the Legal Profession: A Preview of the United States Supreme Court's 2009–2010 Term," *Duke Journal of Constitutional Law & Public Policy* 5 (Sidebar 1) (2009): 1–23, http://www.law.duke.edu/journals/djclpp/index.php?action=showitem&id=150. For the final number of petitions granted cert by the Court, see SCOTUSblog, http://www.scotusblog.com/wp-content/uploads/2010/07/Final-Stats-OT09-0707101.pdf.

22. *Model Rules of Professional Conduct*, Preamble (2010).

23. Markovits, "Lawyerly Fidelity," citing Richard L. Abel, *American Lawyers* (New York: Oxford University Press, 1989), 34–35.

24. *Model Code of Professional Responsibility*, Canon 7 (1969). For discussion of changes in legal rules to decrease the importance of zeal, see Anita Bernstein, "The Zeal Shortage," *Hofstra Law Review* 34 (2006): 1165–1205.

25. David B. Wilkins, "Who Should Regulate Lawyers?" *Harvard Law Review* 105 (February 1992): 799–887. Emphasis added.

26. Markovits, "Lawyerly Fidelity." Markovits adds that the limits on lawyers' partisan zeal fall short of an injunction "to promote truth or justice." But why are these two alternatives (loyalty to client versus loyalty to truth or justice) the only ones available? What about the lawyer's duties to the court or to clients by providing "independent and candid advice" (see *Model Rules of Prof'l Conduct*, R. 2.1)?

27. L. Ray Patterson, "Legal Ethics and the Lawyer's Duty of Loyalty," *Emory Law Journal* 29 (Fall 1980): 909–70.

28. Eli Wald, "Loyalty in Limbo: The Peculiar Case of Attorneys' Loyalty to Clients," *St. Mary's Law Journal* 40 (2009): 909–66.

29. *Model Rules of Prof'l Conduct*, R. 1.2(a).

30. *Model Rules of Prof'l Conduct*, R. 1.2(a) cmt.

31. *Model Rules of Prof'l Conduct*, R. 2.1.

32. *Model Rules of Prof'l Conduct*, R. 1.6(a) (1).

33. *Model Rules of Prof'l Conduct*, R. 1.6(b) (4).

34. Haskell, *Why Lawyers Behave as They Do*, 86. See also Lynn Mather, "Fundamentals: What Do Clients Want? What Do Lawyers Do?" *Emory Law Journal* 52 (Special Edition) (2003): 1065–86.

35. Markovits, "Lawyerly Fidelity."

36. See as examples Simon, "The Ideology of Advocacy"; David Luban, *Lawyers and Justice: An Ethical Study* (Princeton: Princeton University Press, 1988); and Deborah Rhode, "Ethical Perspectives on Legal Practice," *Stanford Law Review* 37 (January 1985): 589–652.

37. Indigent defendants in criminal cases (but not civil cases) are constitutionally entitled to legal representation, and on occasion trial judges will require individual private lawyers to represent them, reminding lawyers that they are "officers of the court." But contrast the highly discretionary practice of lawyer selection of civil clients in the United States with the English rule that requires barristers to accept clients in the order they appear ("cab-rank"). Of course, the fact that many clients with civil law claims in the United States cannot afford legal services weakens the relation between political legitimacy and the court system for these individuals, a point I will return to.

38. The importance of client selection ranks high on any list of ethical advice for lawyers, regardless of their firm size. See Lynn Mather, "How and Why Do Lawyers Misbehave? Lawyers, Discipline, and Collegial Control," in *The Paradox of Professionalism: Lawyers and the Possibility of Justice*, ed. Scott L. Cummings (New York: Cambridge University Press, 2011), 109–31. See also Norman W. Spaulding, "Reinterpreting Professional Identity," *University of Colorado Law Review* 74 (2003): 1–104, arguing that these forces are pushing the legal profession toward what he calls "thick professional identity" in which lawyers intensely identify with their clients.

39. Lynn Mather, Craig A. McEwen, and Richard J. Maiman, *Divorce Lawyers at Work: Varieties of Professionalism in Practice* (New York: Oxford University Press, 2001). Some divorce lawyers reported screening potential clients according to their financial resources, setting a high minimum retainer in order to retain a particular class of clientele.

40. Personal interviews with patent lawyers, on file with the author.

41. Susan P. Shapiro, *Tangled Loyalties: Conflict of Interest in Legal Practice* (Ann Arbor: University of Michigan Press, 2002), 152. As examples of positional conflicts, Shapiro points to disputes over insurance coverage,

environmental pollution, antitrust regulations, employment, professional liability, and banking.

42. See Mather, McEwen, and Maiman, *Divorce Lawyers at Work*; see also Austin Sarat and William L. F. Felstiner, *Divorce Lawyers and Their Clients: Power and Meaning in the Legal Process* (New York: Oxford University Press, 1995).

43. Corey S. Shdaimah, "Legal Services Lawyers: When Conceptions of Lawyering and Values Clash," in *Lawyers in Practice: Ethical Decision Making in Context*, ed. Leslie C. Levin and Lynn Mather (Chicago: University of Chicago Press, 2012), 317–39. See also Ann Southworth, "Lawyer-Client Decisionmaking in Civil Rights and Poverty Practice: An Empirical Study of Lawyers' Norms," *Georgetown Journal of Legal Ethics* 9 (Summer 1996): 1101–56.

44. Robert L. Nelson, "Ideology, Practice, and Professional Autonomy: Social Values and Client Relationships in the Large Law Firm," *Stanford Law Review* 37 (January 1985): 503–52.

45. Philip Lewis, "Aspects of Professionalism: Constructing the Lawyer-Client Relationship," in *The Paradox of Professionalism*, ed. Cummings, 148.

46. John Flood, "Transnational Lawyering: Clients, Ethics and Regulation," in *Lawyers in Practice*, ed. Levin and Mather, 176–96.

47. Jerome H. Skolnick, "Social Control in the Adversary System," *Journal of Conflict Resolution* 11 (Law and Conflict Resolution) (March 1967): 52–70.

48. For summary of research on this point, see Mather, "Fundamentals."

49. Rodney J. Uphoff and Peter B. Wood, "The Allocation of Decision-making between Defense Counsel and Criminal Defendant: An Empirical Study of Attorney-Client Decisionmaking," *University of Kansas Law Review* 47 (November 1998): 1–60.

50. 463 U.S. 745 (1983).

51. Ibid., 761–62.

52. United States v. Kaczynski, No. 99-16531, affirmed by the 9th circuit in 2001. For analysis and critique of the defense lawyers' role in this case, see Michael Mello, "United States v. Kaczynski: Representing the Unabomber," in *Legal Ethics: Law Stories*, ed. Deborah L. Rhode and David J. Luban (St. Paul, MN: Thomson/West, 2006), 139–74.

53. Mather, "Fundamentals," 1075.

54. Mather, McEwen, and Maiman, *Divorce Lawyers at Work*; Sarat and Felstiner, *Divorce Lawyers and Their Clients*.

55. Douglas E. Rosenthal, *Lawyer and Client: Who's in Charge?* (New York: Russell Sage Foundation, 1974).

56. Herbert Kritzer, "Contingent-Fee Lawyers and Their Clients: Settlement Expectations, Settlement Realities, and Issues of Control in the

Lawyer-Client Relationship," *Law & Social Inquiry* 23 (Summer 1998): 795–822; Nora Freeman Engstrom, "Run-of-the-Mill Justice," *Georgetown Journal of Legal Ethics* 22 (Fall 2009): 1485–1548.

57. Herbert Kritzer, "Betwixt and Between: The Ethical Dilemmas of Insurance Defense," in *Lawyers in Practice*, ed. Levin and Mather, 131–51.

58. Carl Hosticka, "We Don't Care about What Happened, We Only Care about What Is Going to Happen," *Social Problems* 26 (1978–79): 599–610.

59. Gary Neustadter, "When Lawyer and Client Meet: Observations of Interviewing and Counseling Behavior in the Consumer Bankruptcy Law Office," *Buffalo Law Review* 35 (Winter 1986): 229.

60. Eve Spangler, *Lawyers for Hire: Salaried Professionals at Work* (New Haven: Yale University Press, 1986), 64.

61. Mark C. Suchman, "Working without a Net: The Sociology of Legal Ethics in Corporate Litigation," *Fordham Law Review* 67 (November 1998): 849.

62. Ibid.

63. Ibid.

64. Kimberly Kirkland, "The Ethics of Constructing Truth: The Corporate Litigator's Approach," in *Lawyers in Practice*, ed. Levin and Mather, 152–75.

65. William Gallagher, "IP Legal Ethics in the Everyday Practice of Law: An Empirical Perspective on Patent Litigators," *John Marshall Review of Intellectual Property Law* 10 (2011): 309–64.

66. Ibid., 335.

67. Patrick Schmidt, "The Ethical Lives of Securities Lawyers," in *Lawyers in Practice*, ed. Levin and Mather, 221–44.

68. Donald D. Landon, *Country Lawyers: The Impact of Context on Professional Practice* (New York: Praeger, 1990); Joel F. Handler, *The Lawyer and His Community: The Practicing Bar in a Middle-Sized City* (Madison: University of Wisconsin Press, 1967).

69. See, for examples, Abraham S. Blumberg, "The Practice of Law as Confidence Game: Organizational Cooptation of a Profession," *Law & Society Review* 1 (June 1967): 15–40; Lynn Mather, *Plea Bargaining or Trial? The Process of Criminal-Case Disposition* (Lexington, MA: D. C. Heath, 1979); Uphoff and Wood, "The Allocation of Decisionmaking"; and Nicole Martorano Van Cleve, "Reinterpreting the Zealous Advocate: Multiple Intermediary Roles of the Criminal Defense Attorney," in *Lawyers in Practice*, ed. Levin and Mather, 293–316.

70. Ronald J. Gilson and Robert H. Mnookin, "Disputing through Agents: Cooperation and Conflict between Lawyers in Litigation," *Columbia Law Review* 94 (March 1994): 509–66.

71. Jason Scott Johnston and Joel Waldfogel, "Does Repeat Play Elicit Cooperation? Evidence from Federal Civil Litigation," *Journal of Legal Studies* 31 (January 2002): 41.

72. Mather, McEwen, and Maiman, *Divorce Lawyers at Work*, 114.

73. Ibid., 115.

74. See, for examples, Suchman, "Working without a Net"; Kirkland, "The Ethics of Constructing Truth"; and Robert Gordon, "The Ethical Worlds of Large Firm Litigators: Preliminary Observations," *Fordham Law Review* 67 (November 1998): 709–38.

75. Gallagher, "IP Legal Ethics," 322.

76. Ibid., 324.

77. Wilkins, "Legal Realism for Lawyers."

78. Lynn Mather and Leslie C. Levin, "Why Context Matters," *Lawyers in Practice*, ed. Levin and Mather, 3–24.

79. Robert L. Nelson, "Trends in the Legal Profession: Demographic, Economic, and Early Careers," presentation to the American Bar Foundation, Chicago, September 2008.

80. John P. Heinz, Robert L. Nelson, Rebecca L. Sandefur, and Edward O. Laumann, *Urban Lawyers: The New Social Structure of the Bar* (Chicago: University of Chicago Press, 2005), 42–43.

81. For diverse perspectives on the rise of pro bono representation and unmet legal needs, see Robert Granfield and Lynn Mather, *Private Lawyers and the Public Interest: The Evolving Role of Pro Bono in the Legal Profession* (New York: Oxford University Press, 2009).

82. Jonathan Casper, *American Criminal Justice: The Defendant's Perspective* (Englewood Cliffs, NJ: Prentice Hall, 1972).

83. Patricia Ewick and Susan S. Silbey, *The Common Place of Law: Stories from Everyday Life* (Chicago: University of Chicago Press, 1998).

84. Martin M. Shapiro, *Courts: A Comparative and Political Analysis* (Chicago: University of Chicago Press, 1981).

85. Marc Galanter, "Why the `Haves' Come Out Ahead: Speculations on the Limits of Legal Change," *Law & Society Review* 29 (Fall 1974): 95–160.

PART III

MILITARY LOYALTY

6

A FRACTURED FIDELITY TO CAUSE

NANCY SHERMAN

As imperceptibly as Grief
. . .
Too imperceptible, at last,
To seem like Perfidy
                                —Emily Dickinson[1]

FIDELITY

The Marine Corps' well-known motto *Semper Fidelis* does not make explicit just what the object of a marine's fidelity is.[2] For most marines, it is unquestionably a commitment to each other and, by implication, to the Corps. But, for many in the Marines and for those in the armed forces in general, there is also loyalty to mission and to the overall cause of war of which the mission is a part.[3] Warriors prepare for war by rallying behind a cause. But what happens when they feel deep ambivalence about the justice of a cause? What happens when the cause for which they fight is not quite the one for which they signed up?

In preparing to write "the true story of GI Joe" for a Hollywood war movie in the early 1940s, Arthur Miller warned that soldiers abhor an ideological vacuum. Unless the American people can "explain and justify this war," they are "going to injure and sometimes destroy the minds of a host of their returning veterans."[4] At issue for Miller was not just how to rally the troops but also how to return

139

them home whole. The rationale for going to war can be motivating, as it was to become for Miller's World War II generation and, too, for a generation of soldiers who enlisted sixty years later in immediate response to the attacks of 9/11. But the rationale to stay at war, as we know all too well from our engagement in Iraq, can shift over time, be more or less rooted in fact, be more or less responsive to the realities on the ground. Cause, unlike camaraderie, can erode a soldier's morale, and soldiers often turn to camaraderie to motivate where cause cannot. "To bring each other home becomes the cause," as lawyer and former Army Reservist Captain Phil Carter said in commenting on this essay.[5] At the time, Phil had recently returned from Iraq, where he had served with the Army's 101st Airborne Division as an adviser to the Iraqi police. Retired Army Reservist Sergeant Dereck Vines put it more bluntly: "You go because you don't want to let your fellow soldiers down."

The sentiment is as old as war. One of the most striking examples comes from Siegfried Sassoon, the English poet and World War I soldier. Even in the face of his own political protest against the war and a growing pacifism inspired by conversations with Bertrand Russell, Sassoon, as a young officer, felt a profound obligation to the men with whom he fought, "shoulder to aching shoulder."[6] And so, after a long psychiatric convalescence at the military hospital Craiglockhardt, outside Edinburgh, which his good friend Robert Graves arranged to stave off possible court-martial for Sassoon's dissent, Sassoon insisted upon returning to the front in France to share the burden of battle with his troops.[7] In Plato's *Symposium*, Phaedrus sings the praises of love in battle. An army of lovers, he insists, is the most courageous kind of army, for shame engendered by love and mutual admiration will check cowardice and self-interest. Plato had in mind homoerotic relations, and Sassoon, to some degree, as well. But the point is a far more general one. Profound mutual love and care are what bind soldiers together and motivate battle. And they are also what heal warriors after war.

But cause has its place, too, in motivating battle and, just as critically, in a soldier's personal sense of accountability for participating in war.[8] Many soldiers, marines, sailors, airmen and -women—draftees, reservists, members of the National Guard, and career military alike—whom I interviewed in the course of writing the book *The Untold War*, on which this chapter draws, insist they are not responsible for the decision to go to war; that is for those at a higher pay grade, they often tell me. And yet those same individuals feel morally accountable not just for how they fight but for what they fight for. They hold themselves accountable for their participation in the collective end that defines a particular war. To a person, they are patriotic and often speak movingly about their responsibilities to do public service and their willingness to sacrifice. Some remind me of the vast public investment in them as soldiers, trained to fight when the call comes. But none want their willingness to serve exploited for a cause that is unworthy or for a war grounded in unjustified fear or waged for a pretext.[9] When they believe that has happened, the betrayal felt is profound. Some view it as a kind of breach in the family, a rupture of the deepest kind of trust and care. They are hurt and angry and also frustrated with themselves for being caught internally between the role of servant and conscientious free moral thinker. For those who are professional soldiers, the tension can feel much greater. They have chosen the military as their careers, and they know well, from years of service and command, the military good of discipline and order. But they also know that a good officer does not obey unlawful or unjust or morally unwise orders. What they are less clear about is how a good soldier should feel when he is uncertain of the justice of a cause or does not trust leadership to take seriously the individual soldier's sacrifices.

How does war feel to individual soldiers who are caught between conscience and obedience to what they reasonably regard as legitimate political authority?[10] How do honorable soldiers prepare themselves for battle when they don't fully embrace the cause of war? How does the duty to take care of each other weigh into the balance? The questions are merged in the minds of soldiers: they fight for each other, but always within specific wars fought for specific causes. The war that they are part of is not something that they can keep separate in their minds, however they may try. They hold themselves responsible for conduct as well as cause, and yet their responsibility for cause is in part, given their limited choices and the cost of resistance, a matter of luck.

These questions are part of a larger project taken on in *The Untold War*. My aim there is to explore the moral *psychic* reality of war.

In the backdrop is Michael Walzer's notion, developed in *Just and Unjust Wars*, that war is a moral enterprise and not just a scourge of tragedy and horrific destruction. "The moral reality of war," as he puts it, meaning by that the experiences of the participants of war as responsible agents and not merely victims, is obviously central to just war theory and its doctrines of just resort to war and just prosecution of war.[11] On his view, fixing war activity as moral and immoral is a casuistic project that turns to historical cases and debates, as well as to general principles of war, philosophy, and law. The dialectic moves in both directions. In my book, I push the casuistry to both a more subjective and an internal place. I explore how soldiers hold themselves accountable for war and its actions, sometimes in a way that is too harsh and doesn't easily track objective culpability, as when soldiers hold themselves responsible for unavoidable accidents or for their lucky survival and their comrades' unlucky death or, as in this chapter, for causes that are not of their choosing and for going to war, in some way, under duress. The idea is to understand moral agency in war, even when it is overimposed. That itself is a soldier's way of reining in the hell of war. It is an antidote to numbing, the armor we are more likely to associate with going to war and bringing war home.

My approach does not diminish the role of psychological therapy and trauma relief. But it doesn't pathologize all psychological injury in war, either. My claim is that philosophy has a place in taking soldiers' narratives beyond the clinician's office into a public space where the moral emotions and moral agency of soldiering become the focus. For soldiers and civilians alike, moral clarity in this area can itself be therapeutic.

My method is unorthodox. With a background in psychoanalysis as well as moral and ancient philosophy, I have interviewed soldiers, listening empathically to their narratives as texts of sorts.[12] What has resulted is a kind of philosophical ethnography, indebted to Walzer but also, always, to Aristotle and to the project of *tithenai ta phainomena*, grasping the particulars embodied in the beliefs or *endoxa* of the many and the wise. In researching the book, I interviewed foot soldiers and officers, noncommissioned and commissioned, about forty in total, most from the wars in Iraq and Afghanistan but also some from the Vietnam War and from World War II. I also interviewed several families of soldiers—spouses, siblings, children, and parents—as they, too, serve and live through war and its aftermath. The sample is not meant to be objective by social science methods. I am more interested in cases and anecdotes, in details that reveal moral salience and help frame a moral taxonomy from the ground up. As such, words and turns of phrases become important, revealing the contours of an individual's conscience in a way that sometimes gets hidden by more abstract or generic terms that are stamped on the phenomena from above. Some of those I interviewed are co-workers or students; I came to know others through my work at military hospitals, academies, and bases. I interviewed most one-on-one but saw some in group settings. No one person speaks for all. The point has been to capture the nuance and the complexity of the inner moral landscape and to fashion a sense of the acute moral agency soldiers assume in war that is often missed in the philosophical tradition of just war theory and that is often oversimplified or merely medicated in clinical practices in an effort to bring relief.

HENRY *V* AND RESPONSIBILITY FOR CAUSE

The issue of a soldier's responsibility for cause is concrete and troubling for Lieutenant Colonel Al Gill, who, at the time of our conversation, was Professor of Military Science at the ROTC program at Georgetown. He framed his remarks by appeal to the famous scene in Act IV, Scene V, of William Shakespeare's *Henry V.* Henry, under wraps, visits the troops the night before battle. "Here are these enlisted guys," says Gill with his deep Tennessee accent. "They don't know who Henry is, and they have these very frank discussions about the rightness of the cause." Henry baits the soldiers: "Methinks I could not die any where so contented as in the king's company; his cause being just and his quarrel honourable." One soldier pleads ignorance of cause: "That's more than we know." Another counsels, "Ay, or more than we should seek after." The soldiers conclude that responsibility for just cause rests with the king and that their own ignorance is not culpable: "For we know enough, if we know we are the king's subjects: if his cause be wrong, our obedience to the king wipes the crime of it out of us." In other words, mere participation in an unjust war is not wrongful action for a soldier. What a soldier is accountable for is conduct, not cause.

Gill puts his own spin on Shakespeare's verses: "I don't know much but I know this. . . . If the cause is not good, then all these guys with their arms and legs chopped off, all these wounded—the king is to blame for that shit." It is spring 2006, and many of Gill's young officers who entered Georgetown's Hoya battalion in the wake of 9/11 are now in Iraq and Afghanistan. "This is the sort of thing cadets need to see," he insists. "There has always been this stuff. As I tell my class, the thing that makes Henry less to blame is that in those days, the king was there with sword in hand. . . . Now we have this situation of guys making decisions for those who have arms and legs cut off, but they themselves have never done this stuff and never will. It's very difficult." The transferred weight of his own responsibility to his cadets hangs heavy.

That ordinary soldiers are not responsible for the cause of war remains a dominant part of traditional just war theory. Walzer famously defends the traditional view: "By and large we don't blame a soldier, even a general, who fights for his own government. He is not the member of a robber band, a willful wrongdoer, but a loyal and obedient subject and citizen, acting sometimes at great personal risk in a way he thinks is right."[13] This implies that soldiers on both sides have "an equal right to kill" and enjoy a kind of "moral equality" on the battlefield.[14] What they are accountable for is how they prosecute war—for conduct free of atrocities and crimes and excessive collateral damage—not for what they fight for.[15]

Francisco de Vitoria, the sixteenth-century Catholic theologian who advised the Castilian crown, put forth the view in one of his lectures. With the Spanish conquest of the New World the catalyst for his remarks, Vitoria argued, "Even though the war may be unjust on one side or the other, the soldiers on each side who come to fight in battle . . . are all equally innocent."[16] Yet, the moral equality of soldiers, Vitoria insists in another lecture, does not preclude a soldier's individual responsibility to conscientiously reflect about what he ought and ought not fight for: "If their conscience tells subjects that the war is unjust, *they must not go to war even if their conscience is wrong*," even if "ordered to do so by the prince."[17] To this, Vitoria adds a rider: *merely* to have doubts is not itself to violate conscience and does not warrant disobedience. Soldiers need more than doubt alone to renege on their obligation to fight.

Vitoria also addresses the moral responsibilities of leadership, with thoughts prescient of our own recent times, where we have witnessed unprecedented executive power. It is not enough, he says, for a leader to believe that war is a just cause and the last resort. "The king is not capable of examining the causes of war on his own, and it is likely that he may make mistakes, or rather that he *will* make mistakes. . . . So war should not be declared on the sole dictates of the prince, nor even on the opinions of the few, but on the opinion of the many, and of the wise and reliable." In the back of his mind is Aristotle's standard of the judgment of the practically wise person. Vitoria critically revises it, with a sharp lesson for our own times: wisdom is not the province of one but rests on the informed deliberation and scrutiny of many, duty-bound to counsel against war and a leader if circumstances demand it. "One must consult reliable and wise men who can speak with freedom and without anger or hate or greed," propounds Vitoria.[18] "If such men can by examining the causes of hostility with their advice and authority avert a war which is perhaps unjust, then they are obliged to do so."[19] Vitoria does not mince his words. He is counseling a monarchy worried about its perilous position as the universal protector of Christendom and Christian values. In a different time and place, he could have been counseling a democratically elected leader about the moral hazards, for a nation and world, of shutting out opinions that do not agree with one's own.[20]

Taken as a whole, Vitoria's remarks actually push us beyond the traditional view that foot soldiers are not accountable for the causes of war for which they fight. True, he grants, foot soldiers, unlike advisers privy to a leader's ears, are limited in their power to prevent a war. Still, given the fallibility of a leader's judgment and the magnitude of the destruction of war, soldiers ought to reflect conscientiously about what, in good faith, they are willing to fight for.[21] The claim has continuing appeal today. It seems plausible to hold that individual citizen soldiers, especially of liberal democracies such as our own, ought to bear *some* modicum of responsibility for the causes of war for which they fight, particularly when they are not conscripts. Given unprecedented access to information and critical debate through enhanced media modes, shouldn't soldiers at the very least be more reflective than they often are about what they are willing to fight for? Moreover, wouldn't such reflection tend to inhibit governments from too casually going to war?

Jeff McMahan has voiced just these concerns, arguing that soldiers act morally wrongly in fighting for unjust wars; they are "unjust combatants" he says, though they are not criminally liable for mere participation.[22] That is, what they do is morally wrong, though excusable.

More specifically, unjust combatants, because of their unjust cause, argues McMahan, cannot satisfy the criterion of proportionality requisite for just conduct in war. In this sense, cause becomes inseparable from conduct. The claim depends on a particular reading of proportionality, that the harm caused by the violence of an act of war must be weighed not simply against the *military* value of the act, that is, the defeat of the enemy (the traditional interpretation), but against the *overall goodness* of that event, that is, the overall importance or good of victory. Combatants who prosecute violence that is disproportionate in this regard are unjust.

In addition to failing to satisfy the just conduct criterion of proportionality, the unjust combatant, on McMahan's view, also cannot satisfy the just conduct criterion of discrimination. Here McMahan relies on a revisionist view of the meaning of discrimination, as well as an argument by analogy with permissible self-defense in ordinary morality. Discrimination, on his view, is not, as conventionally understood, a matter of targeting only military targets or individuals with combatant rather than noncombatant status. Rather, relying on the just and unjust combatant distinction, he argues that discrimination requires that the combatant restrict his targets to those who are morally responsible for unjust threats, namely unjust combatants. The unjust combatant becomes like the abortive bank thief who, in ordinary morality, forfeits his right of self-defense when the bank clerk whom he threatens at gunpoint points a gun back at him in return. The unjust combatant, like the armed thief, argues McMahan, forfeits his rights of self-defense through wrongful action on the battlefield. He is justifiably subject to attack. In this sense, unjust combatants *are* like members of robber bands, contra Walzer. Taken strictly, all those who fight believing their cause is just when in fact it isn't act criminally in their use of force to save their lives and those of their buddies.

Practically speaking, the implications are, of course, absurd and cruel. However much we might like soldiers to be more reflective about the causes for which they fight, we cannot expect them to track and assess from the battleground the shifting rationale for war, puzzling day by day over whether they are justified in their aggression. Rules of engagement are meant to do some of that for them and relieve them, in some measure, of personal responsibility and liability in setting the class of legitimate targets. More critically, militaries work by coercion and command structures. While few good leaders want or expect blind obedience from their troops (and this includes responsible commanders-in-chief with regard to their top brass), they do depend upon mobilized cadres that operate with good discipline and order.[23] This doesn't efface soldiers' individual responsibility to object to unlawful, immoral, and unwise orders, including the ultimate order to go to war, but it does recognize the collectivizing and coercive force of armies and raising armies.[24]

McMahan does not disagree. Despite his insistence that unjust combatants, in principle, act wrongly in fighting, in practice, he argues, they may be excused. His reasons are the familiar ones Aristotle cited long ago as mitigating circumstances for individual moral responsibility: namely inculpable ignorance and duress. In the case of duress, a host of ordinary circumstances coerce choice and limit options, including conscription, the call of patriotism and duty, the moral authority the state is believed to have or its persuasive powers in defending a rationale for going to war, or the paucity of socioeconomic and educational benefits for some outside the military. Once in uniform, soldiers face the credible constraint of the threat of harsh military punishment for resisting orders.[25]

In fact, McMahan ultimately denies the practical import of his arguments: the thesis of the inequality of combatants is an ideal conception "at the level of basic morality."[26] At the level of actual practice, the moral equality of combatants remains in place. Thus, with regard to real wars, McMahan concedes his theory is "self-effacing" and yields to a conventional account of the laws of armed conflict. Walzer sums up McMahan's position in a pointed remark: "What Jeff McMahan means to provide . . . is a careful and precise account of individual responsibility in time of war. What he actually provides, I think, is a careful and precise account of what individual responsibility in war would be like if war were a peacetime activity."[27]

Some observers sympathetic to McMahan's general concerns have argued that it makes sense to have exit options that allow citizen soldiers to refuse to fight specific wars they believe unjust, without the imposition of crippling penalties. To deny soldiers reasonable exits, they claim, is to hold the liberal state ransom to the military.[28] However, it is easy to see the practical problems with selective conscientious objection. Especially in the case of a volunteer army, it would be hard to raise troops for unpopular wars. Doubt about the cause of war might mushroom into rationalizations for not fighting. The defense needs of a country would be left to the discretion and motivation of each soldier. Still, this may be an unnecessarily gloomy picture. It is not inconceivable that selective exit policies could be designed that were at once neither overly punitive nor overly permissive and incentivizing. Under such a policy, recruitment numbers could be met while still allowing those who are truly conscientious objectors about certain conflicts to refuse to fight without being subject to excessive disciplinary punishment.

But, exit options aside, we still have reason to ask, in a more general way, how good soldiers responsibly reflect about the causes for which they fight. What I found throughout my interviews is that soldiers do struggle hard with their individual accountability for participating in a war of others' making. But it is often an internal moral struggle, rather than a matter of being externally judged by others. True, the boundaries are not always sharp. What others think and say is sometimes reflected in self-assessments. But what I observed is that often the debate goes on largely inside, as a soulful struggle with conscience. Few soldiers think in the abstract terms of just war theory or its legacy in international law and United Nations doctrine—that justified wars are conducted only to fend off attack or in the face of "immediate and imminent" attack.[29] Most don't worry, as theorists and political, legal, and military advisers do (and did in the run-up to the war in Iraq), about whether fending off "immediate and imminent" attack allows not only preemption but also prevention. But what they *do* worry about is whether they are going to war on a pretext that camouflages other, actual causes. In a deep and personal way, they worry about whether they are being betrayed or manipulated by leadership and how they can serve honorably in those circumstances. As we shall see, this is the worry of Dereck Vines, who served in Iraq in an intelligence unit. It is the worry of Bob Steck, who served in the army in Vietnam, and of Hank McQueeny, who was a naval officer in that war.

Put more globally, soldiers worry about the goodness of the ends of their wars and whether those ends will outweigh the destruction. I get insight here from my father. Seymour Sherman, a veteran of World War II, wrestled hard with that question over and over again, when he was reading the papers and following the wars in Iraq, Afghanistan, and Gaza, as he had some forty years ago, in the Vietnam War era. He looked on, often, through the eyes of a soldier, as the army medic he was. Somewhere in his reveries, he is back on the *Queen Elizabeth I,* Cunard's luxury line that was refitted as a U.S. Army transport and hospital. He is zigzagging across the Atlantic some sixteen times on a slow five-day journey to Gourock, Scotland, in the Firth of Clyde, and then on to Normandy. In his case, he does have time to think, and he wonders whether the fight is worth the horrific ruin and devastation he anticipates and then sees up close in dying men and mutilated bodies. That image of his own responsibility for the specific war he fights is there, whether or not he talks about it openly. The worry is about proportionality, the ratio between the moral good anticipated and all the carnage. Is it worth it? In the war he fought, he believes it was, then and now, as most do. But the point I am making is that the moral oversight is internal. Yes, it is about not just what he did as an individual soldier, in his case, administering inoculations and relief to the war-torn and maimed. It is also about the war he was in. That frames his perspective and his responsibility. Perhaps, at some level, there is also appreciation of the role of luck in arranging for which war was his to fight and the fact that moral luck is not itself equitable.

My experience is that my father's worries are shared by many of the soldiers I have interviewed, whether they are engaged in Iraq and Afghanistan or served in Bosnia or Vietnam. They carry on their shoulders the burden of the wars they fight, and not just their individual conduct in those wars. But the debate is often internal and inchoate, never fully verbalized or articulated.

Philosophers often miss this inner debate. And it's not just because they don't talk to soldiers. It is in part because of a long philosophical tradition that casts morality in terms of our praise and blame of others: the address is "second personal" and legal.[30] A conversation between McMahan and a soldier who fights for an unjust cause might be reconstructed along these lines: "Your participation is unjustified. But, because you may have been coerced, deceived, understandably afraid of the authority of the state, or because of the unfeasibility of trials (Who would conduct such a trial? It would certainly not be the state that demands you fight. And if the trials fall under the jurisdiction of international courts, then neither would it be their courts, given their already overextended dockets and underfinanced budgets.), you are not held individually responsible or culpable. Given the mitigating factors and pragmatic consequences of holding you and others like you liable, you are excused for your participation."

But telling soldiers that they have a blanket excuse in case war is unjust does not always help them.[31] Many continue to worry about the justification itself, both about the immorality of fighting in an unjust war and the immorality of dissent, when there is only doubt about the injustice of the cause and fear that giving in to such doubts would become acts of cowardice, a desertion of one's country in its time of need, and, in the case of the professional soldier, a failure to put to use all the money and resources the state has invested in preparing one to be ready when called.[32] For many soldiers, being excused doesn't mitigate their own need for moral accountability for the cause for which they fight. They engage in inner moral debates often framed in terms of virtue and cowardice, certainty and doubt about cause, and obligation to fellow soldiers and to country.

The irony, as Ryan Balot has implied in his insightful comments on this chapter, is that McMahan's worries about the deep morality of just cause are not, in fact, irrelevant to soldiers in a practical way. Soldiers often internalize the moral debate, at times reproving themselves more harshly than outsiders would but also anguishing over just how manipulated they are by authority, duty, and patriotism and how helpless they feel as a result. They don't easily excuse or forgive themselves for the luck of their cause, even if they recognize how limited their options are and how coercive their circumstances.

Indeed, many soldiers I have spoken to hold themselves accountable for the wars they fight in, whether they feel proud or

tainted, accomplished or disillusioned, compromised or sacrific-
ing and sacrificed. The feelings are typically mixed and muted,
with a sense of agency and a sense of being used immorally often
bleeding into each other. Some soldiers try to compartmentalize
their portion of war as a way of fending off more complicated feelings. It may be true that traditional just war theory is too limiting,
because it too neatly pries apart cause from conduct. But it is also
too limiting because it doesn't invite us to listen to soldiers' own
struggles with that for which they are asked to fight.

Moral Psychic Realities

So let us begin again to listen to and frame the inner moral debate
as soldiers themselves experience it. Even if war can be a "tyrannical enterprise" that "overrides individuality," as Walzer has put
it,[33] soldiers nonetheless struggle to maintain their own senses of
autonomy in the face of what can seem overwhelming constraints
and the faithful servitude that is at times abused. They suck it up
and are stoic, as I have argued elsewhere,[34] in sticking with the mission and its personal sacrifices. They detach from losses and attachments, both as an automatic, adaptive response to traumatic
stressors and as part of the cultivated warrior ethos of getting on
with the job. But, despite stoic fidelity and loyal service, conflicts
about individual complicity and personal responsibility for participation in collective ends don't easily disappear.

In what follows, we hear from four soldiers, three whom I have
interviewed and the fourth a literary character who lays bare the
soul of his author, a World War II soldier. For each, specific moral
emotions become leitmotifs, emblematic of bearing the cause of
war ambivalently.

"Tainted"

Bob Steck got his greetings to go to Vietnam a few days after he
turned twenty-six.[35] At that point, he was too old to be drafted,
but the letter from his Texas draft board had been postmarked
before his birthday. Officially, he was still eligible. "There was a
sense of the absurd," Bob said. "It was 1970, and I was against the
war at the time." He had recently finished graduate course work in

philosophy at Yale and was teaching at Washington and Lee University in Virginia. He even hired the firm of Boudin, Rabinowitz, and Standard, New York attorneys well known at the time for their opposition to the war. The strategy was to test his orders to go to war as illegal, on the basis of his assertion that the war was illegal. "It was a way of trying to bring cause to the courts." The case didn't go very far, and ultimately he faced, as many drafted did, an existential crisis. Canada was not much of an option for him. It was jail or going into the army: "I decided to go to the army because I didn't think it was a one-step inference from 'I don't believe in this war' to 'I won't serve in this war.' I reasoned, if I don't go, someone else will, who is maybe younger without my resources or someone who would be less likely to keep his wits and be more tempted to commit atrocities. It was very difficult, obviously. Maybe it was all rationalization. I never was entirely confident with my decision. Also my dad had died five years earlier, and my mother was on her own. My going to jail would have been terribly hard on her."

Bob served in Vietnam for a little less than a year as a radio operator with the Army Air Cavalry ("A" Troop, 3/17), keeping networks open so that helicopter teams could communicate with each other. I first met him in 2005 at a discussion of my book, *Stoic Warriors*. During the question-and-answer session, he was one of the first to speak. Then in his early sixties, Bob briskly stepped up to the mike but then choked with emotion as he tried to talk. When he regained his composure, what followed was a fairly dry academic question: "Can you distinguish the justness of a war from the justness of a warrior?" he asked. But it was clear that there were layers underneath.

I hadn't addressed the issue in my talk, so I was a bit taken aback. As I paused, he offered his own answer. "Those of us who became antiwar veterans about Vietnam used to insist that we could—that we must—distinguish the war from the warrior." Some thirty-five years after his war in Vietnam, Bob had to believe that the cause for which he had fought and his conduct in fighting were separate if he was to make peace with himself. Still, believing that was not easy.

As I was to learn later through many conversations with Bob over the past several years, the wars in Iraq and Afghanistan have led him and scores of other Vietnam vets to relive some of their worst war trauma. Some have returned to therapy; others, including Bob, have regularly visited hospitals, like Walter Reed Army Medical Center in Washington, D.C., to share their own hard-won lessons with returning, war-torn soldiers. (One such vet who has been public about his returning depression is Max Cleland, former U.S. senator from Georgia and a decorated Vietnam veteran and triple amputee.)[36] In Bob's own case, what weighs heavily is a felt impotence at not being able to save soldiers from the suffering he went through.

This was on his mind as I interviewed him in February 2007. "I think my works and days are kind of marinated in a sort of melancholy," he said soberly. He himself had felt betrayed by World War II veterans who did not really tell him the truth about going to war—what it feels like, what it requires of soldiers, and what it does to them. The commitment he has carried since Vietnam and his activism in Vietnam Veterans Against the War is not to betray a future generation of soldiers.

Bob reflects on an incident early in his military career that was formative. He was standing in chow line in basic training when a drill sergeant "came down" hard on an African American soldier for being dressed sloppily. "He kicked the hell out of his leg and then kicked him again when the guy flinched. . . . I was just livid," says Bob. But maybe that's how you have to make an army, he rationalized. Maybe that's how you have to prepare for "the contours of what combat was really like." But the anger really never subsided; neither did the resentment that he had been kept in the dark about the true price of combat: "Why in heaven's name didn't the combat veterans from the Second World War come back and tell us, even though theirs was a war worth doing: 'Hey folks, here are the prices of this kind of thing. We don't go into this stuff lightly. We don't go into wars of choice. We don't go in on a bet or a theory. We go in if we have to stop Nazi Germany.' Why didn't they tell us? So one of the things I sort of resolved for myself standing in that chow line out in Fort Lewis, Washington, was that I'm not going to let people forget. I am not going to let this be just passed over."

Returning to the present, he says with disbelief, "I thought we had talked enough. I thought we had talked enough. I thought we had talked so much people had gotten tired of it. I thought at least they knew."

Bob is visibly anguished about his own generation's ultimate
failure to inoculate future generations of soldiers. He is a man of
strong moral sensibilities, well read, knowledgeable, and an activ-
ist. (He has returned to Vietnam several times to heal himself and
fellow vets, on one occasion riding on a bike tour from Hanoi to
Saigon on a tandem with George Brummell, a vet a who lost his eye-
sight from an explosion during the war, seated behind.) Over the
past thirty-five years, Bob has not taken his mission lightly. Part of
the anguish comes from the sense of political impotence, part from
the underlying fact that he can't psychologically or morally fully separate himself from the war he fought. Wars and warriors don't easily
come apart, even if they do in some theoretical formulation.

Shortly after Veterans Day in 2007, Bob told me in a phone
conversation that he had gone down to the Vietnam Memorial to
commemorate the day. At the time, I was trying to understand the
notion of shame some soldiers feel for their engagement in war,
and so we began to talk about that. In his case, he said, the predominant feeling wasn't shame but a sense of taint. "We *all* felt
a sense of taint," even those who were in the nursing corps, who
were "on the side of the angels in that they did not carry weapons."
Steck tells me that Michael Herr puts his finger on the feeling in
his famous memoir of his years as a war correspondent in Vietnam:
"I went to cover the war, but the war covered me."[37]

Taint implies contamination by what's toxic. In the Vietnam era,
returning soldiers sometimes met jeering crowds who yelled "baby
killer" and "murderer,"[38] even though the enlightened public, and
probably many of the jeerers, knew well that not all returning soldiers had committed those atrocities and that many (such as Bob)
had fought hard to prevent them.[39] Still, honorable soldiers felt
vulnerable to the criticism, for they viewed the shaming remarks as
commenting not only on *how* they fought the war but on the fact
that they fought the war. Being blamed for conduct was a way to
really get at the fact that they fought at all. The soldiers were seen
as, in some way, complicit, even if the preponderance of public
criticism was reserved for those higher up and, in particular, the
civilian administration.[40] By fighting in Vietnam, the soldiers had
become tainted.

Taint is a feeling seldom discussed in the philosophical or psychological literature (though it does figure in the work of some

anthropologists, such as Mary Douglas).[41] Philosophers tend to write about moral feelings like guilt and shame, remorse and regret, indignation and moral protest. Some with a more legal bent write about complicity. Taint is rarely mentioned. So what does Bob have in mind when he says that he feels tainted?

"Taint" implies pollution, staining, fouling. There is a kind of guilt by association. If complicity figures in the account, it is often of the mildest kind. In Bob's case, it's clear that, as a young soldier, he was far from the center of power, where decisions were made and policies formulated with regard to why the war is fought or continued. He was a draftee, who went even though he was opposed to the war. Like most foot soldiers, he participated at the extreme periphery of a collective end, and he is, by any measure, far less complicit than the top civilians and brass who called the shots.[42] Yet, Bob feels tainted—not corrupted or sullied. Those words are too strong, and not his. In his mind, there is a passive yet pervasive association with a policy that was wrong or unjust. The tinge spread, irrespective of his moral protest. What was toxic permeates his being. In that physical metaphor, taint so fills the pores that cleansing and purification seem impossible.

Bob tells me the taint was reinforced when people later said to him that, as a member of the Vietnam Veterans Against the War movement, "you are not in a position to criticize the war, since you fought in it." Taint mingles with the shame of internalizing something you don't really believe but that "has traction"—that you are guilty of hypocrisy. Some fellow veterans worried precisely about the risks of open dissent. So, he noted, veterans who did not join the movement (perhaps some of whom would later become part of the "Swift Boat" attack on John Kerry's 2004 presidential bid) may have privately felt that they fought an ill-conceived and unjust war, but they "did not want to make it public because it would cast shame on veterans" for being less than patriotic.

As Bob describes it, the taint moves from the outside in. Others (and the circumstances of his war) stick it on him. Yet it sticks. This veteran was and forever will be part of a war he didn't believe was just. There will always be that felt lack of confidence about his moral position because, in the end, he agreed to fight. "Maybe it's all rationalization?" he muses. "I will probably go to my grave not knowing if I made the right decision." But his own doubts are exacerbated when others see him as part of an undifferentiated force that prosecuted a misguided war. He is implicated, not for some specific action or accident but because of bad, circumstantial luck that caught him in its snare. In a different war, in a different generation, he might have come home from war feeling pride and a sense of courage for having put his life on the line for the sake of what is noble. Instead, because of the war he fought, he feels contaminated. His assessment of himself and the way others assess him are wrapped up with moral luck and a kind of coerced choice.[43]

In a sense, Bob Steck internalizes Jeff McMahan's notion of the deep morality of war and its claim that cause is inseparable from conduct. But, for Bob, that moral stance isn't at all self-effacing; quite to the contrary, he carries the weight of unjust cause with him and is tainted by it. He doesn't easily excuse himself, and feels the shame of what he was a part of. Moral repair, on his view, is requisite and comes in the form of educating future soldiers about the seepage of cause into the very soul of a soldier. What he wants desperately is that soldiers be saved from the lasting melancholy that that seepage can cause. But, just as he felt betrayed by those who served before him, he now feels that, despite his best efforts and for all his candid talking, he still can't protect soldiers (or, for that matter, a nation) from the moral injuries that come from fighting unjustified wars. He feels a kind of perfidy, a soldier's treachery, in his impotence.

"SUCKERED"

The theme of betrayal runs deep in soldiers' narratives. Some of that sense of betrayal comes from failing to protect buddies, whether through the generations, as Bob Steck feels it, or side by side on the battlefield itself. To betray is to breach a trust, in these cases to make vulnerable the fidelity soldiers place in each other. But that vulnerability is felt not just at the level of horizontal bonds but also at the level of vertical bonds, especially bonds that go upward.

Relevant here are multiple interviews I conducted with Dereck Vines.[44] Vines is a veteran of Bosnia and Iraq who served in the army reserves in both wars. In his early fifties at the time we talked, he deployed to Iraq at the age of forty-five, with the 404th Reserve

Unit from Fort Dix, New Jersey, as a civil affairs sergeant in an intelligence unit. He retired at the rank of army sergeant first class. I met Dereck at the Woodrow Wilson Center, where he was on the tech staff and I was a research fellow. When he learned about my project on soldiers, he asked to sit down with me to chat. We talked in the spring of 2007 several times and again, a few times, in late 2008, on one occasion with his family.

Each time we spoke, Dereck compared his experiences in Iraq and Bosnia. Bosnia was a war he could believe in and that he felt good about being part of. He went feeling he had a mission and came home feeling proud. "In Bosnia we had a purpose. The Serbs were about to wipe out the Bosnian people altogether. If we or the UN hadn't stepped in, it would have been a catastrophe," he says. The start of the war in Afghanistan, too, had a mission he said he could rally around and did when his unit was put on an alert roster to go there. "I felt the importance of the mission in Afghanistan, to try to find Bin Laden and to get back at them for their attacks. Otherwise, we'd be suckered. We'd let them just get us." But orders shifted, and his unit was deployed to Iraq. "Iraq was the complete opposite of Bosnia," he says. It was a war he just couldn't believe in.

The word "suckered" jumped out at me. It had come up before, the first time we talked. In fact, it was the theme of that interview. In going to Iraq and in serving there, *he* felt "suckered." Dereck wasn't talking about a public that had been suckered or blinded into going into war. And he wasn't analyzing a history of America or other countries "suckered" into war by blind patriotism or the beating of the war drums by effective propaganda.[45] He was talking painfully about his own feelings, the notion that his life might have been squandered on a pretext, a mission whose purpose he couldn't believe in and still believes was ill formed: "The whole thing with the weapons of mass destruction. Did we ever find any? And that's what we always say—did we ever find any weapons of mass destruction? All of the chemicals and stuff that Iraq was supposed to have—and we never found any. . . . It's just like: 'Okay, I've been suckered.'"

"I try not to think about it," Dereck says in his quiet, but angry voice. "The more and more you hear in the commissions, that this was false information and that was false information. You're sitting there. You're just like, 'Okay, I was almost killed. I was almost not here and they haven't really given me a clear reason.' You hate to be against the president and I don't care if he's a Republican or a Democrat or whatever. But for your upper echelon to really sucker you—that's kind of a hard pill to swallow."

What Dereck Vines means by being suckered is that he feels duped, deceived, toyed with by those in charge to whom he had sworn fidelity and for whom he put his life on the line. To be sure, like many soldiers, Vines is adamant about his patriotism: "When you are feeling these thoughts [of being suckered], pride in America and the uniform—that's what kind of holds you together," he says. But what fractures that pride is the sense of betrayal, the feeling of being abandoned, misled, unsupported, manipulated by those who have put you in danger's way. Even those terms are too abstract to capture Vines's feeling. The betrayal is raw and existential: "I was almost killed. I was almost not here."

The words are a soldier's shorthand for traumatic moments imprinted in his psyche—in this case, images of picking up and bagging body parts of buddies caught in a fire bombing, of watching his convoy get severed by a bomb that thrust him against the windshield of his armored vehicle, of being medevaced, half-conscious, to a hospital. The memories are seared in his mind and return intrusively. But the trauma is exacerbated by moral anguish and resentment that his trust was misplaced and abused. The shock and the disappointment are tangible as he speaks. To be suckered by "your upper echelon" (top military and civilian leaders, he means) is almost unfathomable to him. "You serve your country," he says passionately. "You don't want to let your fellow soldiers down." In his case, there was never the thought that he wouldn't go. But still he felt duped. He wanted and felt morally owed wiser leadership and better analysis of the intelligence from the military and government agencies. The teachings of Vitoria are relevant here: a leader cannot examine the causes of war on his own, nor can an insulated coterie of advisers. The likelihood of making a mistake is too great. The wisest and most reliable must deliberate and provide counsel. Again, in Vitoria's words, "If such men can by examining the causes of hostility with their advice and authority avert a war which is perhaps unjust, then they are obliged to do so."[46]

Betrayal is a word not to be taken lightly in military contexts. If we turn to the Oxford English Dictionary for instruction, we find that the first definition of "betrayal" is "a treacherous giving up to an enemy." Next is "a violation of trust or confidence, an abandonment of something committed to one's charge." The definition of the verb "to betray" again puts the military context first: "to give up or place in the power of an enemy by treachery or disloyalty."

The military connotation is suggestive, but it doesn't tell the full story. It is not, at least in Dereck's case, that he was given up to the enemy. Rather, what counts as the betrayal for him is that a sacred bond of trust was broken: a "sacred band," like those Plato and Plutarch wrote about, founded on military honor, loyalty, and a sense of shame.[47] For some, the betrayal is experienced as the rupture of the most basic caring bond: there is a rupture of the family that a soldier becomes part of when he or she joins the military. The reciprocal caring from those cared for and served breaks down. The betrayal is experienced profoundly, as perfidy. Here it is critical to remember that bonding in the military is not just horizontal, shared with comrades, brothers and sisters in arms, though that undoubtedly is the most intense attachment. Bonding also runs vertically, up chains of command: soldiers give allegiance and respect to superiors with the trust that their service and sacrifice won't be squandered. Their trust is betrayed when a country and its soldiers are duped into going to war.[48]

The attachment element in military life cannot be underestimated. Many young recruits, just out of high school, join the military in search of a new family. What they have at home may no longer satisfy or, for some, never did. They want new role models that give them something to believe in and to idealize. They want to be part of something bigger than themselves, where there is community and caring if you are willing to work for them. Others don't so much seek a new family as find it through the radical socialization process of boot camp. Markers of old attachments (first name, easy contact with home and family, civilian clothes and hair, comfort objects and personal styles) are removed and replaced with new attachments and look-alike images that stamp the recruit with a new family identity. Boot camp is about molding a new self but also about becoming a part of a new family, with all its aspirations and its promise of care.

The Marine Corps' *Semper Fidelis,* again, speaks volumes. To be betrayed by this new family is devastating, especially for those who have sought it out because of earlier betrayals or traumas within their families of origin. A psychotherapist who has worked with scores of patients at Walter Reed Hospital once commented, anecdotally, that those who are wounded psychologically by war often experience an element of betrayal. The attachment bond has been snapped and, with it, the belief that fidelity ought to be reciprocated by support and care and empathic leadership. It is a betrayal often not easily resolved, given the distance between ranks and the implausibility of "working it out" in the way individuals do in healthy families or marriages, face-to-face. The betrayal may just have to be accepted as a fact, a bitter fact.

The soldier's implicit wish, voiced by Dereck Vines, is that commanders not betray subordinates' willingness to serve and make sacrifices. When commanders do, they act with treachery and perfidy. Dereck went to war as a graying noncommissioned officer (NCO). He was "Pops" to his troops, no naive, wide-eyed boy. Yet he feels suckered, taken for a fool. He is angry at others but also angry at himself for being gullible. If called again, knowing what he now knows, he tells me, he'd still go. That is what he signed up for. Like many enlisted and reserved soldiers, he is willing to fight because he accepts that responsibility as part of his job. But still he feels betrayal—a sense that his willingness to make the ultimate sacrifice for his country and comrades ought to be mirrored by the gravest of sense of responsibility on the part of higher-ups. If betrayal is about the rupture of trust, perfidy and treachery are about the risk and danger to which abuse of trust exposes one.

Shakespeare's Henry V again makes the point, though this time from the perspective of the compassionate commander and more from the stance of his own entitlements than from that of just cause. If *I* live to see the king ransomed, says Henry in disguise to his troops (imagining his possible defeat and the private "life boat" that will rescue him), "then I will never trust his word again."[49] Henry projects his wishes onto the soldiers: he desperately wants them to have faith in him, to believe that he won't be ransomed or lose the war. He wants them to feel that their fighting will not have been in vain and to believe that they will not be exploited or seen as expendable. But the soldiers can't and won't share the luxury of his lofty fantasy.

They are, after all, just subjects. Ransomed or not ransomed won't make a hoot of difference once they are dead, they say. They are (or in death will have been) just the king's instruments. But Henry wishes they were more and he were less. In the shadow of soliloquy, he deflates his own "farced" (stuffed) pomp and title, which inspires "awe and fear in other men." Still, deflation in status is just for the sake of a "proud dream," a wishful fantasy that he might share the weight of his responsibility for war. But the moral reality is that he remains the king and calls the shots. At the end of the day, the soldiers still take his orders and die for his causes. They can only hope that their faithful service is not abused.

Dereck Vines carries that feeling of being someone else's instrument. What smarts is that he is no king's subject. He votes. He is informed. He now works in a Washington policy institute, whose head he much admires and feels special affection toward—Lee Hamilton, the former Indiana congressman who with James Baker headed up the Iraq Study Group in 2006 to advise on American policy in Iraq. Vines never uses the word "tainted," as Bob Steck does. For Vines, Iraq is not toxic in the way Vietnam felt and feels to many veterans of that war. Vines was not a draftee. He did not feel coerced to serve in the way many draftees who went to Vietnam did. He went willingly, as part of his duty. But he still felt "suckered." That feeling of having been lied to and of having let himself be lied to is what tears him up.

Again, this is not just a tale of a tragic victim. It is a tragic victim of the Aristotelian sort, as Aristotle outlines in the *Poetics*, where there is choice, *hamartia* (literally, a missing of the mark), but constrained and coerced or duped choice.[50] And, because of that choice, in Vines's case, the choice to serve patriotically and not to abandon comrades, there is personal responsibility and no easy self-absolution. Vines has plenty of moral anger toward the brass, but he is also angry at himself and what he allowed them to do to him. As we talk, the anger simmers rather than boils, but it is unmistakable when he utters the word "suckered." He let himself be suckered, and they suckered him. Selective conscientious objection was not and is not part of Vines's live options; it is not part of his ingrained and socialized expectations of obedience and loyalty. Still, he is angry that he could be duped and angry that he was willing to sacrifice so much for what he thinks was a lie.

"DISILLUSIONED"

Hank McQueeny is a retired naval officer who served in Vietnam and always wanted to be in the navy.[51] Of all the military uniforms, navy summer whites, officer summer whites, "dress whites with the stiff neck and the bridge cap" were those he loved best. He also loved battleship grey "and the smell of the ship oils and resins and paint and the sea all mixed together." As a young boy, he could remember himself saying, "By God, if I'm in the service when I grow up, I want to be in the navy." Growing up in Boston, there was also a local naval hero—John F. Kennedy, the young lieutenant and captain of the PT-109 that was ripped apart by a Japanese destroyer in August 1943 in the Solomon Islands. For Hank, the navy called. And so, in 1960, after graduating from Boston College, Hank McQueeny was commissioned, went to intelligence school, survived simulated POW training, and was assigned as a junior officer to a squadron in fleet. By 1964, he was aboard the USS *Ticonderoga* off the shores of Southeast Asia.

But it wasn't long before disillusionment set in. His disillusionment centered on the ruse that led to the Gulf of Tonkin Resolution (August 5, 1964), in which Congress, in a near unanimous vote, authorized President Lyndon Johnson to use "all necessary measures" to repel armed attacks against U.S. forces in Vietnam.[52]

The surrounding incidents are well known (and were narrated to me earlier by another officer on board the *Ticonderoga*, Vice Admiral Jim Stockdale, who one year after the Tonkin incident was shot down in Vietnam and who was held as a POW for seven and a half years in the Hanoi Hilton).[53] The circumstances are these, as Hank narrates the events: two U.S. destroyers were ordered to enter the claimed sovereign waters of North Vietnam. "The idea was to prompt the North Vietnamese to send small vessels . . . —the little fast PT boats—against the destroyers to have them back away from their port. . . . That would be an excuse, a reason to accelerate the war."

From the *Ticonderoga*, two A-1s (single-seat aircrafts) were sent overhead to inspect the damage. "But they saw no PT boats. They saw nothing" and reported as much through their command structure up to the Pentagon. All they saw was "the flash of the weapons aboard the destroyers shooting aimlessly against the presumed target." As one of the skippers of the aircraft told Hank at the time, "Hank, there's nothing up there, no shit, nothing up there." In Hank's sober words, "They said that the ships were attacked, falsely said that, and they used that as a ruse, manufactured a ruse, to thereby enlarge the war. That was a big disillusionment. . . . Everybody on the ship knew the truth, or practically everybody," even if many accepted it as the cost of moving the war forward. But, for Hank, the reality of what happened loomed large in his consciousness.

His disillusionment is a brooding anger in being deceived, toyed with, made party to a deception. The treachery is a kind of triple abuse of respect and dignity: you are lied to (or at least what you know to be true is denied) in order for you to play a role in a public deception (the ruse), which then puts you at great risk (the war's acceleration through the Gulf of Tonkin Resolution).[54] "I was disillusioned. I thought, I still think, that this country ought not to be above ordinary standards." From then on, as he puts it, "there was just a sense of going down a slippery slope real quickly." His way of coping, like that of many soldiers in all wars, was self-medication and avoidance: "We did a lot of drinking, carousing, a lot of running around. We played bridge." Drugs would come later in the war, after Hank's time.

The general tenor of this narrative is familiar to those for whom the Vietnam era was formative. But the point that emerges over and over again in my interviews is that combatants internalize their conflicts about the justification of war, suck it up, truck on, keep fighting, and perhaps only later, if they are reflective and empathically supported, expose their anger and ambivalence. Like Dereck Vines, Hank McQueeny clings to the uniform as something that idealizes his service and helps him tolerate his disillusionment. "I used to enjoy my uniform," he says tenderly. "I used to greatly enjoy my uniform. I still have dreams about my uniform." He confides on a lighter note that he once failed to show up in his dress uniform because he refused to spend a hundred dollars on a ceremonial sword that was a mandatory part of the dress code. He chuckled as he relived the moment of youthful defiance: "I stood up the guy who wanted me to wear a sword to the party!" Musing about this and his mention of dreams, I coyly asked if he ever dreamt about his sword. "No, that's too phallic," he shot back. "I never dreamed about that!"

Of course, in Hank's case, if there hadn't been the uniform, there wouldn't be the disillusionment. For what he is saying is that there is a still an important place in him for the military at its best—for the ideal of the military and the protection and support it represents, captured for him in the gleam of bright summer whites. Holding onto that idealized object removes some of the taint, alienation, and loss in service to a cause he fears may not have been worth it and in service to leaders who may not have deserved his trust.

To my ears, Hank McQueeny's disillusionment is conceptually, morally, and psychologically distinct from Dereck Vines's feeling of being suckered. True, Hank feels betrayed, but what hurts most is the *deflation* of himself and his ideals. What he imagined he stood for in his whites got drained of meaning, and with that loss he also lost his image of self, defined by commitment to worthy public service and sacrifice. The disillusionment is the deflation that follows upon the betrayal. It is that deflated self that is so hard to reconcile with who he envisions he was in uniform and who he was supposed to be.

Of course, this kind of deflation needn't be specific to military service. Idealization and failures to meet ideals or destruction of ideals by sober thought or cruel awakenings are the stuff of growth and moral development, especially in late adolescence. But *this* deflation is mixed with all the suffering of war, of thousands upon thousands of deaths and one's own sense of complicity in the killing fields. To see the lie being woven about the need to escalate a war that will cause more unjustified sacrifice is to feel disarmed in one's patriotism. It is to feel naked, to be stripped of sailor whites, in a fully vulnerable moment. It is moral disillusionment, of the deepest kind, about the justification of service for a cause. To be fully conscientious, perhaps Hank ought to have abandoned his post and ceased participation, at whatever cost. But this isn't how he assumed moral responsibility. Instead, like many soldiers, he internalized the conflict and struggled all these years, living with a hollowed out sense of patriotism.

THE CESSPOOL OF NAPLES

As a public, we tend to idealize World War II and have a tendency to think that American soldiers and the Allies that fought in that war, by and large, did not have to struggle with the anguished feelings I have been describing. They went to war rallying not just for one another but also for a cause that was popular. The evil of Nazism and Hitler's tyranny was real. Defending homeland and allies against attack was justified. The internal doubts and conflicts were, on the whole, fewer. Perhaps that is so for most of those who fought. But consider one soldier's voice from that war. The voice is from John Horne Burns's underread World War II novel, *The Gallery*.[55] Written in 1947, it is more memoir than novel. The setting is North Africa and Naples, and the "gallery" in the title is the Galleria Umberto Primo, a bombed-out glass arcade that was "the unofficial heart of Naples," where Americans, British, and Neapolitans commingled in sin.

Through Burns, we see again the internal tensions soldiers experience in fighting wars that they have come to lose faith in. Though World War II is by most portrayed as a war to save the world from evil, Burns, writing with fresh eyes just three years after the war, paints a picture that is not so noble. Whatever he felt going to war soon evaporated in war. Naples was a cesspool of soldiers selling their rations for an hour at a brothel, of child-pimps with their prostitutes, of Neapolitan ladies showing up en masse at a public concert in winter coats sewn from purloined Army issue blankets, of army freighters, tanks, and wheels of military vehicles stolen by a population that was bombed out and starving.[56] This, we might say, is an indictment not of the cause of war but of how it is prosecuted and the reality of postbellum occupation. But it is also about cause. For Burns, a writer schooled at Andover and Harvard, the lofty rationale for World War II never fully stuck. What he saw daily was war's corruption, "its annihilation of everything" that "the sensitive, shy, and gentle" stand for, and the fury of those who die, who leave "this life angry, but not hurt," some wrestling "with the larger issues" when it is not even clear if they can read or write.[57]

Many of the soldiers he wrote about see themselves as participants in the grotesquerie and hold themselves liable. They are their own persons, not just marionette-servants of someone else's decision to go to war. It is *their* war. It frames what they do and their engagement. Disconnecting from their feelings about the war comes at too great a psychological price, though some will pay the price for the protection.

Hal is a character in one of Burns's "gallery portraits." He has crossed the Atlantic to arrive in the "gummy city" of Oran, Algeria. He visits the bars, as he used to in New York, from Central Park to Greenwich Village. There, he had been a looking glass in which others could feel understood and enlightened. But here, after ten minutes, conversation with the "Joe" next to him freezes in a sub-conscious sense of shared complicity that indicts them all:

> Hal found it difficult, after a few drinks, to look them straight in the eye. There was some vast and deadly scheme in which they were all working; only they didn't know it. Hal himself had an inkling of what was upsetting him. Casting about for a rational explanation of why he felt so *odd*, he decided it was because the war was beginning to seep into his bones. This war was the fault of everyone, himself included.[58]

To read Burns is to feel the nausea, booziness, loneliness, and fear young boy-men experience as they leave home for the first time and steam across the world. But it is also to feel the ache of searching to justify the violence of war with a worthy cause, a fine and noble end that will ensure that courage is genuine, as Aris-totle might put it. And when such an end isn't easily found (and when war sucked of its glory is seen at best as just the least immoral option), characters like Hal turn war inward and line up enemy positions inside. The corruption of soul becomes war's collateral damage: "Something in him seemed to be chasing another part. Often this hunt between sections of himself became so vicious that he had to put his head between his hands, as a man with a hangover expects his heart to stop in the very next moment, and prays for even the distraction of a bowel movement."[59] Ghoulish incubi inhabit his mind "with no bodies or faces," scuttling around "squeaking in furry voices of doubt and doom." "Hal knew that actually they were playing with him—that each of these vague ani-mals was himself in pieces."[60] But knowing this did not relieve the self-persecution and fragmentation.

This is where deep conflicts about the reasons for which a sol-dier fights can recede—to an unsavory interior, where a soldier turns the battle inward and relives unresolved battles of betrayal, complicity, and taint. From ancient Greek and Roman philosophy to contemporary philosophers like Harry Frankfurt, the moral and psychological quest is often about becoming a unified or har-monized psyche, "wholehearted,"[61] the enemy "beat back" at the gates, as Seneca put it in a Stoic plea for tight self-control and he-gemony.[62] But, for most of us and certainly for soldiers who some-times see themselves as fighting others' wars in large tyrannizing bureaucracies, Freud seems more convincing. Battles are turned inward. Psyches fracture, and self-empathy with the warring parts can be in short supply. There is a sense of accountability for one's part in collective ends but also a sense of being manipulated, be-yond easy control, to carry out others' mistakes or deceptions.

Soldiers are good at compartmentalizing, I've been told over and over. But as the stories I have related attest, conflicts about one's own complicity and about others' betrayal of one's service and loyalty do not just vanish. Often, those conflicts are displaced, deferred, put on hold until soldiers find the safety and the trust they need to express their personal doubts and torments. As em-pathic listeners, civilians can play a role in that social healing. Wars may be fought by soldiers, but those wars are not theirs alone.

CONCLUSION

There are lessons to be learned here about going to war with frac-tured fidelity to the cause and about moral self-assessment that can both seem to fall short of taking responsibility for one's part in war and yet exaggerate that responsibility, given the constraints of socialized patriotism, economic coercion, and the sheer pressure of the drum beat. With today's unprecedented suicide rates in the military, it is hard these days to underestimate the psychic toll of war.[63] But the *moral* nature of that suffering is still not fully appre-ciated. It is easy to think that the moral anguish has primarily to do with the dissonance of becoming a killer. To be sure, "cracking the shell" of moral disgust, as one Marine colonel put it to me, is hard at first. After the initial kill, killing comes easier.[64] For some, it comes too easily. But for those who kill discriminately, at least by conventional doctrines of just war, and take due risks to limit col-lateral damage, what is often more dissonant than killing is suffer-ing betrayal by those whose office it is to protect or support you in the line of service. That is something that live-artillery training and desensitization to blood and gore don't prepare you for. Given the hierarchical power structure of the military, protesting those be-trayals can be extremely costly. Many settle for "sucking it up" and getting on with the mission. But, while stoic armor can work in war, it often cracks when the uniform comes off. And then the dis-sonance of betrayal and ruptured fidelities becomes unbearable. Part of the anguish, of course, is that the betrayal is not just from outside. It is a self-betrayal, too, of sorts, a reluctance to be more forgiving (and excusing) for participating in a war that one may not have wholeheartedly chosen to fight.[65]

NOTES

1. Emily Dickinson, "As Imperceptibly as Grief," in *The Complete Poems of Emily Dickinson, with an Introduction by Her Niece, Martha Dickinson Bianchi* (Boston: Little, Brown, 1924).

2. This essay is an adaptation of ch. 2 of my recent book, *The Untold War: Inside the Hearts, Minds, and Souls of our Soldiers* (New York: W. W. Norton, 2010).

3. For an historical account of loyalty to cause (and comrade) see James M. McPherson, *For Cause and Comrades: Why Men Fought in the Civil War* (New York: Oxford University Press, 1977).

4. "You cannot make a true picture of this war until you make up your mind as to what this war is about. And the reason Hollywood has not so made up its mind is that the American people have been carefully prevent-ed from making up their mind. And, movie making aside for a moment, until they do come to agreement on some basic credo which will explain and justify this war, they are going to injure and sometimes destroy the minds of a host of their returning veterans." Arthur Miller, *Situation Normal* (New York: Reynal & Hitchcock, 1944).

5. At meetings of the American Society for Political and Legal Philoso-phy at the Eastern division of the American Philosophical Association, De-cember 2007. Ryan Balot was also a commentator. I am grateful to both for their insightful responses.

6. Siegfried Sassoon, "Banishment," in Sassoon, *Counter-Attack and Other Poems* (New York: E. P. Dutton, 1918).

7. For a fictional casting of Sassoon's story, see Pat Barker's *Regenera-tion* trilogy: *Regeneration* (New York: Penguin, 1992); *The Eye in the Door* (New York: Plume, 1993); *The Ghost Road* (New York: Plume, 1995). For Sassoon's memoirs, see Paul Fussell, ed., *Siegfried Sassoon's Long Journey: Selections from the Sherston Memoirs* (New York: K. S. Giniger, 1983).

8. For the most part I use the term "soldier" in this chapter (and in the book) to cover all members of the military, though I am very mindful that each branch of the service has its own distinctive nomenclature and that there exist interservice rivalries.

9. On just cause and the current wars in Iraq, see May, Rovie, and Viner's helpful introduction to their anthology on the morality of war, in Larry May, Eric Rovie, and Steve Viner, eds., *The Morality of War* (Upper Saddle River, NJ: Pearson/Prentice Hall, 2005), xi.

10. See David Estlund's insightful piece "On Following Orders in an Unjust War," *Journal of Political Philosophy* 15 (June 2007): 213–34.

11. Michael Walzer, *Just and Unjust Wars: A Moral Argument with Historical Illustrations* (New York: Penguin, 1977), 15.

12. A caveat is in order: I am not a clinician and do not see patients. I am a research graduate in psychoanalysis from the Washington Psychoanalytic Institute, where I studied for five years and maintain ongoing affiliations, including occasionally teaching there.

13. Walzer, *Just and Unjust Wars*, 38–39.

14. Ibid.

15. Some might reasonably argue that this is too broad; not all governments have legitimate political authority. It is only in regimes that are considered legitimate that we tend to think a soldier who fights for an unjust cause is not a criminal. See Estlund, "On Following Orders," on this important point.

16. Francisco de Vitoria, "On the Law of War," 3.5–6, par. 48, in *Political Writings/Francisco de Vitoria*, ed. Anthony Pagden and Jeremy Lawrance (New York: Cambridge University Press, 1991). Note, though, that Vitoria seems to contradict his earlier claim (par. 22) that if a war seems patently unjust, then killing in that war is like killing an innocent man, and this is unlawful. The combatant who fights for an unjust cause is not the moral equal of the one who fights for a just cause. The first is like a murderer, he says.

17. Ibid., 2.1–2, par. 22–26.

18. Ibid., 2.1–2, par. 21.

19. Ibid., 2.2–3, par. 24.

20. For a detailed account of this pattern in the later years of the George W. Bush White House, see Bob Woodward, *The War Within: A Secret White House History 2006–2008* (New York: Simon and Schuster, 2008).

21. Vitoria, "On the Law of War," 2.2–3, par. 22–26.

22. Jeff McMahan, "The Ethics of Killing in War," *Ethics* 114 (July 2004): 693–733. See also McMahan, "Liability and Collective Identity: A Response to Walzer," *Philosophia* 34 (January 2006): 13–17, and "Killing in War: A Reply to Walzer," *Philosophia* 34 (January 2006): 47–51. In addition, see McMahan, "The Morality of War and the Law of War," in *Just and Unjust*

Warriors: The Moral and Legal Status of Soldiers, ed. David Rodin and Henry Shue (Oxford: Oxford University Press, 2008).

23. On this, again see Woodward's account in *The War Within* of George W. Bush's reliance on a like-minded retired military general for counsel about the proposed surge of troops in 2006 and his shunting out of the loop those who strongly opposed that action, including the chairman of the Joint Chiefs of Staff, Admiral Michael Mullen, and General George W. Casey, the commanding general in Iraq from 2004 to 2007.

24. For a debate on this, see Walzer and McMahan's 2006 exchange in *Philosophia*. Michael Walzer, "Terrorism and Just War," *Philosophia* 34 (January 2006): 3–12; McMahan, "Liability and Collective Identity"; Walzer, "Response to Jeff McMahan," *Philosophia* 34 (January 2006): 19–21; McMahan, "The Ethics of Killing in War," *Philosophia* 34 (January 2006): 23–41; Walzer, "Response to McMahan's Paper," *Philosophia* 34 (January 2006): 43–45; McMahan, "Killing in War."

25. See McMahan in the *Philosophia* 2006 exchange.

26. "The Ethics of Killing in War: The Uehiro Lectures," manuscript from author, 4.

27. *Philosophia* 2006 exchange.

28. See David Garren, "Soldiers, Slaves, and the Liberal State," *Philosophy and Public Policy Quarterly* 27 (Winter/Spring 2007): 8–11. He presented an earlier version of the article (for which I was a commentator) at the meeting of the American Philosophical Association, December 2006. Israel is sometimes mentioned in this context, and specifically the disposition of military courts in some cases not to punish harshly conscripts who selectively refuse to serve in the occupied territories. See Chaim Gans, "The Refusal to Serve in the Occupied Territories in the Second *Intifada*," *The Jurist*, http://jurist.law.pitt.edu/forum/forumnew109.php (submitted 23 May 2003). Also, see Amnesty International's positions on this: http://web/amnesty.org/library/print/ENGMDE151692002.

29. In the words of Hugo Grotius, *The Law of War and Peace: De Jure Belli ac Pacis Libri Tres*, trans. Francis W. Kelsey (Oxford: Oxford University Press, 1925), and as cited by May, Rovie, and Viner, eds., *The Morality of War*, xi. For further discussion of preventive war, see David Luban, "Preventive War," *Philosophy & Public Affairs* 32 (Summer 2004): 207–48.

30. For a recent account, see Steven Darwall, *The Second-Person Standpoint* (Cambridge, MA: Harvard University Press, 2006).

31. I thank Paul Woodruff for help in framing the point this way.

32. I am here paraphrasing remarks made to me by Army Colonel Tony Pfaff, former military attaché to Kuwait, and a Ranger and infantry officer who served twice in the current conflict in Iraq. I disclose here that he is a Ph.D. student of mine at Georgetown.

33. Walzer in the *Philosophia* 2006 exchange with McMahan.

34. See Nancy Sherman, *Stoic Warriors: The Ancient Philosophy behind the Military Mind* (New York: Oxford University Press, 2005).

35. This discussion is drawn from numerous ongoing conversations with Robert Steck between June 2005 and January 2009.

36. Max Cleland spoke publicly about the resurgence of his symptoms of postwar trauma at a discussion after the premier of Sean Huze's play *Sandstorm*, about marines in Iraq, in the fall of 2005, in Alexandria, Virginia.

37. Michael Herr, *Dispatches* (New York: Knopf, 1977).

38. From testimony of a veteran speaking at the Vietnam War Memorial, Washington, D.C., November 2007, covered by NPR's *All Things Considered*.

39. Here, I am reminded of Hugh Thompson, the helicopter pilot who interceded in the My Lai massacre and yet was viewed by many fellow soldiers, long after the war, as a traitor. For my interviews with Thompson, see Sherman, *Stoic Warriors*, 64, 93–95, 105–7.

40. See H. R. McMaster, *Dereliction of Duty: Lyndon Johnson, Robert McNamara, the Joint Chiefs of Staff, and the Lies That Led to Vietnam* (New York: HarperCollins, 1997).

41. I am grateful to Michael Byron for reminding me of this important connection. See, for example, Mary Douglas's classic, *Purity and Danger: An Analysis of Concepts of Pollution and Taboo* (New York: Routledge and Kegan Paul, 1966).

42. On this, see Christopher Kutz's helpful spatial metaphor for assessing an onlooker's response to others' relative complicity in a collective end. Kutz considers a vice president of sales, an engineer, and a shipping clerk who are part of an ethically irresponsible international arms company that manufactures and sells mines. Though all participate in achieving the end, the vice president more directly and knowingly engages with the harm, since he arranges for sales and lines up a schedule of production. In the spatial model, he is at the core of the activity and identifies with its success and uses. He must promote the product, advertise its benefits, and deflect social criticism. Even if ethically conflicted, in his role as an effective vice president of sales, he backs the product, views it as reliable, and is its spokesman. The engineer is further from the core. He needn't really care if the mines are ultimately sold, though he does care that the individual products he makes work and are technically well designed. The shipping clerk is at the extreme periphery. He puts objects in boxes without a commitment to sales or technically sound products. Granted, says Kutz, all have "participatory intentions" in the collective end that defines their engagement. But, given the workers' different functional roles with

172 **Nancy Sherman**

respect to the product, we as onlookers weigh their participation differently. While a shipping clerk may be criticizable for compartmentalization or
indifference if he doesn't think much about the ultimate end of his labor,
in terms of participation in the collective end, he is not as complicitous as
those at the core. Christopher Kutz, *Complicity: Ethics and Law for a Collective
Age* (New York: Cambridge University Press, 2000), esp. 157–65.

43. I thank Ryan Balot for pressing the connection between moral luck
and the specific war in which a soldier may participate. For further discussion of soldiers' guilt and what I call "accident guilt," "luck guilt," and
"collateral damage guilt" (guilt that is felt despite the sufferer's having
committed no apparent wrongdoing or unjust conduct), see ch. 4 ("The
Guilt They Carry") of *The Untold War.* I make the point in that chapter
that "agent-regret," Bernard Williams's term for the moral "bad" feeling
of being causally responsible for accidents (though not morally culpable),
does not capture the depth and the pain of the subjective feeling that
soldiers typically experience in such cases, nor the wish to reinsert *moral*
agency, often squeezed out in war. In this sense, "guilt" does a better job
and does have a kind of reasonableness. For the literature on moral luck,
see Bernard Williams, *Moral Luck* (New York: Cambridge University Press,
1981); Thomas Nagel, "Moral Luck," in his *Mortal Questions* (New York:
Cambridge University Press, 1991); and Marcia Baron, "Remorse and
Agent-Regret," in *Ethical Theory: Character and Virtue,* ed. Peter A. French,
Theodore E. Uehling Jr., and Howard K. Wettstein (Notre Dame: University of Notre Dame Press, 1988). For a reading of Greek literature and phi-
losophy in terms of moral luck and dependence on externals, see Martha
C. Nussbaum, *The Fragility of Goodness: Luck and Ethics in Greek Tragedy and
Philosophy* (New York: Cambridge University Press, 1986).

44. Interviews with Dereck Vines, May 31, 2007 and several times later
that summer and during 2008.

45. For a discussion of American propaganda and the beating of war
drums, I am grateful to Richard Rubenstein of George Mason University
in a lecture delivered to Kehila Chadasha in Bethesda, MD, on October
5, 2008.

46. Vitoria, "On the Law of War," 2.2–3, par. 24.

47. Plutarch describes the "Sacred Band" founded by Gorgides at Thebes,
around 378 b.c.e. Within this sacred band, homoerotic ties bind individual couples. (See also Phaedrus's speech in Plato's *Symposium* on an "army
made up of lovers," 178d.) But the motivational point goes beyond homo-
erotism: honor, loyalty, and protective shame and fear of dishonor keep
soldiers fighting. See Plutarch, *Pelopidas,* trans. John Dryden, in *Plutarch's
Lives,* vol. 2, ed. A. H. Clough (Boston: Little, Brown, 1906), 14ff. For other related sources, see Thomas Hubbard, ed., *Homosexuality in Greece and*

Rome: A Sourcebook of Basic Documents (Berkeley: University of California Press, 2003). For further discussion of Roman ideas of masculinity, see Craig Williams, *Roman Homosexuality: Ideologies of Masculinity in Classical Antiquity* (New York: Oxford University Press, 1999).

48. I am grateful to Tony Pfaff for help in strengthening the point.

49. I thank Paul Woodruff for pressing clarification here.

50. For an account of *hamartia* in the *Poetics*, see Nancy Sherman, "Virtue and Hamartia," in *Essays on Aristotle's Poetics*, ed. Amélie Oksenberg Rorty (Princeton: Princeton University Press, 1992).

51. From an interview with Hank McQueeny on February 16, 2006. I recently learned that Hank McQueeny died shortly before *The Untold War* was published. His wife told me he died of symptoms related to Agent Orange, to which he was most likely exposed during his service in Vietnam.

52. The vote was unanimous in the U.S. House of Representatives for the Gulf of Tonkin Resolution; in the Senate, only two senators—Wayne Morse of Oregon and Ernest Gruening of Alaska—voted against it.

53. For an interview with Jim Stockdale, see Sherman, *Stoic Warriors*, and chs. 1 and 6 of *The Untold War*.

54. I am indebted to Alisa Carse for discussion of this point.

55. I am grateful to Janet Spikes, head librarian at the Woodrow Wilson International Center for Scholars, for bringing this work, as well as many others, to my attention.

56. See Paul Fussell's introduction to John Horne Burns, *The Gallery* (New York: New York Review of Books, 2004). For further background on the period, see Norman Lewis, *Naples '44* (New York: Pantheon, 1978).

57. Burns, *The Gallery*, 87–88.

58. Ibid., 77.

59. Ibid., 75.

60. Ibid., 78.

61. Harry G. Frankfurt, *The Reasons of Love* (Princeton: Princeton University Press, 2004).

62. See Sherman, *Stoic Warriors*, 96.

63. Rates of suicide in the army have traditionally been lower than rates for civilians in the corresponding age groups. However, in 2009, the rates exceeded the comparable civilian rate, sounding alarm bells within the military. As a *Wall Street Journal* military correspondent, Yochi Dreazen, made the point to me in a broadcast by Diane Rehm on mental health in the military, the military viewed itself as fighting three wars—the war in Iraq, the war in Afghanistan, and the war against suicide: http://thedianerehmshow.org/shows/2009-11-19/mental-health-us-military. On rising suicide rates in the military, see "Army Suicide Study Kicks into Gear," http://www.nimh.nih.gov/about/director/2010/army-suicide-

study-kicks-into-gear.shtml. In the fall of 2008, the Department of Defense initiated DCoE, Defense Centers of Excellence for Psychological Health and Traumatic Brain Injury, in response to the pressing need for better mental health care treatment of returning troops and their families.

64. On military training to overcome the aversion to killing, see Lieutenant Colonel Dave Grossman, *On Killing: The Psychological Cost of Learning to Kill in War and Society* (Boston: Little, Brown, 1995). For a description of one of his training sessions that I attended, see Sherman, *The Untold War,* 11–12.

65. I am grateful for the comments of *NOMOS* editors Sandy Levinson, Paul Woodruff, and Joel Parker on earlier drafts of this essay.

7

THE PSYCHOLOGY OF JUST AND UNJUST WARS: RESPONSE TO SHERMAN

RYAN K. BALOT

Nancy Sherman's chapter explores the psychic trauma associated with fighting for unjust causes. In the background of Sherman's essay is her wish to rethink, with Jeff McMahan and others, the traditional distinction between the "right to make war" (*ius ad bellum*) and "right in [conducting] war" (*ius in bello*).[1] Sherman asks whether this traditional distinction can be maintained at a psychological level, which she calls the soldiers' "moral psychic realities." Can soldiers coherently or authentically dissociate their moral evaluations of the larger causes for which they fight from their own particular, day-to-day conduct in war? Sherman's answer is no. First-person accounts show that soldiers habitually struggle with the justice of the cause. Whatever the judgments of just war theorists, soldiers hold themselves responsible for the justice or injustice of their nations' war efforts. They take responsibility upon themselves even when their choices are limited and constrained and even when their opportunities to exercise moral agency have been sharply reduced, if not entirely eclipsed. Soldiers feel internal pressure to be loyal to their causes, even when they harbor moral criticisms of those causes. Such thoughts lead to obvious psychological dissonance, which Sherman productively identifies as a "war within" the soldier's soul or self-image. Sherman argues that this "war within" is a morally relevant fact of soldiers' psychology, which is better explained by Freudian theories of interior fragmentation than by quixotic ancient or modern ideals of psychic harmony.

Sherman's work is unusual in combining rigorous philosophical analysis with the psychological interpretation of narrative and first-personal accounts.[2] This enlarged, synthetic approach enables her to isolate and grapple with entire continents of ethically relevant experience—experience that is too often and too easily suppressed in our typically more anodyne philosophical modalities. Like John Keegan and Victor Hanson, whose accounts of the "face of battle" have guided a generation of readers through the foul smells, burnt hair, and other banalities of warfare's evil, Sherman makes vivid for us the heart-rending, if not downright ugly, psychological "faces of battle" disclosed to soldiers in their own frightening inner lives.[3] Sherman's provocative research significantly illuminates the present volume's theme of loyalty; it sheds light on the soldier's psychological experience as a problem of moral luck; and it may suggest political ways of healing the soldier's internal fragmentation.

Taking fidelity to one's comrades as familiar within and essential to military life, Sherman focuses on recent debates over fidelity to cause or mission. In the first half of her essay, Sherman intervenes in debates over just war theory; in the second half, she analyzes the shame and disillusionment of real soldiers. What is the relationship between these two apparently disconnected moments? Why does Sherman "begin again," as she says, roughly at the midpoint? The answer is that Sherman aspires to render problematic the relation of objective evaluation to subjective experience. The implication is that just war theorists usually do not ask the most important psychological questions—which may be the most important questions of all. This does not imply, however, that they ask the *wrong* questions altogether; their questions answer to the obviously necessary effort to maintain a universalizing, impartial, objective legal domain for the evaluation of social conduct.

Yet, it does imply that the efforts of contemporary just war theorists are inadequate to their own purposes. Hence, Sherman's work should refine or enlarge the traditionally limited perspectives of just war theorists. Her own sharply focused psychological account should encourage third-party observers to be more merciful or compassionate in their ethical evaluations of soldiers, particularly in military courts, where Sherman's account directs attention to our own epistemic deficiencies. We—especially *qua* judges—can never attain a God's-eye view of another's soul or adequately take into account the contingencies or psychological pressures that derive from our soldiers' previous life experiences and socioeconomic circumstances, not to mention their native talents or even their "talents of the heart" that is, their natural ethical dispositions. Recognizing that third-party evaluation, such as court work and performance evaluations, must go on, we should move slowly and sympathetically and with enlarged psychological horizons in rendering moral or legal judgment on the behavior of combatants.

To put these points differently: fighting loyally in an unjust cause gives rise, in an especially acute manner, to problems of moral luck.[4] I am using the term "moral luck," perhaps loosely, to designate situations in which individuals are held morally responsible, by themselves or others, for actions, events, character states, contingent traits or dispositions, and outcomes that are beyond their control.[5] Because Sherman's chapter is focused on first-personal self-assessment, I also concern myself chiefly with cases in which individuals hold *themselves* morally responsible for actions, events, and so on that are beyond their control. Prototypically, at least, moral luck comes into view in circumstantial cases: individuals feel guilty and punish themselves, for example, for automobile accidents that they sought strenuously to avoid, as when cars slip on ice with catastrophic consequences, without any negligence or imprudence on the driver's part. Even in such manifestly "unlucky" circumstances, drivers usually feel responsible. By virtue of constitutive luck, on the other hand, we all inhabit inner worlds shaped by contingent traits, unchosen attributes or dispositions, and ascribed social identities that we do not wholeheartedly endorse. We feel shame and punish ourselves vigorously for these contingencies, even if we are misguided in doing so. In an often excruciating way, loyal adherence to an unjust cause raises questions of both circumstantial and constitutive luck.

Reflecting upon the different experiences of soldiers in World War II and in the Vietnam War helps to bring out the significance of circumstantial luck. Soldiers in each of these wars may have been equally courageous, equally loyal, and equally committed to their comrades and their cause, but their psychological experiences and their anxious evaluations of their own behavior depend almost entirely on the year of their birth. As Sherman's vivid interviews reveal, soldiers feel "tainted" merely by participating in an unjust war, even before weapons are fired; they feel doubly ashamed when they fire weapons in an unjust cause; and they feel triply ashamed when they are called hypocrites for returning home, like Bob Steck, to campaign politically against their unjust wars. They feel guilt and shame even as they carry out the orders of their commanders, limit their fighting to other combatants, and strictly observe the requirements of just war "proportionality."

Constitutively, soldiers have been socialized to be loyal to particular nations. Patriotism may be a mistake or even a double mistake, but patriotism is part of the elementary socialization of virtually all citizens of modern nation-states.[6] Loyalty to our nations is a contingent and constitutive (though admittedly not immutable) feature of our self-image. Patriotism tends, moreover, to be one of the strong emotional bonds connecting soldiers with one another and with their particular missions.[7] One of the psychological problems that soldiers face is that their socially cultivated patriotism— their comparatively abstract commitment to their countries—can come into conflict with their moral evaluations of the particular causes for which they must fight, not to mention their day-to-day activities on the battlefield. This situation, too, creates cognitive dissonance and thus feelings of shame, "taint," and guilt, as soldiers morally question or condemn the particular behaviors seemingly demanded by their loyalty to their nations.

What are the specific psychological mechanisms at play in this process? These mechanisms come to sight readily, I believe, when we examine the tensions and ambiguities brought out by Sherman's critique of McMahan. McMahan argues that combatants are unjust in virtue of their promotion of unjust causes; the "deep morality" of war implies that soldiers fighting for unjust causes cannot satisfy proportionality or discrimination, two criteria essential to just war theory. This holds true, McMahan argues, even when soldiers are compelled to fight through conscription or ignorance. In these cases, soldiers are excused from responsibility but not justified. As Sherman points out, however, we would confront substantial difficulties in assessing real soldiers on the basis of this purportedly "deep morality." Moreover, and more importantly, Sherman criticizes McMahan for excessive abstraction and legalism. In fact, she imaginatively attributes to McMahan the following accusatory address to soldiers fighting in unjust campaigns: "Your participation is unjustified. But, because you may have been coerced, deceived, understandably afraid of the authority of the state, or because of the unfeasibility of trials (Who would conduct such a trial? It would certainly not be the state that demands you fight. And if the trials fall under the jurisdiction of international courts, then neither would it be their courts, given their already overextended dockets and underfinanced budgets.), you are not held individually responsible or culpable. Given the mitigating factors and pragmatic consequences of holding you and others like you liable, you are excused for your participation."[8] Sherman emphasizes that this accusation is "second-personal" and "legal," as distinct from the first-personal voices she recovers.

My goal is neither to strengthen nor to qualify Sherman's critique of McMahan; nor do I suggest that settling their controversy will explain why soldiers feel shame and guilt. Whatever else needs to be said, however, consider that Sherman and McMahan agree in rejecting the traditional distinction between *ius ad bellum* and *ius in bello*, Sherman at a psychological level, and McMahan at a conceptual level.[9] This observation raises the following hermeneutical opportunity: what if we were to read the accusation that Sherman attributes to McMahan not as second-personal and legalistic but rather as the record of one soldier's internal psychological conversation with himself?[10] In other words, what if we were to read McMahan against the grain and to construe his moral assessment as a psychological description? As the soldier wrestles with questions of morality and personal responsibility, he might well say to himself: "Your action is condemnable; it is unjustified. . . . [Yet] you are not individually responsible. . . . You are excused for your participation." These accusations and absolutions make perfect sense if they are understood as part of an *interior* dialogue. The soldier is psychologically susceptible to these accusations; they have traction within him. As a result, the soldier will work effortfully to argue down the accusatory voices within. Like Bob Steck, who tried to separate the war from the warrior, the soldier tries to gain psychological release from his own self-condemnation. We should read McMahan as uncovering the "deep morality" that exists, not only out in the world but also *within* our soldiers' own moral psychology. Thus, despite his own intentions, McMahan's deep morality in fact provides a deep grammar of individual character, moral psychology, and fragmented subjectivity.

Subsuming McMahan's analysis within Sherman's study of military psychology enables us to see continuity between the two movements of Sherman's essay. The social perspective is always already present within the individual perspective; the polis is prior to the individual. To understand the soldier's psychology adequately, therefore, we must also understand the second-personal legal and social evaluations that exist out in the world. Since soldiers have been socialized from birth into the ethical life of their civilian communities, they will inevitably assess themselves according to civilian standards. In this respect, McMahan's work can be read—to repeat, against the grain, or at least in a way not apparently intended by McMahan—as helpfully analyzing arguments that operate not only within the abstract legal or philosophical domain but also within the soldier's own psyche.

Such a process of internalization explains why even the World War II novelist John Horne Burns found warfare to be so psychically destructive. World War II was paradigmatically the "good fight," the just war. Yet, human beings are typically not prepared to act the part of killers even in a just cause. (This, of course, raises another question of circumstantial luck: one would be better off not having to go to war at all than being forced to go to war even in the most unambiguously just cause.) Our emotional life has been socially constructed so as to produce fear, horror, and grief when other human beings die painful deaths. And, in particular, we cannot willfully abandon the deeply internalized commandment "Thou shalt not kill" whenever we wish—for example, whenever we walk onto a battlefield. As a symptom of this internalized commandment, we may point to the well-known difficulties encountered in training newly enlisted soldiers to become killers, even of enemy soldiers, and even in the ostensibly morally insulated "safe space" of war (even an unequivocally just war).[11] Soldiers never completely repress their human sympathies for other combatants, who are, like themselves, sons or daughters of particular mothers, brothers or sisters of particular siblings, friends of particular fellow soldiers, and so forth. They recognize themselves in the people they strive to kill. Having once been internalized, though, the "war within" is again *externalized* when soldiers recognize other combatants as equally human, moral, social beings whose lives matter deeply to them(selves)—and who are perhaps equally uncertain about the justice of their own cause, equally subject to the larger forces of power that initially brought them onto the battlefield. (Note that the traditional effort to barbarize the enemy is a reaction against this "recognition" of one's enemy as a fellow human being; such barbarization is, in its own right, a well-known intensifier of PTSD.)[12]

If we believe that soldiers experience psychic conflict because they have internalized conflicting voices about what they should do, who they are, and where their loyalties lie, then we can grasp the shame experienced by so many soldiers for events that are beyond their control and even for accusations unjustly leveled against them. One of the most interesting sections of Sherman's essay concerns the elusive social emotion of shame, which she explores through Bob Steck's vocabulary of being "tainted." According to Steck himself, his "predominant feeling wasn't shame but a sense of taint," which, Sherman says, "implies pollution, staining, fouling" and is, she agrees, distinct from the moralistic vocabulary of shame utilized by philosophers.[13] Without doubting Steck's authority to describe his own experience in his own way, I wonder whether "shame" does not adequately or even more fruitfully accommodate the experience of being "tainted" by the injustice, betrayal, cruelty, and suffering known to soldiers on the battlefield and to soldiers returning home to a hostile or rejectionist public. Where, indeed, should their loyalties lie?

The relationship between shame and "taint" is important, not only at a terminological level but also (and more significantly) at a sociological level. Shame includes "taint" but goes beyond it in social and cognitive ways. The reason is that the quasi-ethical emotion and disposition of "shame," as opposed to the more immediate or "raw" feeling of "being tainted," helps to explain the claim or hold or traction that others' evaluations, even manifestly unjust evaluations, have on our psyches. As Sherman rightly points out, it was unfair of jeering crowds to taunt returning Vietnam veterans with accusations of being "baby killers." But it proved difficult, if not impossible, for those veterans to shake off the painful feelings of shame aroused by such damaging taunts, even when everyone concerned clearly grasped their inappropriateness.

Why is that? The answer is that the soldiers were vulnerable because they had internalized and had themselves felt the force of the rejectionist critique of the war embodied in the crowds' taunts. They saw themselves through the critical eyes of their civilian fellow-citizens, even though they had not literally killed infants. Shame includes the feeling of being tainted, to be sure, but the salient point is that "shame" denominates the social emotion through which our ethical sense of ourselves is linked to the communities of evaluation in which we have been socialized. Accordingly, shame produces an inescapable fidelity or loyalty to those communities of evaluation—inescapable, that is, unless we are (*per impossibile*) utterly to transform the people we have been constituted or socialized to be. (Shame's grip on us, in fact, is intensified by the following consideration: that, by definition, *we* could have no reason to want to achieve an *utter*, as opposed to a partial, transformation of ourselves, for what would such a transformation seek to realize, apart from our own ideals?) One's sense of oneself is, in its own right, dialogic; we have already internalized the voices of others whose moral and aesthetic evaluations we endorse.[14] This explains why shame, a preeminently social emotion, is also intimately tied to our self-image and our sense of self-respect.[15]

Hence, soldiers typically feel shame even when no one else "catches" them in misbehavior, even, perhaps, when they are alone and even, as Sherman points out, for behaviors or contingent attributes that are not of their own making. Having been raised to be loyal to a particular government is just such a contingent attribute. We can be simultaneously ashamed at our loyalty to a government that unjustly makes war and ashamed at our failure to fight loyally and courageously for *our* government, whatever the justice of its cause. In this light, we can appreciate that, contrary to their intentions, Sherman and McMahan have offered us the perfect expression of a sequence of psychological events in which a soldier experiences shame as a result of being condemned by "others" whose voices have become, through socialization, his own and in which, subsequently, the soldier tries to "rebut" those voices through bringing forward considerations of choice and intentionality.

When we consider Sherman's case studies from the perspective of shame and moral luck, it is hard to avoid connecting these ethical and psychic dilemmas with questions about how one might live a flourishing human life. In her conclusion, however, Sherman contrasts Freudian descriptions of interior fragmentation with the traditional philosophical exhortations to pursue psychic integrity or "wholeness." Sherman favors Freud's account and finds it more realistic. But it is more accurate, I would say, and also more fruitful, to reject this contrast and to envision fragmentation and wholeness as polarities along a spectrum of human psychological possibilities. The ancient eudaimonists, such as Plato and Aristotle, were similar to Freud in their extensive familiarity with psychic disorder. They were also, like Freud, zealous exponents of psychological health, construed as a kind of rational self-governance. Both the ancients and the moderns understood that implicit in everyday misery and inner fragmentation, not to mention the misery and struggles of combat soldiers, is the longing for psychic integrity. The only question is whether psychic integrity is possible when properly socialized human beings are forced to kill others.

The answer is probably no, especially for today's soldiers. Here, in fact, is where the contrasts between ancient and modern life take on special interest. Today's soldiers are enmeshed in a command-and-control structure that divorces their agency on the battlefield from any meaningful context of decision making, self-direction, and choice. Because of the severe hardships associated with conscientious objecting or refusing to obey, soldiers are, psychologically, like characters in a Greek tragedy—forced to take responsibility for themselves when their circumstances, their moral frameworks, even their own psychologies are not of their own devising.

If we are not to fantasize about the disappearance of war altogether, then is it possible at least to reduce our soldiers' level of psychic fragmentation? Sherman is right to remind us of Shakespeare's *Henry V* in this context, because, from the perspective of our soldiers' moral experience, our own commanders in chief might as well be kings of war, or warlords. Is there any other political model that might possibly limit the psychic damage caused by war or heal it more completely *post eventum*? Is there any way of conducting politics that might more fully reduce moral luck or more closely align our loyalties and constitutive attachments with our choices and our actual behavior?

A possible answer is more complete democratization. As Sherman points out, one of McMahan's central ideas is that soldiers (especially in a democracy) should make every effort to think through their own decisions carefully and to act accordingly. They should not be unreflectively loyal to their leaders or their countries. But how can such an observation be realized politically? If we grasp and truly accept the idea that young enlisters must cope with innumerable social, emotional, legal, and financial pressures, then we can appreciate the difficulties of achieving genuinely self-directing behavior in our present circumstances.

Nevertheless, we might find enlarged possibilities for self-direction if we look to past democracies, particularly that of classical Athens, an ancient Greek polis that was home to a direct democracy of roughly forty-five thousand citizens. We must always have reservations in treating Athenian democracy as a model for us, because (among other things) of its slaveholding and its exclusion of women from political participation. Moreover, we should ever be mindful of the reservations about direct democracy expressed by "Publius" in *The Federalist*: beyond the familiar question of what Publius calls the "turbulence" of direct democracy, there lies the pressing structural problem of the immense scale of the modern republic.

Even so, time travel to classical antiquity can still be useful for us. By comparing and contrasting the ancient Athenians with ourselves, we can see more clearly that and how our institutional design and political ideologies have involved particular choices and benefits, as well as significant losses and exclusions. By contrast with our modern, large-scale democratic republics, which were initially designed in order to "tame" democracy,[16] Athens provides a well-documented historical example of a stable, direct, and highly militarized democracy, the cardinal ideals of which (freedom, equality, patriotism) were remarkably similar to our own. While Arendtian nostalgia for the ancient polis is undoubtedly misguided, it is nonetheless possible to make significant gains in self-understanding by reconsidering the ancient Athenian example.

As Lieutenant Colonel Gill from Georgetown would appreciate, the chief difference between modern and ancient Athenian warfare is that Athenian citizen-soldiers themselves, in their own persons, took decisions to go to war. They did so after listening to opposed viewpoints, revising their own outlooks, framing their thinking in publicly acceptable ways, and arriving at decisions through a vote. They idealized consensus while recognizing their inability to achieve it without remainder. They understood that their deliberative practices, which (by contrast with most contemporary models) explicitly engaged substantive questions of the human good, would result in the fullest subscription to collective decisions.[17] They were emboldened by their feeling of having left no question unasked in taking the initial decision to go to war. They also maintained tight interconnections among their political decisions, the city's implementation of those decisions, and the eventual execution of those decisions. Athenian citizens played an integral role in shaping and creating the ideals to which they could then be faithful.

The result was that, across the board, democratic decisions had greater "uptake" than those produced by any other known regime at the time or among today's democratic nation-states. The resort to war was more completely voluntary in democratic Athens than in other known regimes, including those of the liberal democratic variety. Accordingly, processes of democratic decision making made all Athenian citizens more fully responsible for the justice or injustice of their city's initial resort to war. This made Athenian soldiers on campaign less susceptible to paralyzing doubts about the justice of their cause; on the contrary, it made them more loyal to the city's causes, because they themselves had voted for them.[18] Democratic deliberation also helped to inform the Athenians' expressions of courage with practical understanding of the demands of this mysterious virtue, seen in light of the Athenians' overall conception of a flourishing human life.[19] Altogether, the Athenians' robustly democratic practices helped them to heal the supposed rift between *ius ad bellum* and *ius in bello* that has exercised contemporary just war theorists and their critics.

But the Athenian democracy did not simply create a psychologically healthier and thus more efficient and destructive military force. Democratic political structures also had potentially positive ethical consequences. It is arguable that, by rendering individual judgments on the decision to go to war, Athenian democrats made decisions that were not only more prudent but also more just than they would have been otherwise. As McMahan has hypothesized, "It seems that by exercising their own judgment rather than deferring to that of their leaders, soldiers would be substantially less likely to participate in unjust wars."[20] This is a quasi-empirical claim that cries out for further empirical and normative exploration; it is also undoubtedly a controversial claim. But the historical experience of classical Athens may support the point. Even though Athenians were highly bellicose by modern standards, they were, as I have argued elsewhere, less likely to resort to war than their pugnacious ancient Mediterranean neighbors, and they were more likely to fight for just causes when they did resort to war.[21]

In voting for war and in implementing their decisions, the ordinary Athenian soldiers' sense of voluntary action and thus of responsibility, fidelity, and justice was enhanced by other allied democratic practices. The common soldiers' endorsement of the cause was strengthened, for example, by the Athenians' democratization of military leadership. Generals were democratically elected for one year at a time. There was a board of ten generals, an institution that placed limitations on the authority of any particular leader. Athenian generals had to justify their use of public funds to the entire citizenry. They were held accountable for their military decisions, both for mistaken choices (whether justified at the time or not) and even occasionally for bad luck. They fought in person with their troops, and their regalia made them special targets for enemy attack; they were most decidedly not, to use Vietnam-era slang, REMFs.[22]

Widespread subscription to democratic causes was also enhanced by the Athenian democracy's egalitarian and communal practices of military commemoration. The entire demos, not any particular general or hero, won glory from victory.[23] The yearly funeral orations, of which Pericles' speech is simply the most famous, effaced any social or military hierarchies and praised individuals chiefly for their loyalty and service to an exceptional city. Public funerals at state expense provided a formal ritual to honor those who had loyally dedicated their lives to the city's efforts to maintain and defend itself with integrity.

One might say, therefore, that more complete democratization led to political loyalty that was more voluntary, more fully self-chosen, and less contingent than the forms of political loyalty with which we are most familiar. Above all, the loyalty demanded of ancient Athenian soldiers did not create the intense problems of moral luck faced by modern soldiers.

Even more important for Sherman's essay, the Athenians practiced an unusual sort of public and ethical therapy after war. Like us, the ancients, too, appreciated the horrors and sufferings of war, except in a more immediate way, because all families had members who fought for the city. Even when all democratic political cylinders fired correctly, the Athenians knew that the psychic trauma of war was inevitable. The Athenians' response was to democratize their soldiers' posttraumatic "grief-work," that is, the social processes of remembering, mourning, and reconciliation that help to restore psychological health to combatants.[24] Prior to the advent of Athenian democracy, grief-work was aristocratic; Homeric soldiers as a servile collectivity mourned the death of Patroclus, for example, in order to promote the grief-work of Achilles. In the Athenian democracy, by contrast, grief-work was democratic and egalitarian. It was accomplished through communal practices such as public funeral ceremonies with funeral orations and funeral games and, above all, through religious festivals in which tragedy and comedy held center stage.

Consider, with Jonathan Shay, the possibility that Athenian tragedy was a form of grief-work. Imagine the experience of Athenian combat veterans—and virtually every citizen in Athens was a long-time veteran of foreign wars—sitting in the Theater of Dionysos watching Herakles come home from war only to go insane and destroy his family (Euripides' *Herakles*), or watching Agamemnon return from the Trojan War only to be slain by his wife, who had fallen into another man's arms during his absence (Aeschylus's *Agamemnon*), or watching the madness of the heroic Ajax, who thought himself unjustly deprived of the rewards of heroism (Sophocles' *Ajax*).[25] Theater was the vehicle through which Athenian democrats collectively explored the trauma, anxieties, and hopes associated with their service as combatants. This is why, for example, the U.S. Marine Corps has recently begun to incorporate Greek tragedy into its efforts to heal the catastrophically rising numbers of soldiers returning home with PTSD.[26] The Athenian democrats were far superior to their American counterparts in publicly recognizing, accepting, and addressing the psychic traumas of war. Instead of hiding caskets from TV cameras, the ancient Athenians put them up on stage and publicly mourned and honored them as they deserved. By doing so, they not only paid a debt to the fallen but also helped to relieve their own psychic suffering.

The Athenians resorted to war and conducted war in a democratic and, arguably even if paradoxically, healthy way. Of course, their emotional health may sometimes have made them stronger and more efficacious imperialists. There is no end to the ambiguities of warfare as a social practice. So long as war exists, in fact, there will also be no end to psychic trauma, even in the most just causes; nor will there emerge any way to evade the tensions between objective evaluation and subjective experience that Sherman has unearthed. We can at least enlighten ourselves by recognizing warfare as a peculiarly intense domain of moral luck—a domain in which the city and man are related in uncanny and more than metaphorical ways. And we can perhaps learn something about loyalty, democracy, and military psychology by looking at ourselves, all over again, in the distorted mirror of classical antiquity's most famous democracy, the imperial city of Athens.

NOTES

This is a lightly revised version of the response I delivered at the initial panel sponsored by the American Society for Political and Legal Philosophy, held at the American Philosophical Association meeting in Baltimore in December 2007. I have chosen not to take fully into account the changes Professor Sherman has made to her essay in the meantime.

1. For modern discussions of this traditional distinction, see Michael Walzer, *Just and Unjust Wars: A Moral Argument with Historical Illustrations* (New York: Basic, 1977), 21–47, and the essays in Terry Nardin, ed., *The Ethics of War and Peace: Religious and Secular Perspectives* (Princeton: Princeton University Press, 1996). McMahan's critique can be found in "The Ethics of Killing in War," *Ethics* 114 (July, 2004): 693–733.

2. Apart from Walzer's pioneering work, other good examples of this trend include Nancy Sherman's own *Stoic Warriors: The Ancient Philosophy*

behind the Military Mind (Oxford: Oxford University Press, 2005); William Ian Miller, *The Mystery of Courage* (Cambridge, MA: Harvard University Press, 2000); and Douglas N. Walton, *Courage: A Philosophical Investigation* (Los Angeles: University of California Press, 1986).

3. Victor Davis Hanson, *The Western Way of War: Infantry Battle in Classical Greece* (New York: Oxford University Press, 1989); John Keegan, *The Face of Battle* (New York: Penguin, 1976).

4. As I will suggest later, fighting loyally in a just cause also gives rise to problems of moral luck.

5. The origins of the "moral luck" literature can be found in Bernard Williams, "Moral Luck," in Williams, *Moral Luck: Philosophical Papers 1973–1980* (Cambridge: Cambridge University Press, 1981), and in Thomas Nagel, "Moral Luck," in Nagel, *Mortal Questions* (Cambridge: Cambridge University Press, 1991); the literature is now extensive, but a good overview can be found in Daniel Statman, ed., *Moral Luck* (Albany: SUNY Press, 1993). An important exploration of this concept in classical Greek thought can be found in Martha C. Nussbaum, *The Fragility of Goodness: Luck and Ethics in Greek Tragedy and Philosophy* (Cambridge: Cambridge University Press, 1986).

6. On the morality of patriotism, see, among others, George Kateb, *Patriotism and Other Mistakes* (New Haven: Yale University Press, 2006). For a critique of patriotism as it relates to courage, see my essay "The Dark Side of Democratic Courage," *Social Research* 71 (Spring 2004): 73–106. For an appreciation of the "givenness" of our social identities and loyalties, see the discussion of Gertrude Himmelfarb, "The Illusions of Cosmopolitanism," in Martha C. Nussbaum, *For Love of Country?*, ed. Joshua Cohen (Boston: Beacon, 2002), 72–77, along with these essays in the same volume: Nathan Glazer, "Limits of Loyalty," 61–65; Charles Taylor, "Why Democracy Needs Patriotism," 119–21; and Nussbaum's "Reply," 131–44.

7. For an historical example emphasizing loyalty to cause (though without ignoring loyalty to fellow soldiers), see James M. McPherson, *For Cause and Comrades: Why Men Fought in the Civil War* (New York: Oxford University Press, 1997).

8. Nancy Sherman, "A Fractured Fidelity to Cause," this volume.

9. Here is one point that the discussion might obscure: McMahan's professed goal is to encourage military personnel "to consider with the utmost seriousness whether any war in which they might fight is just and refuse to fight unless they can be confident that it is." McMahan, "The Ethics of Killing in War," 733. This is an optimistic and profoundly demanding democratic goal. Its attraction, of course, is that McMahan summons citizens to reflect and to act independently and with moral sensitivity. Yet I have serious concerns over how realistic or attractive McMahan's account

can be, if he intends soldiers—or anyone else, for that matter—to be confident of their own justice. This confidence carries with it on one hand the danger of rigid self-certainty amid messy and uncertain circumstances; on the other hand, McMahan's pressure to attain moral confidence fails to do justice to the common experience, among thoughtful and introspective individuals, of moral uncertainty within our rapidly changing and never fully intelligible political world.

10. Here I thank Professor Sherman for her conscientious reaction to my own response to her original essay—and, in particular, for taking into account, in the revised version of her essay, my emphasis on moral luck; my efforts to read McMahan's account against the grain, as internal and psychological, rather than second-personal, legalistic, and accusatory; and my comments on her original discussion of shame, autonomy, and heteronomy.

11. The most interesting recent discussion of our resistance to killing other human beings in combat is Dave Grossman, *On Killing: The Psychological Cost of Learning to Kill in War and Society* (New York: Back Bay, 1996), which builds on the pioneering work in this area conducted by S. L. A. Marshall.

12. See Jonathan Shay, *Achilles in Vietnam: Combat Trauma and the Undoing of Character* (New York: Simon and Schuster, 1994), 103–19.

13. Sherman, "A Fractured Fidelity to Cause."

14. On the dialogic conception of the self, see the helpful analysis of Christopher Gill, *Personality in Greek Epic, Tragedy, and Philosophy: The Self in Dialogue* (New York: Oxford University Press, 1996).

15. My discussion of shame builds upon those of Gabriele Taylor, *Pride, Shame, and Guilt: Emotions of Self-Assessment* (Oxford: Clarendon, 1985), and Bernard Williams, *Shame and Necessity* (Berkeley: University of California Press, 1993).

16. On this point, see Sheldon S. Wolin, *The Presence of the Past: Essays on the State and the Constitution* (Baltimore: Johns Hopkins University Press, 1990).

17. For an analysis of the Athenians' "deliberative democracy" and its bearing on decisions to make war, see my essay ""Free Speech, Courage, and Democratic Deliberation," in *Free Speech in Classical Antiquity*, ed. Ineke Sluiter and Ralph M. Rosen (Leiden: Brill, 2004), 233–59, along with the essays (especially Hanson's essay) in *War and Democracy: A Comparative Study of the Korean War and the Peloponnesian War*, ed. David R. McCann and Barry S. Strauss (New York: M. E. Sharpe, 2001).

18. There will, of course, still have been the problem of dissent among those who had voted against a particular decision to go to war, but, like modern deliberative theorists, the Athenians recognized the connections

between subscription to a cause and the previous opportunity to speak one's mind and discuss the issues. For a general discussion of dissent in democratic Athens, see Josiah Ober, *Political Dissent in Democratic Athens: Intellectual Critics of Popular Rule* (Princeton: Princeton University Press, 1998). And we should ever keep in mind the relative homogeneity of ancient democracy by contrast with the diversity of modern nation-states; for an enlightening treatment of the latter, see William E. Connolly, *Pluralism* (Durham, NC: Duke University Press, 2005).

19. On the novel and highly developed epistemological underpinnings of Athenian democratic courage, see my essay "Pericles' Anatomy of Democratic Courage," *American Journal of Philology* 122 (Winter 2001): 505–25.

20. McMahan, "The Ethics of Killing in War," 703–4.

21. For those familiar with Thucydides' account of the Athenian Empire, this will perhaps be a counterintuitive point. To appreciate the point, we must remind ourselves of the highly bellicose ancient Mediterranean context. When we compare Athens to Sparta, Rome, Macedon, and Persia, we can see that the Athenians were, indeed, more peaceful, more tolerant, and more just than others of their time. On these points, see my essay "Democratizing Courage in Classical Athens," in *War, Democracy and Culture in Classical Athens*, ed. David M. Pritchard (Cambridge: Cambridge University Press, 2010), 88–108.

22. "Rear-echelon m***** f******."

23. Democratic practices of honoring and commemorating should be contrasted with the heroic ones depicted in the Homeric epics; on the latter, and on the ethos surrounding heroic commemoration, see Hans van Wees, *Status Warriors: War, Violence, and Society in Homer and History* (Amsterdam: J. C. Gieben, 1992).

24. My discussion of combat trauma and grief-work is indebted to Shay, *Achilles in Vietnam*. On the implications of Shay's reading of the *Iliad* for the possibility of democracy, see pp. 180–81. Within his discussion of the healing power of narrative (ch. 11), Shay suggests that theater might have been a way for combat veterans to communalize grief (194, 230 n.14). For further commentary and bibliography, see also my "Dark Side of Democratic Courage."

25. On the theme of the veteran's difficult return to society, see Jonathan Shay, *Odysseus in America: Combat Trauma and the Trials of Homecoming* (New York: Scribner, 2002); on theater and the arts, see pp. 152–53.

26. For one report, see http://www.msnbc.msn.com/id/26203463/ns/us_news-military. This article refers to Shay's *Achilles in Vietnam* as the inspiration for the plays' director, Bryan Doerries.

8

FOR CONSTITUTION AND PROFESSION: PARADOXES OF MILITARY SERVICE IN A LIBERAL DEMOCRACY

PAUL O. CARRESE

The American constitutional order launched in 1789 has never suffered a military coup d'état or even a serious attempt, even as we have evolved from few professional forces to the world's largest military. Is this a fortunate accident or the product of civic education among citizens at large and professional education of soldiers, marines, sailors, and members of the air force? If our political liberty is the fruit of civic and professional education, it suggests that citizens and military professionals conceive of loyalty in constitutionalist and professional terms, not only in the more individualist terms of moral agreement with every war, president, or policy. There is much evidence that this is an achievement of education and civic commitment, but it is extraordinary and fragile nonetheless. Indeed, today there is much less understanding or appreciation of George Washington, the great military leader who established the principle of civilian control of the military, than there was in our first two centuries, even among today's professional military. We take the principle and its advocate for granted, as part of the standard furniture of democracy, when in fact neither is automatic or natural. Moreover, we less frequently study the warnings of two great observers of America's young constitutional democracy, Abraham Lincoln and

Alexis de Tocqueville, about the tendencies of democratic politics to undermine commitment to the rule of law and to formal ideals of rules and professionalism. They shared a particular concern about a greater commitment to "the people" or to moral indignation expressed by citizens than to abstract, seemingly elitist ideals like law or professionalism. Democracies also favor current public opinion and egalitarian or progressive causes that serve the majority at the expense of constitutional commitments to respect the decisions of elected officials. Lincoln and Tocqueville anticipated, that is, that the democratic view of military loyalty would emphasize the experiences of individual soldiers and the aggregate of such feelings in the ranks. Democracy also would emphasize immediate public opinion about the justice or expediency of a given war or strategy. They argued, however, that these were self-destructive traits and that they would vindicate the authoritarian view that democracies cannot sustain the order and wisdom needed to avoid anarchy, civil war, or defeat. These admirers of popular government echoed, in fact, Washington's argument from the American founding era that civic and professional education must temper these traits so that loyalty to constitutional government perpetuates liberal principles of individual rights, liberty, and order. Moreover, this complex constitutional structure—giving space to not-so-democratic offices like the presidency and the Senate (as originally conceived) on matters of war and foreign affairs—has to be studied to be loved; it probably won't be loved by the people spontaneously.

Washington, Tocqueville, and Lincoln point us toward considering, therefore, several paradoxes about loyalty in constitutional liberal democracy and about liberal democracy itself. If a constitutional democratic republic is to be liberal and sustainable, civic education must emphasize principles that moderate democratic choice and public opinion. This is a perpetual dilemma for Americans, given our origins in popular protest (the Boston Tea Party) and revolution and our history of war protests ranging from New England's dissent in the War of 1812, to the New York City draft riots in the Civil War, to more recent opposition to the Vietnam and Iraq wars. This larger set of dilemmas amplifies the more particular paradoxes of military service and professionalism in democratic republics. The latter include these tensions: that one risks one's life to defend the natural rights to life and liberty of others;

that one kills to defend these rights to life and liberty; and that one chooses to subordinate one's freedom to duties to constitution and profession.[1]

Shakespeare's classic depiction of these tensions in *Henry V*—is this a just war I fight? who is morally responsible for the suffering, the supreme commander or the officers and soldiers who actually inflict it?—is rightly a staple of ethical and professional study. We also should study, however, the classic reflections on America's principles of civil-military relations and loyalty to constitutional liberty.[2] George Washington's conduct as commander in chief in the revolutionary war and, later, his advice in his Farewell Address provide a foundation for the reflections by Lincoln and Tocqueville about the duties and dilemmas of citizen-soldiers who serve a constitution. Recent controversies about the justice of serving in wars in Iraq and Afghanistan suggest that the insights of these American classics are salient today. These sources also anticipate the dilemmas faced by senior officers who have a duty to critique the policies of presidents and civilian superiors while ultimately obeying civilian authority. Indeed, once we reflect on tensions between civilian and military leaders during the recent wars in Afghanistan and Iraq, we can recall forerunners in the Balkan wars of the 1990s, during Vietnam and the Cuban missile crisis, and back toward the Second World War; Lincoln faced a general in McClellan who perhaps was as much of a menace to Lincoln as to Confederate armies. Few Americans, however, recall that, as the Revolutionary War ended, Washington faced a military coup from below and that his response shaped our national character. It is worrisome that the citizenry at large tends to overlook these questions, but academics and other citizens can appreciate the weight of these evergreen dilemmas. The paradoxes and tensions will continue, and we will not negotiate them safely unless we study them.

CITIZENS, SOLDIERS, AND THE ETHICS OF CONSTITUTIONAL DEMOCRACY

Citizens who have not served in the military—in our day, that is most of us—probably take for granted this exceptional record of America's constitutional democracy. Many popular governments past and present have suffered coups, and, of course, many governments throughout human history have been established or marked by the rule of strongmen, but how is this record relevant to America? I number myself among the once-complacent. I had only occasionally studied our extraordinary constitutional achievement of civil-military relations before finding myself, a civilian with no military service, teaching at a military academy. I had studied and taught for years the theory and practice of liberal democracy and the principles of American politics and law from the founding to the present, and yet I largely assumed the perpetual existence of this ethical, professional, and constitutional principle of civilian control of the military. Not to be too hard on myself and fellow citizens, one can note that the success of the civil-military ethic and of loyalty to the Constitution has led us toward complacency—for isn't it countries far away in the nondemocratic or less developed world, countries like Pakistan or Libya or Chile, that suffer military coups? The closest experience many Americans might recall is General MacArthur's public insubordination to President Truman over the strategy for prosecuting the Korean War. This was a perilous moment for a not very popular president in handling a famous and popular general, but this test of constitutionalism at least never reached the point of rebellion by intrigue or force. When Truman ended the dispute by removing MacArthur from command in 1951, the general obeyed, although he did not fade silently. The Civil War is our closest encounter with a military revolt since the enactment of the Constitution; putting aside Lincoln's difficulty with McClellan, it is striking that many West Point graduates did secede with the Confederate States in 1861 to fight against Constitution and Union, Robert E. Lee being the most famous. Nonetheless, that crisis was largely a political revolt that attracted the support of military professionals, not an attempted military takeover of the government.

While officers and cadets today understand our constitutional ethic of civil-military relations better than do the civilians they serve, most also tend to assume that this extraordinary political achievement is like gravity. They dutifully study its theory, and few question it, but most don't fully appreciate how exceptional the conduct of their profession and their fellow citizens has been since the American revolutionary war. Nor do many officers study or appreciate as adequately as they might how to perpetuate this principle, given its fragility. Fortunately, there is a small but thriving study of civil-military relations and professional ethics within military institutions and civilian academia, which examines the fundamental political and moral principles involved as well as historical cases and recurring tensions.[3] Moreover, perhaps no other profession requires study of ethical professional conduct more regularly and more thoroughly than the American military. Given this core repository of expertise and debate within the military and among some civilian scholars, we might say in our third century as a constitutional republic that the complacent view of most civilians and of many officers and enlisted in fact indicates the depth and strength of the profession's attachment to the principle.

Nonetheless, free governments have a long history of leaders warning of complacency about basic civic principles. Lincoln's 1838 address "On the Perpetuation of Our Political Institutions" observes a growing tendency toward lawlessness in pursuit of political and moral aims, whether abolitionism, or anti-abolitionism, or another cause. It also is prescient about greater violence on the horizon, as arose in subsequent decades with Bloody Kansas, the John Brown raid, and other steps toward civil war. Tocqueville's nearly simultaneous observations in *Democracy in America* similarly forecast that the moral superiority of constitutional democracy would not solve endemic human problems with ambition, passion, and erroneous views of justice. The fact that many West Point graduates chose to follow their own judgment about what the Constitution required and thereby helped to launch the Civil War, rather than following the judgment of the Congress and the president who had been elected in 1860, suggests that Lincoln and Tocqueville were addressing a basic dilemma, rather than indulging patriotic hyperbole. Certainly, from the perspective of those duly elected constitutional authorities, the secessionists fought for comrades and cause, rather than Constitution, as the rebellion raged for years. Lee, Jefferson Davis, and other West Pointers who served in the military or elsewhere in the Confederacy followed their own moral and political judgments at the cost of disobeying their oaths to support the Constitution, as well as (for the officers) the legal orders of superiors, including their civilian commander in chief.[4]

In our post–Vietnam War era, when Americans worry about failure by subordinates to question immoral or unwise orders of their military or civilian superiors, it is important to note that this republican or constitutionalist conception of loyalty does not conflict with but rather reinforces what we now call the Nuremberg principle. Officers and enlisted must follow only lawful orders, with the understanding that laws and rules of engagement embody moral principles defined in terms of the just war tradition and human rights.[5] A focus on ethical conduct in battle (traditionally termed *jus in bello*) can obscure the fact, however, that this principle echoes the premise of constitutional government itself, as many of America's founders argued and as Lincoln reaffirmed in the crisis leading to the Civil War. Institutional forms and rules serve the moral principles enunciated in the Declaration of Independence and the Preamble to the Constitution and the various entrenchments of rights in the Constitution and its amendments. Lincoln borrowed a metaphor from the book of Proverbs to argue that these moral principles were the "apple of gold" that the Constitution seeks to serve and protect as a "frame of silver" around its precious object.[6] Still, Lincoln's affirmation of an ethical politics helps to indicate why the paradoxes posed to citizen-soldiers by loyalty to constitution and to profession are as subtle and as difficult to address as the moral and professional quandaries involved with war crimes or violations of rules protecting noncombatants or captured combatants. The "apple of gold" for the American tradition of international relations and military professionalism—at least through the founding and the nineteenth century, before the rise of Teddy Roosevelt and Woodrow Wilson—is its aim to avoid the rival extremes of an amoral militarism and a moralistic pacifism. The Declaration of Independence captures this balanced or moderate aim when it states that all human beings have not only a "right" but a "duty" to throw off governments that violate natural rights and also in its closing invocation of the "sacred honor" in fighting for a just politics. This kind of moderation between extremes of ruthless violence and righteous passivity is one reason why the American Revolution was a rebellion but was not as radical and self-destructive as the French Revolution. The traditional American view explicitly calls for prudential rather than categorical judgments about justice and affirms established moral and social principles even while calling for rebellion against a particular government.

Much political analysis now assumes that the American founders strike this balance about justified rebellion on the basis of a
Lockean social contract, with individuals calculating the costs and
benefits of obeying or opposing a political order. This is one aspect of America's founding moment, but—to focus on the views of
political leaders, rather than those of ordinary folk—the framers'
moderate view of war and politics presupposes another principle
of balance, that between individual liberty and the rule of law. The
American Revolution occurred through elected representatives
(the Continental Congress) and was promulgated in a Declaration that reads like a legal filing in court, not a utopian manifesto.
Indeed, in the middle of the bill of indictment against king and
parliament, the representatives declare that the British have imposed acts and laws "foreign to our Constitution." This was written eleven years before other delegates proposed a constitution
to replace America's first attempt at a basic law. The constitution
invoked in 1776 is the partly written and partly unwritten common
law derived from Britain and instantiated in the colonies, which
entrenched rights and principles of free government.[7] The Americans thus rebelled in the name of law-as-justice and defined their
liberty in its terms; the British were the lawbreakers. Moreover, the
American leaders drew these ideas of balance not only from the
common law but also from a constitutionalist and republican tradition that developed from Aristotle, through the medieval era, to
Montesquieu. It is this complex French philosopher, who declared
moderation as the main point of his work *The Spirit of the Laws*, who
was cited more than any other philosopher in America's constitutional debates of the 1780s and 1790s, much more so than Locke.[8]
After the failed Articles of Confederation, which, in Locke's spirit,
so distrusted government that the Confederation had no powers to govern, the leading framers adopted Montesquieu's view
that individual and collective liberty not only require law but are
defined by it. In this conception of a republican constitution,
"[l]iberty is the right to do everything the laws permit; and if one
citizen could do what they forbid, he would no longer have liberty
for the others likewise would have this same power."[9] Indeed, constitutional government at its best is devoted to liberty or embodies
ordered liberty, for only in such a constitution is it true that "no
one will be constrained to do the things the law does not oblige

him to do or be kept from doing the things the law permits him to do."[10] The 1787 Constitution strikes these balances—avoiding militarism and pacifism, authoritarianism and anarchy—by establishing a single commander in chief whose powers, in turn, are qualified substantially. This constitutional executive takes an oath to the Constitution (the only part of the document in quotation marks); commands troops who swear to serve the Constitution and, therefore, a range of constitutional offices, rather than the president alone; and has the power to make war but not initiate it, since only Congress has the legal power to declare or initiate full state-to-state warfare.

In our more democratic era, however, we tend to focus less on these republican and constitutional conceptions of liberty, which for the framers included the duty to serve duly authorized efforts that defend or seek justice. When we do study military service, we tend to bring a more egalitarian and individualist lens that focuses on the moral quandaries of individual officers and common soldiers or, alternately, the majority's fatigue with and moral doubts about war. One of the great books of the twentieth century about the ethics of war, recommended by no less a figure than Hannah Arendt, is the meditation by the philosophy professor Glenn Gray on his service in the Second World War. Gray's focus on the warrior's alienation from self and humanity during industrial-scale "total" war concludes that the moral wounds to and the doubts that press upon the individual weigh against the justice of any modern conflict. This is so even for a war against Nazi Germany, since evil and inhumane acts are committed by all sides in such wars.[11] Gray's existentialist rejection of total war is a variation upon Kant's declaration in *Perpetual Peace* of a moral imperative condemning the inhumanity and the antidemocratic character of modern-scale warfare.[12] Our more democratic and individualist sensibilities are reinforced by these kinds of antiwar or pacifist philosophies. They encourage us to elevate the feelings of ordinary soldiers, the momentum of majority public opinion—that is, when it is disgusted with or fatigued by war—or the progress of egalitarian and humanitarian causes above the constitutionalist ideals of loyalty and professionalism in military service.

The point of noting this change in our ideas of war and service during two centuries is not to settle the debates among schools of realists, liberal internationalists, pacifists, and just war theorists in international relations theory and the ethics of war. It is, rather, to note that our constitutional order incorporates a modified version of the medieval just war theory, as adapted by Montesquieu and other modern philosophers, which aims to achieve a principled middle position between realism and liberal internationalism by blending elements of each. America's first foreign policy, forged by George Washington, was a principled blend of realist and liberal idealist ideas that drew upon Montesquieu's philosophy of international relations and the principles implicit in our constitutional structure.[13] Moreover, this attempt at balance on the one hand has kept America largely safe from foreign attack and conquest into its third century and on the other has allowed philosophers, ethicists, and other scholars and citizens the freedom to question the justice of any particular war or, more generally, America's growing military power. This same fundamental moderation also produces the requirement that soldiers and officers serve law, not any party, cause, or leader, and teaches them that they fight not for conquest or any will to power. Those who are skeptical about traditional republican views of constitutional loyalty, or who are more pacifistic about war, might be less severe in their criticisms if they appreciated the balanced tradition of civil-military affairs and military power that protects their freedom to criticize. This political tradition is more balanced and moderate, arguably, than that of any other power of similar magnitude in history. Moreover, those who either overlook or criticize republicanism and constitutional loyalty might also pause to appreciate the extraordinary effort it took to achieve this moral and constitutional balance, before taking for granted the freedom and moderation it has yielded.

WASHINGTON, CONSTITUTIONAL REPUBLICANISM, AND THE NAPOLEONIC TEMPTATION

George Washington is less appreciated by his countrymen now than during the first two centuries after his singular role in America's founding. Few of our civic educators today—professors, teachers, writers, and other opinion shapers—find him an exemplar of principles worthy of serious study. His best known writing is his "Farewell Address," declaring to "Friends, and Fellow-Citizens" his retreat from public life at the end of his second term as president.

He relinquished near-absolute power when equally ambitious yet less principled men usually have grasped for more. Indeed, after Napoleon Bonaparte had lost a crown and a continent, he said that "they wanted me to be another Washington"—but himself disdained such quaint republican ideals of service and citizenship.[14] Washington's deeds and his statements of principle about them led his countrymen to rank him with an ancient Roman renowned for relinquishing absolute power once the threat to his country passed: Washington was the American Cincinnatus. The American general and president, however, had earned this title not only from his final farewell but from his initial resignation, when, as the victorious leader of the American revolutionary war, he retired to his farm in 1783 once peace was secure.

Washington's loyal service to republican principles, including subordination to civilian authorities, marked him from the opening of the war. In his "General Orders" of July 9, 1776, he ordered the new Declaration of Independence read to all the troops, so that they might understand from Congress "the grounds and reasons" of the war.[15] This is striking, as, generally, throughout history liberty has never arisen or has been short lived because military despots have crushed genuine politics or the rule of law. All liberal democracies today owe to Washington the principle that a professional military is necessary to protect liberty *and* can be safely subordinate to laws and civil authority. John Marshall, the great Chief Justice of the U.S. Supreme Court who was a young officer under Washington, further concluded that, without his character, the American cause likely would have failed or ended in rule by the conquering military hero as had befallen republics from Rome to Cromwell's England. Indeed, Washington showed himself loyal to republicanism not only in moments of near-defeat early in the war but also when prospects brightened and temptations of power arose. After the victory at Yorktown, in 1781, an American colonel suggested that Washington should be king, an offer that might have tempted a general deeply admired by his army and—like a Caesar, Cromwell, Napoleon, or Benedict Arnold—also ambitious himself. The temptation might have been strengthened given how disorganized Congress was during the war, how often Washington had proposed executive offices to remedy this, and the daily wants he witnessed in supplies, equipment, and pay for his men and cause. Colonel Lewis Nicola exploited these points, proposing that chaos in Congress and suffering in the army proved to all "the weakness of republicks, and the exertions the army has been able to make by being under a proper head"; hence, many in the army would support him as a king.[16] Washington replied immediately, expressing "abhorrence," "astonishment," and "painful sensations" upon learning of "such ideas existing in the Army." To be sure, "no Man possesses a more sincere wish to see ample justice done to the Army," but he would pursue this only "as far as my powers and influence, *in a constitutional way* extend" (emphasis added). He turned Nicola's regard for him against such a plan, connecting principles to the character needed to animate them: "Let me conjure you then, if you have any regard for your Country, concern for yourself or posterity, or respect for me, to banish these thoughts from your Mind."[17] Under a weak government that deemed itself "Articles" as if between foreign powers, Washington stuck to genuine constitutionalism precisely at the moment he could have exploited such weakness.[18]

Washington already had supported military discipline and civil authority during two troop mutinies early in 1781 over lack of pay and supplies. To Marshall, these threats to civil authority and military command "threatened the American cause with total ruin," and he contrasted the "miserably defective" organization of the Confederation Congress that caused such problems with the good fortune that America's one effective executive had restored order and then pressed, yet again, for reform measures.[19] Perhaps the most dangerous episode, however, arose in 1783, at the war's end, with a peace process under way that might disband the army before paying it its due. Officers at Washington's headquarters in Newburgh, New York, thought he might finally support a threat of mutiny against Congress. Their grievances were obvious and compelling. The states would not pay the funds requisitioned by Congress, and the latter had no powers to compel them, so the army suffered. An anonymous letter in March summoned all the officers to a meeting and suggested they seek the support of their "Illustrious Leader" for this plot.[20] Washington denounced that meeting but called an official one at which "mature deliberation" should develop "rational measures" for Congress to consider.[21] He implied he would not attend; the element of surprise was his when, as the meeting began, he entered. His speech contrasted the "unmilitary" character and "blackest designs" of the plot with the "rules of propriety" and "order and discipline" more fitting to "your own honor, and the dignity of the Army." Ultimately, "the calm light of reason" and "moderation" must control "feelings and passions," for "sowing the seeds of discord and seperation between the Civil and Military powers" would undermine "that liberty, and . . . that justice for which we contend." To support these principles, he invoked their longstanding affection for him, since no one had been more "a faithful friend to the Army."[22]

It is further striking that Washington not only invoked military honor but also defended Congress as an "Hon[ora]ble Body." He likely drew on his experience as a Virginia legislator to insist that Congress should not be distrusted just because, "like all other Bodies, where there is a variety of different Interests to reconcile, their deliberations are slow." His final appeal was to both reason and emotion and to ideas from the Declaration of Independence: "let me conjure you, in the name of our common Country, as you value your own sacred honor, as you respect the rights of humanity, and as you regard the Military and National character of America," to reject this plot to "overturn the liberties of our Country" through a military coup and civil war. Steadfastness now would prove them models of "unexampled patriotism and patient virtue" and "afford occasion for Posterity to say . . . 'had this day been wanting, the World had never seen the last stage of perfection to which human nature is capable of attaining.'"[23] Washington sealed his efforts with another dramatic gesture, again using the army's devotion to him not for his own advantage but to promote loyalty to the rule of law and liberty. He began to read a letter from Congress and then stopped: "Gentlemen, you will permit me to put on my spectacles, for I have not only grown gray, but almost blind, in the service of my country."[24] Some of the officers, no longer rebellious, were in tears. After he left, they unanimously repudiated the plot and reaffirmed their allegiance to civil authority.

Washington's influence achieved a narrow escape from disaster and a lasting principle. The main doctrinal statement of the U.S. Army today opens by recounting "Washington at Newburgh: Establishing the Role of the Military in a Democracy," finding in these deeds and words "a fundamental tenet of the American military profession."[25] Principled to the end, Washington disbanded the army once the peace was official. His last "Circular Address," to the states in June 1783, recommended policies for the future and endorsed efforts to reform and strengthen the Articles. His final orders to the army, in November 1783, gave further political advice, including his urging that all veterans "prove themselves not less virtuous and useful as Citizens, than they have been persevering and victorious as soldiers."[26] He resigned his commission before Congress in December 1783, professing "honor" at being present to "surrender into their hands the trust committed to me" and asking "the indulgence of retiring from the Service of my Country." With repeated recognition of "the interposition of Providence" that had secured America's independence and gratitude for the support of countrymen and trusted aides, he bade farewell: "Having now finished the work assigned me, I retire from the great theatre of Action; and bidding an Affectionate farewell to this August body under whose orders I have so long acted, I here offer my Commission, and take my leave of all the employments of public life."[27] Jefferson soon wrote to him: "the moderation and virtue of a single character has probably prevented this revolution from being closed as most others have been, by a subversion of that liberty it was intended to establish."[28]

Washington's protégés in military and civilian life, including Hamilton and Madison, drew him out of retirement to play a leading role in the constitutional reform movement of the mid-1780s. After serving as president of the 1787 constitutional convention in Philadelphia and de facto role model for its bold innovation of an independent executive office, he was again drawn from retirement upon his unanimous election as the first president under the new Constitution. Washington sought to retire at the end of his first term and had Madison draft an address, but he was pressed by many leading figures to submit to a second term, to which he was again unanimously elected. However, near the end of that term, Washington published a statement refusing further service—in mid-September of 1796, to mark the anniversary of the constitutional convention's close in 1787. Later termed his "Farewell Address" and addressed to "Friends, and Fellow-Citizens," it opens by invoking republican virtue and civic duty; patriotic devotion to the common good; gratitude to Heaven for the country's blessings and prayers for continued Providence; and the need for prudence and moderation among citizens and government to sustain such goods. He pledged "unceasing vows" that America and the world would enjoy further blessings, including that "our Union and brotherly affection may be perpetual" and that "the free constitution, which is the work of your hands, may be sacredly maintained."[29] The bulk of the address comprises "disinterested warnings of a parting friend" on domestic and foreign policy and the foundations of a political culture of ordered liberty. Among the counsels is an adherence to separation of powers and the rule of law over populism, passion, and partisanship. Washington's suggestion that his parting guidance be the subject of "frequent review" by future citizens perhaps inspired Jefferson and Madison to place it on the curriculum of the new University of Virginia. Indeed, the address called for new educational institutions (Washington himself had endowed, among other institutions, the school that would become Washington and Lee University): for "[i]n proportion as the structure of government gives force to public opinion, it is essential that public opinion should be enlightened."[30] The last letter he wrote on politics, just before his death, in December 1799, more particularly addressed professional schooling for a portion of the citizenry. He commends Hamilton's plan for a federal military academy and recalls that, while president, he had repeatedly urged such an institution on Congress as "an Object of primary importance to this Country."[31] Whether or not Washington would be amazed at the staying power and growth of the republic he founded, he certainly warned of the challenges it would face in its early years and beyond. Among these was the need to provide a range of educational institutions that would inculcate principles of the rule of law and adherence to a complex constitutionalism in the citizens at large and in the professional military. He was to be joined in such anxious reflections by two astute observers of American constitutional democracy, both of whom admired Washington's practical wisdom and example.

Tocqueville and Lincoln on Civic Character and Constitutional Liberty

Abraham Lincoln's record of balancing liberty and order is suspect to some, especially civil libertarians, given his forceful use of executive power during the Civil War and especially his suspension of the writ of habeas corpus. Leading scholars even have categorized his actions as a kind of dictatorship—not the full version from ancient Rome or modern autocratic states but a narrower exercise of extralegal powers that seeks to preserve a constitutional order from grave threats.[32] Responses to this characterization (or indictment) of Lincoln cite his insistence upon holding the elections of 1864, especially given his dire electoral standing during most of the year before that election—and the easy excuse he could have cited of postponing elections during a raging rebellion.[33] If Lincoln had sought to crush liberty by invoking constitutional order, he presumably would have deployed such a cynical stratagem in the most self-interested case. Further doubt about the view of Lincoln as illiberal autocrat or as any kind of dictator arises from the fact that he had publicly warned of such temptations two decades earlier. In his first great political address and while still obscure, in 1838 he emphatically urged loyalty to law above power. Just when the sectional controversy and the conflict over slavery began to boil, Lincoln's "Perpetuation" address of 1838 warned that all sides of those quarrels or any other quarrels must resist the urge to resort to violence lest the fabric of ordered liberty be damaged beyond repair. It is striking that his address twice names Napoleon, citing the putative republican and military leader as one who used the excuse of anarchy and succumbed to the temptation of national glory to override republicanism, and that he concludes by invoking the anti-Napoleon, George Washington.[34] Lincoln's opening premise is that any existential danger to the American republic a half-century after its constitutional founding would arise not from military invasion (such as a Bonaparte might attempt) but from within, given "the increasing disregard for law which pervades the country."[35] There is always some moral cause that is cited to justify indignant violence or vigilante justice, from opposing gambling, to avenging murder, to upholding one side or other in the moral conflicts over slavery and racial segregation. Lincoln argued that it is not only immediate victims but all citizens who "fall victim to the ravages of mob law." One such act disposes citizens to tolerate or undertake others—"and thus it goes on, step by step, till all the walls erected for the defense of the persons and property of individuals, are trodden down, and disregarded."[36] Given the violence the country did increasingly inflict on itself in the coming decades, this seems a prescient warning that "the lawless in spirit" can easily become "the lawless in practice," rather than an alarmist trick of invoking a slippery slope for tactical political gain.

For academics and other professionals who are educated to prize dissent, Lincoln's argument that "lovers of liberty" must swear "never to violate . . . the laws of the country" seems an over-reaction and its own source of danger. It sounds more authoritarian than not to urge that "reverence for the laws, be breathed by every American mother, to the lisping babe, that prattles on her lap—let it be taught in schools, in seminaries, and in colleges . . . let it be preached from the Pulpit . . . in short, let it become the political religion of the nation."[37] Lincoln's rationale is in part the traditional republican concern for vigilance, that civic education and commitment to the rule of law must be explicit and active, rather than passive, if republican liberty is to survive in a dangerous world. In this view, fifty years of successful perpetuation of the Constitution is no answer: "We hope that dangers may be overcome, but to conclude that no danger may ever arise, would itself be extremely dangerous." As evidence for his concern, beyond the growing trend toward violent political action Lincoln adds the record of human affairs that any educated citizen should know, including a self-taught rustic like himself:

> It is to deny, what the history of the world tells us is true, to suppose that men of ambition and talents will not continue to spring up amongst us. And, when they do, they will as naturally seek the gratification of their ruling passion, as others have done so before them. The question then, is, can that gratification be found in supporting and maintaining an edifice that has been erected by others? Most certainly it cannot. [Those] whose ambition would aspire to nothing beyond a seat in Congress, or a gubernatorial or presidential chair . . . belong not to the family of the lion, or the tribe of the eagle. What! think you these places would satisfy an Alexander, a Caesar, or a Napoleon? Never! Towering genius disdains a beaten path. It seeks regions hitherto unexplored. . . . It thirsts and burns for distinction; and, if possible, it will have it, whether at the expense of emancipating slaves, or enslaving freemen.[38]

Lincoln insists that it is only reasonable to expect that "some man possessed of the loftiest genius, coupled with ambition sufficient to push it to its utmost stretch" will arise in America, and when this happens, "it will require the people to be united with each other, attached to the government and laws, and generally intelligent, to successfully frustrate his designs."

Some observers have argued that Lincoln, wittingly or unwittingly, spoke of his own ambition. It is less presumptuous to note that many historians who have studied him consider him a genius—and yet, as noted, either he was a fool not to seize power when the stage was set (the 1864 elections) or he was truly committed to republicanism.[39] Further support for the latter point of view arises from two points in the closing of the Perpetuation address. Lincoln states that, a half-century after the founding, his era faces what all future generations will confront—the need to embrace the constitutional order, not from emotional patriotism or personal memory of founders and events but from choice. "Reason, cold, calculating, unimpassioned reason, must furnish all the materials for our future support and defense"—and this must lead to a national commitment to "general intelligence" and "sound morality" as foundations for "a reverence for the constitution and laws." This echoes the republican ideal of an educated citizenry in Washington's Farewell. Not surprisingly, then, the second mark of Lincoln's early commitment to constitutionalism arises through the one statesman he invokes as counterexample to leaders who are not republicans or who betrayed their republic. Only his countrymen's continued "reverence for the constitution and laws" would be worthy of "our WASHINGTON."[40] Lincoln's admiration for the founder was abiding, for in brief remarks two decades later, when departing Illinois as president-elect, he looked back to gauge the tests ahead: "I now leave, not knowing when or whether ever I may return, with a task before me greater than that which rested upon Washington."[41] The task—or, put differently, the cause—was to save Union and Constitution, whether achieved at the moral cost of allowing slavery to continue (but not spread) or by abolishing slavery.[42] Frederick Douglass eventually endorsed this moderate strategy of putting Constitution first as providing the only plausible path to rally a majority of whites to eventually support abolition.[43] What Washington, Lincoln, and Douglass shared, then, was a commitment to the constitutional rule of law as the safest ark in the continual storms of political life, however deficient an instrument it might seem when measured against a particular moral test or crisis.

Lincoln did not know, when delivering his 1838 address, that, a few years earlier, a French observer had similarly praised Washington for founding and sticking to constitutionalism. In the first volume of *Democracy in America*, Tocqueville notes Washington's presiding role at the constitutional convention, an assembly of "the finest minds and noblest characters that had ever appeared in the New World."[44] He admires the Constitution's complexity, specifically its placement of the powers of war and foreign affairs in an executive and a Senate, neither of which reflects the immediate views of the people.[45] As shocking as this seems to sensibilities that now are more democratic or populist (at least in some ways), Tocqueville emphasizes that this constitutional structure and Washington's use of it as president served to keep America out of a war it would have been foolish to enter—the Anglo-French war of the 1790s that followed the French Revolution and led to Napoleon's rise. He commends the Farewell Address, "the political testament of that great man," for counseling America to avoid great-power quarrels in Europe and to balance the claims of national interest and justice when deciding about alliances and wars. By sticking to these principles, despite the unpopularity of his neutrality policy, Washington had "succeeded in keeping his country at peace when all the rest of the universe was at war."[46] Tocqueville insists, however, that the complex structure of the Constitution was the indispensable framework:

> The sympathies of the people in favor of France were . . . declared with so much violence that nothing less than the inflexible character of Washington and the immense popularity that he enjoyed were needed to prevent war from being declared on England. And still, the efforts that the austere reason of this great man made to struggle against the generous but unreflective passions of his fellow citizens almost took from him the sole recompense that he had ever reserved for himself, the love of his country. The majority pronounced against his policy; now the entire people approves it. If the Constitution and public favor had not given the direction of the external affairs of the state to Washington, it is certain that the nation would have done then precisely what it condemns today.[47]

Tocqueville's deeper point is to warn democracies they will be "decidedly inferior" to other states in matters of war and foreign policy unless they can balance and structure their constitutional orders to compensate. The "everyday practical wisdom" of individuals and groups fostered by "democratic freedom" is perfect for domestic politics, but relations between states will require constitutional democracies, like all states, to "coordinate the details of a great undertaking, fix on a design, and afterwards follow it with determination through obstacles." The new democracies also must be capable of formulating measures "in secret" and of "patiently awaiting their result." Tocqueville worries, however, about the democratic tendency "to obey sentiment rather than reasoning in politics, and to abandon a long matured design to satisfy a momentary passion."[48] Moreover, between Washington's struggles against popular opinion in the 1790s and his posthumous vindication in the 1830s lies an episode that Tocqueville omits here, although he discusses it elsewhere—the disastrous War of 1812. America declared war against a superpower in a fit of popular fury, to discover that its earlier popular policy against a standing army and navy exposed it not only to infringements of its sovereignty (as with British impressments of American seamen, a grievance for war advocates) but to having its capital invaded and burned in 1814.

It makes sense, then, that Tocqueville also discusses the American view of patriotism or "public spirit" as a strength of its political culture. America's constitutional order asks soldiers and citizens to respect the republican and nondemocratic structures of an indirectly elected president and Senate (in the original design) as the primary authorities on foreign affairs. True, it balances this principle by including the more democratic House in funding and regulating the armed forces and by sharing the power to declare war between House and Senate to the exclusion of the president. Still, this is a constitutional order that, in its complexity and insistence upon balance and in the space provided for not-so-democratic offices, must be studied to be loved in a democratic era. Tocqueville finds that Americans understand this with their "reflective patriotism" rooted in a calculation of the individual benefits gained by supporting national well-being and a constitution, in contrast to the "instinctive" or passionate patriotism that marked predemocratic times.[49] Similarly, in the second volume of *Democracy in America*, Tocqueville discusses the danger of military coups in democracies and argues, seemingly in echo of Washington and Lincoln, that civic education is the best way to ensure the stability of the constitutional order: "Have enlightened, regulated, steadfast, and free citizens, and you will have disciplined and obedient soldiers."[50] If the "peaceable and regular spirit of the country" evident in the "national mores" is both "enlightened and energetic," then the soldiers and officers will defend the country without endangering civilian command, the rule of law, and peaceful aims.[51] He reinforces this theme by discussing the kind of discipline characteristic of democratic armies, which cannot be the "blind, minute, resigned" obedience to superiors that marks aristocratic armies. Rather than trying to "negate the free flight of souls," a democratic discipline should "aspire to direct it" so that obedience is "less exact, but more impetuous and more intelligent."[52] He notes as a model for modern liberal democracies the "fraternity" between officers and soldiers in the ancient Greek and Roman citizen-armies as captured in Plutarch's *Lives of the Noble Greeks and Romans*: that "soldiers speak constantly and very freely to their generals, and the latter listen willingly" and respond, leading "by words and examples much more than by constraint and chastisements."[53]

Tocqueville's conception of a moderate military discipline accords with his earlier praise for the balance of liberty and order in America's complex constitutionalism, and he returns to this theme as *Democracy in America* closes. Moderate discipline, with some liberty for independent thinking and judgment by soldiers, is still discipline. Similarly, the political culture of America should continue to appreciate the balance of liberty, equality, and constitutional forms that brings order but does so by providing a diversity of channels for action, expression of views, and decision. Tocqueville commends this model of complex constitutional forms, in fact, to all new constitutional democracies. Democratic peoples "do not readily comprehend the utility of forms" and in fact feel "an instinctive disdain" for anything that is prescribed by tradition or authority or that slows down the march of majority opinion.[54] However, we should appreciate the rules and structures that "slow down" our debates and give room in the not-so-democratic branches for long-term thinking about complex issues. In accord with his praise for Washington's constitutional capacity to check a stampede toward war, Tocqueville presents this complex chain of authority from individual officers and soldiers up through Congress, including particular direction from a Senate and a president, as the best way to achieve the substantive aims that Washington counseled for America. This hierarchical, complicated system would not negate the moral judgment and liberty of soldiers and citizens nor give scope to "presidentialism" or elites disposed toward war. Rather, its structure would regularly balance the claims of national interest and universal human justice in making decisions about whether and how to fight wars, make alliances, and enact treaties. This complicated system also embodies a division of labor between political branches of government and between civilian leaders and military professionals that is meant to strike that right balance whether the policy be in the realm of grand strategy, or normal political-military affairs and diplomacy, or crisis management.[55] Leaders and thinkers such as Washington, Lincoln, and Tocqueville also remind us, however, that the right civic character is needed in citizens and leaders in order to perpetuate both the constitutional order and the liberty it serves.

CIVIC AND PROFESSIONAL EDUCATION FOR NAVIGATING THE PARADOXES

The oath to the Constitution does not relieve officers or soldiers of the need for moral and legal judgment or for critical and adaptive thinking. For military professionals, the paradoxes inherent in the oath are all the more real today given the experiences of the Second World War and Vietnam, which provoked reaffirmations of individual responsibility and reiterated the moral and legal parameters to obedience in the chain of command. Moreover, in a post–Cold War era in which American professionals face the full spectrum of threats from conventional to unconventional war, there is still greater need for judgment by junior officers and soldiers, let alone higher commanders.[56] Nonetheless, as professionals, these individuals, as well as their institutions, cannot be full-time moral philosophers or grand strategists, for this would separate them from a constitutional chain of command and also render them less effective or even dangerous. They cannot transcend the paradoxical balance of law and liberty, obedience and independent judgment—for this paradox defines their profession in a constitutional republic. This is why our dilemmas of military ethics and war should be studied within the context of constitutional principles and classic reflections on them. Literary views or personal reflections by active-duty, retired, or separated soldiers and officers are important, too, but such inquiries should illuminate rather than escape from our constitutional framework and the professional realities it entails. Immediate views about desired policies, which can more readily admix passion than reason amid the fog and the friction of debates about whether or how to fight a war should not skew the basic principles and character of our largely successful and long-enduring constitutional order.

For example, recourse to the scene in *Henry V* where the king, in disguise, discourses with common soldiers before the battle of Agincourt can be used to deny the paradoxes of professionalism rather than to prepare us to cope with them. Huntington would simply adopt the view of the soldiers that the war's justice is the king's business and is more than they can "know" or "should seek after"; this fits with his theory that the larger ethical and political questions lie strictly with the civilian authority so that the military remains a safe, effective instrument of the state. Sherman adopts the opposite view, that we should heed Shakespeare's apparent focus on the moral burden of the soldier and adopt a more egalitarian approach that empowers individuals to dissent not only on tactics but also on operations and strategy (the larger "cause" or war aims).[57] These rival interpretations omit, however, Shakespeare's depiction of the complexities that face governments and individuals bound by law and ethics. These include Henry's initial deliberations on whether the war is just; his command as the campaign opens to obey the law of war by respecting French property and civilians, despite the bluster he employs at the siege of Harfleur to goad the town to surrender; the king's erasure at Agincourt of the line between commoners and nobility, foreshadowing a constitutional monarchy in which all are citizens under law; and the French massacre at Agincourt of noncombatants, viewed against the English command's consideration of—but apparent restraint against—killing their many prisoners to prevent being overwhelmed by remaining French forces.[58] *Henry V* can be studied, that is, for prefiguring the complex balance of principles about just war and professionalism in a constitutional republic and the range of burdens placed upon soldiers, officers, and the national command.

Moral and professional standards in a constitutional democracy do not place the primary burden on the soldier or junior officer to assess the justice of the cause (*jus ad bellum*) or to set rules of engagement for operations (*jus in bello*). This falls on the constitutional order, in all its complexity. The Nuremberg principle does not require otherwise. That principle holds military professionals responsible for the *legality* of orders, understood to include very broad and obvious moral standards that the modern law of armed conflict codifies, but not for the wisdom or moral purity of every strategic or tactical choice in war. It is true that the burdens of implementing the modern law of armed conflict require professionals to develop the moral and practical judgment they will need in actual operations.[59] It also is true that soldiers and officers can vote and participate (within limits) in political debate, so they can affect the choice of leaders who formulate national security policy. On the other hand, conscientious objectors or pacifists mostly do not join the all-volunteer force in our era, giving military and civilian authorities justification to insist that soldiers and officers obey the constitutionally authorized national authority in ordering them to war. As noted, that command authority is as complex as any that a great power has ever imposed upon itself: the shared war power between Congress and president; legislative and executive (not exclusively executive) regulation of the military and its code of justice; congressional oversight of the services, their operations, and rules of engagement; and, in recent years, the addition of real-time monitoring of battle operations by judge advocate general (JAG) officers for legal compliance. Moreover, a free press and citizenry monitor and debate this complex command authority, even elements of this system legally deemed secret. This complex system of constitutionalism and professionalism does not ensure that senior civilian or military leaders will avoid errors or injustices, as dissenting views about the recent Afghanistan and Iraq wars would note. It does incorporate, however, the premise of some degree of "culture gap" between military or national security professionals and the civilian citizenry they serve and protect—so as to cultivate and preserve the kind of distinct professionalism the nation needs to cope with a dangerous world, but to do so as a constitutional republic.[60]

In this light, there is a burden on military professionals that is more pressing than the broad morality of war—the tensions of supreme command, between senior generals and civilian leaders, regarding the practical wisdom of particular decisions on whether or how to wage war. Is an officer ever loyal to the Constitution by resisting civilian commanders on questions of grand strategy and policy, or does the principle of civilian control require that officers have a limited opportunity for dissent and critique but in the end must follow civilian policy? Eliot Cohen's recent scholarship captures the complexities of these relationships and criticizes Huntington's drawing of bright lines between civilian and military roles. Constitutional democracies require—and at their best have achieved—an "unequal dialogue" between strategically serious officers and the strategically serious civilians who, in the end, they must obey.[61] This debate between various theories of civil-military relations points to the competing views in our political discourse about how generals should act if they have grave concerns about the wisdom of civilian decisions, which usually is a harder call than the legality of a policy. The military must report to, in different ways, the president, the secretary of defense, Congress, and the courts. Legislative reforms in the 1980s sought to clarify these relationships but also complicated them in some ways.[62] For example, a theater commander (e.g., in Afghanistan) can express concerns to the general who is the combatant commander of the region, who in turn reports directly to the secretary of defense and the president—but both the combatant (regional) commander and the secretary report not only to the president but also to Congress in certain ways. In addition, the chairman of the Joint Chiefs of Staff is the senior military adviser to the president and has direct access, even while informing the secretary of defense of concerns, and this can provide another channel for combatant command or field generals to reach the president. Further, presidents are explicitly authorized by recent statute, apart from any claim made about inherent executive authority, to reach down directly to the combatant commander or field commander, and even to the members of the Joint Chiefs of Staff who are not in the statutory chain of command.

These are the complex relationships within the executive branch as directed by Congress, apart from Congress's power to compel testimony by generals—be they theater or combatant-region commanders or on the Joint Chiefs, in public or in secret session. Officers, civilian officials, journalists, and academics should study this complexity, and one could add this maxim: the more insistent their opinions about whether this system is broken or working, the more studious they should be. This would moderate a significant tendency in public and academic debates since the Vietnam era, in which a given president or secretary of defense is criticized for suppressing dissent by generals, while another president or secretary is criticized for allowing military insubordination to civilian control. The reactions and standards offered by members of Congress, executive officials, the press, academics, or retired or active-duty officers are not consistent across different wars and decades or regarding hot issues like gays in the military. Is the problem overbearing civilian leaders, or is it insubordinate generals gaming the system's multiple access points in order to shirk and "slow roll" in resisting a civilian policy? Should we admit, alternately, that contentious policy views about a particular war or issue tend to drive judgments about the appropriate supreme command relationships between a president and generals and about whether the system is broken or functioning as designed?[63] Our pronouncements should be cautious given the divergent views of experts about various episodes of the "revolt of the generals" phenomenon in the last half-century, beginning with the Truman-MacArthur conflict and continuing under every president since but especially the lopsided support for dissent against George W. Bush and Secretary of Defense Donald Rumsfeld.

The regularity of these episodes and the difficulty of the judgments involved indicate that these tensions are intrinsic to our complex constitutional structure, to the legislation or policies subsequently developed, and to the challenges of national security in a globalized world. We should assess each new episode with greater equanimity but also sobriety given the constitutional pedigree of these tensions.[64] Moreover, some recent views of serving and retired officers overlook the corrosion to the professional culture and ethic likely to follow if the publicly dissenting general we praise today proves to be of the ilk of McClellan or MacArthur or if praise for such conduct prepares (intentionally or not) future professionals to consider such a path. A prominent military journal recently featured the ill-considered views of an officer who insisted that there are circumstances in which an officer is required, given the "moral autonomy" granted by the officer's oath and professional status itself, to disobey a legal order the officer considers likely to yield great harm to the nation, the military, or subordinates.[65] Arming every officer with a policy veto in light of his or her own standard of wisdom or grave harm would clearly violate the military's fundamental professional tenet. This would be true in every era of America's constitutional history, but it is all the more true in the era of the all-professional military. With fewer citizens serving in uniform and fewer elite educational institutions hosting ROTC programs or having other contact with the armed services, military professionals should be more deeply concerned about the wrong kind of "gap" between civilians and soldiers—the civilian concern about a praetorian guard serving its own identity and interests, rather than the Constitution through its duly elected and appointed authorities. Our principles and our experience show that we need field and region commanders or members of the Joint Chiefs to appropriately and discreetly challenge their civilian commanders about the tactical or strategic wisdom of particular decisions but without threatening or even seeming to threaten ultimate civilian control and responsibility.

One does not have to like war or be blind to the cruelties it inexorably proliferates upon combatants and innocents alike—Thucydides, himself a general, observed two millennia ago that war is a stern master or cruel teacher—to accept that republics cannot escape the necessity of preparing for and conducting wars. America's complex constitutional order tries to provide this capability while serving our ultimate moral aims and principles. This requires continual judgment from civilians, officers, and soldiers throughout the system, as well as continual debate about the rights and wrongs of various judgments and decisions. This does not mean that constitutional design and the statutory refinements of it are displaced by prudential judgment. Amid these pressing yet perpetual debates, we must take time to recall the fundamental principles and structures of our complex order of civil-military relations and constitutional politics. There is a particular burden on military and civilian national-security professionals to be well educated and continually educated about the classic sources and current debates in the domains of professional ethics, civil-military relations, political-military affairs, grand strategy, and crisis management. That education must begin before officers are commissioned and continue throughout a career, especially given the complexities of modern technology and the range of threats and the kinds of warfare liberal democracies face in the twenty-first century.[66] Indeed, this essay has tried to capture the kinds of literature and issues that professionals, military or civilian, must regularly confront and study. A further word about current education and training at one of the federal service academies may clarify these issues, as well as the difficulty of preparing officers to understand and navigate the paradoxes of constitutional loyalty.[67]

The overarching program for education, military training, athletic fitness, and leadership at the U.S. Air Force Academy is currently defined as the Officer Development System. Its main document prominently identifies the Academy's main mission as preparing officers to understand and live by their oath to the Constitution.[68] Aristotle isn't cited therein, nor do most cadets or faculty know of him much beyond the required course in ethics in the cadet curriculum, but the basic approach derives from the *Nicomachean Ethics*, suitably adjusted in light of the disciplines of the modern university, the practices of the modern military profession, and the principles of American constitutionalism. That approach is to educate leaders of character by combining intellectual, moral, physical, and habitual or experiential dimensions of excellence (formerly known as virtue), in a comprehensive program across eleven months a year for four years. The military professionals who founded and have shaped the program at the national academies for two centuries have not placed all the eggs in any one basket, judging that a blend of education, training, and other kinds of habituation is the best way to forge a professional identity and ethic, and the cadets simultaneously receive a bachelor's degree and an officer's commission at graduation. Habituation of mind, body, and experience makes for a busy schedule. It is not surprising that both military and civilian faculty have long worried that this atmosphere might not provide sufficient motivation and support for the intellectual development needed by officers in a constitutional republic. This is especially true for the adaptive, critical thinking and the professional judgment expected of the middle and higher officer ranks, particularly regarding civil-military relations and political-military affairs.

That said, the arguments, issues, and literature addressed in this essay are presented to all cadets to at least some degree in several courses of the required curriculum, in American government, ethics, military history, law, and military strategic studies, among others. They are explored in greater depth in several of the majors cadets can choose, such as political science, history, military strategic studies, law, and behavioral science and leadership. Running throughout the curriculum, as well as the daily training under the military commandant and the athletic programs, is the Honor Code, which is inculcated in and enforced primarily by the cadets. The Academy identifies the core values for all professionals in the Air Force as "integrity first, service before self, and excellence in all we do." To enforce these high aims, the Honor Code requires all cadets to affirm that "we will not lie, steal, or cheat, nor tolerate among us anyone who does." The cadets are charged with monitoring conduct by self and others (that is, self-reporting violations or reporting on others) and, further, with enforcing the Code by investigating and adjudicating cases of alleged violation (with oversight by officers, to include judge advocate general officers as legal advisers). The non-toleration clause places a burden on individual cadets and on the system, but this is seen as a way for cadets to practice and habituate honor and thus to prepare for being an officer who must enforce the Uniform Code of Military Justice and other regulations—including the norms of civil-military relations. Cadets and permanent staff continually debate how to balance the benefit of inculcating honor through cadet enforcement with the cost posed by the perception or the reality that a cadet jury will be more lenient with one of its own than an officer or faculty member would be. As noted, similar assessments and efforts at striking the right balance mark the internal debates about the professional development program as a whole. Whatever its flaws and despite the continual arguments by civilian and military professionals about how to improve it, it has produced and perpetuated a military professionalism that has avoided grave threats of insubordination while encouraging officers to articulate their policy judgments and expertise in advising civilian superiors.

America's constitutional experience indicates that it is the civic and professional judgment of well-educated officials, officers, and citizens that allows our system of law to be flexible enough to work in the service of our principles. There may be states in history with a better record of balancing immense power with extraordinary commitment to free debate about and ethical monitoring of the use of such power, but there are not many. This paradoxical system is our law, but it is not a law like gravity, as the reflections of Washington, Lincoln, Tocqueville, and other voices all urge us to consider. It will not sustain itself. Two further paradoxes we must accept are that, to enjoy and obey it, we must continually study and debate it and that such debate within the constitutional order can be its own kind of loyalty.

NOTES

I am grateful for instructive comments by my colleagues Damon Coletta and Schuyler Foerster and by Sandy Levinson. This essay does not represent the views of the U.S. Air Force Academy or the U.S. government.

1. Two quite different responses to the paradoxes of military loyalty in a republic are Nancy Sherman, "A Fractured Fidelity to Cause," in this *NOMOS* volume, and Eva Brann, "The Paradox of Obedience," originally delivered at the U.S. Air Force Academy in 2004 as the Reich Lecture in War, Morality, and the Military Profession and reprinted in Brann, *Homage to Americans* (Philadelphia: Paul Dry Books, 2010). I have benefited from the provocations in Sherman's essay, but my approach and conclusions are more indebted to Brann's views.

2. Samuel Huntington discusses *Henry V* in his classic *The Soldier and the State: The Theory and Politics of Civil-Military Relations* (New York: Random House, 1957), 73; Sherman discusses similar themes about just war from the play in "A Fractured Fidelity to Cause." Walter Berns grapples with the paradoxes of educating citizens in a free society and analyzes Tocqueville and Lincoln, among other classic American sources, in *Making Patriots* (Chicago: University of Chicago Press, 2001).

3. In response to Huntington's argument in *The Soldier and the State* for a division of labor between civilian authorities who set strategy or policy and military professionals with near-autonomy over operations and tactics, Morris Janowitz argues for a more dynamic relationship and more political awareness by officers in *The Professional Soldier: A Social and Political Portrait* (Glencoe, IL: Free Press, 1960). Two collections that provide an excellent introduction to the range of debate in subsequent decades are Peter D. Feaver and Richard H. Kohn, eds., *Soldiers and Civilians: The Civil-Military*

Gap and American National Security (Cambridge, MA: MIT Press, 2001), and Suzanne C. Nielsen and Don M. Snider, eds., *American Civil-Military Relations: The Soldier and the State in a New Era* (Baltimore: Johns Hopkins University Press, 2009).

4. The oath of office taken by all U.S. military officers when commissioned and upon promotion in rank is prescribed by statute and varies mostly in identifying the branch of service; the U.S. Army oath, since 1959, reads: "I, _____, having been appointed an officer in the Army of the United States, as indicated above in the grade of _____ do solemnly swear (or affirm) that I will support and defend the Constitution of the United States against all enemies, foreign or domestic, that I will bear true faith and allegiance to the same; that I take this obligation freely, without any mental reservations or purpose of evasion; and that I will well and faithfully discharge the duties of the office upon which I am about to enter; So help me God." See http://www.history.army.mil/faq/oaths.htm.

5. See Malham M. Wakin, "The Ethics of Leadership," *American Behavioral Scientist* 19 (May/June 1976): 567–88, reprinted in Wakin, *Integrity First: Reflections of a Military Philosopher* (Lanham, MD: Lexington Press, 2000).

6. Lincoln, "Fragment on the Constitution and Union" (ca. January 1861), in The Abraham Lincoln Association, Springfield, Illinois, *Collected Works*, vol. 4, ed. Roy P. Basler (New Brunswick, NJ: Rutgers University Press, 1953), 168–69.

7. See James R. Stoner Jr., "Behind the `Facts Submitted to a Candid World': Constitutional Arguments for Independence," in his *Common Law and Liberal Theory: Coke, Hobbes, and the Origins of American Constitutionalism* (Lawrence: University Press of Kansas, 1992), 179–96.

8. See Donald Lutz, "The Relative Influence of European Writers on Late Eighteenth-Century American Political Thought," *American Political Science Review* 78 (March 1984): 189–97. I discuss the blending of liberal and republican ideas in "Montesquieu's Complex Natural Right and Moderate Liberalism: The Roots of American Moderation," *Polity* 36 (January 2004): 227–50.

9. Charles de Secondat baron de Montesquieu, *The Spirit of the Laws*, trans. and ed. Anne M. Cohler, Basia Carolyn Miller, and Harold Samuel Stone (New York: Cambridge University Press, [1748] 1989), Book 11, ch. 3, 155; see also Book 29, ch. 1, 602.

10. Ibid., Book 11, ch. 4, 156.

11. J. Glenn Gray, *The Warriors: Reflections on Men in Battle* (Lincoln: University of Nebraska Press, [1959, 1970] 1998); Sherman does not cite Gray's work, but the spirit of her essay is similar. Gray particularly discusses loyalty at 39–51.

12. Immanuel Kant, "Perpetual Peace: A Philosophical Sketch" (1795), in *Kant: Political Writings*, 2nd ed., ed. Hans Reiss, trans. H. B. Nisbet (Cambridge: Cambridge University Press, 1991), 93–130; see also John Rawls, *The Law of Peoples* (Cambridge, MA: Harvard University Press, 2001).

13. I argue this in "American Power and the Legacy of Washington: Enduring Principles for Foreign and Security Policy," in *American Defense Policy*, 8th ed., ed. Paul J. Bolt, Damon V. Coletta, and Collins G. Shackelford Jr. (Baltimore: Johns Hopkins University Press, 2005), 6–16; see also Felix Gilbert, *To the Farewell Address: Ideas of Early American Foreign Policy* (Princeton: Princeton University Press, 1961), 4–6, 16–8, 135–36, and Nicholas G. Onuf, *The Republican Legacy in International Thought* (Cambridge: Cambridge University Press, 1998), 233–46, 262.

14. See Richard Brookhiser, *Founding Father: Rediscovering George Washington* (New York: Free Press, 1996), 103. Other studies of Washington's republicanism include John Marshall, *The Life of George Washington: Special Edition for Schools*, ed. Robert Faulkner and Paul Carrese (Indianapolis: Liberty Fund, [1838] 2000); Glenn Phelps, *George Washington and American Constitutionalism* (Lawrence: University Press of Kansas, 1993); and Jeffry H. Morrison, *The Political Philosophy of George Washington* (Baltimore: Johns Hopkins University Press, 2009).

15. John Rhodehamel, ed., *George Washington: Writings* (New York: Literary Classics of the United States, 1997), 228. This section draws on my discussion in "Liberty, Constitutionalism, and Moderation: The Political Thought of George Washington," in *History of American Political Thought*, ed. Bryan-Paul Frost and Jeffrey Sikkenga (Lanham, MD: Lexington Press, 2003), 95–113.

16. Rhodehamel, ed., *Washington: Writings*, 1106 n.468.31; spelling as in the original in all selections.

17. Ibid., 468–69.

18. A recent analysis of Washington's influence on shaping American civil-military relations is Christopher P. Gibson, *Securing the State: Reforming the National Security Decisionmaking Process at the Civil-Military Nexus* (Aldershot, Eng.: Ashgate, 2008), 30–36, 64–65.

19. Marshall, *Life of George Washington*, 245–48.

20. Rhodehamel, ed., *Washington: Writings*, 1107–9 n.490.13-4.

21. Ibid., 490.

22. Ibid., 495–500.

23. Ibid., 498–500.

24. Ibid., 1109 n.496.12.

25. Department of the Army, *The Army, Field Manual 1* (Washington, DC: Department of the Army, 2005), 1–4 and section 1-15. See also Douglas V. Johnson and Steven Metz, "Civil-Military Relations in the United States," in *American Defense Policy*, 7th ed., ed. Peter L. Hays, Brenda J. Vallance,

and Alan R. Van Tassel (Baltimore: Johns Hopkins University Press, 1997), 495–96.

26. Rhodehamel, ed., *Washington: Writings*, 544.

27. Ibid., 547–48.

28. Jefferson to Washington, 16 April, 1784, in *Thomas Jefferson: Writings*, ed. Merrill D. Peterson (New York: Literary Classics of the United States, 1984), 791. Compare Marshall's extraordinary tribute in *Life of George Washington*, 301.

29. Rhodehamel, ed., *Washington: Writings*, 963–64.

30. Ibid., 964, 972.

31. Ibid., 1051.

32. The classic work is Clinton L. Rossiter, *Constitutional Dictatorship: Crisis Government in the Modern Democracies* (Princeton: Princeton University Press, 1948); for a more recent view see Sanford Levinson and Jack M. Balkin, "Constitutional Dictatorship: Its Dangers and Its Design," *Minnesota Law Review* 94 (June 2010): 1789–1866.

33. See Herman Belz, *Lincoln and the Constitution: The Dictatorship Question Reconsidered* (Fort Wayne, IN: Louis A. Warren Lincoln Library and Museum, 1984).

34. Lincoln, "The Perpetuation of Our Political Institutions," Address to the Young Men's Lyceum of Springfield, Illinois, January 1838, in Basler, ed., *Collected Works*, vol. 1, 108–15.

35. Basler, ed., *Collected Works*, vol. 1, 109.

36. Ibid., 111.

37. Ibid., 112.

38. Ibid., 113–14.

39. Two recent books praising Lincoln's brilliance, among many others one could cite, are Gary Wills, *Lincoln at Gettysburg: The Words That Remade America* (New York: Simon and Schuster, 1992), and Doris Kearns Goodwin, *Team of Rivals: The Political Genius of Abraham Lincoln* (New York: Simon and Schuster, 2005).

40. Basler, ed., *Collected Works*, vol. 1, 115 (emphasis in original).

41. Lincoln, "Farewell Address at Springfield," February 11, 1861, in Basler, ed., *Collected Works*, vol. 4, 190–91.

42. Lincoln states this most succinctly in his letter of August 22, 1862, to the abolitionist Horace Greeley: "I would save the Union. I would save it the shortest way under the Constitution. . . . My paramount object in this struggle *is* to save the Union, and is *not* either to save or to destroy slavery. If I could save the Union without freeing *any* slave I would do it, and if I could save it by freeing *all* the slaves I would do it; and if I could save it by freeing some and leaving others alone I would also do that" (emphases in original). Basler, ed., *Collected Works*, vol. 5, 388–89.

224 PAUL O. CARRESE

43. Frederick Douglass, "Oration in Memory of Abraham Lincoln," 14 April, 1876, in *The Life and Writings* of *Frederick Douglass,* vol. 4, ed. Philip S. Foner (New York: International Publishers, 1950–55), 309ff.

44. Alexis de Tocqueville, *Democracy in America,* vol. 1, trans. and ed. Harvey C. Mansfield and Delba Winthrop (Chicago: University of Chicago Press, [1835] 2000), Part 1, ch. 8, 107.

45. Ibid., Part 2, ch. 5, 217.

46. Ibid., Part 2, ch. 5, 217–18.

47. Ibid., Part 2, ch. 5, 220.

48. Ibid., Part 2, ch. 5, 219.

49. Ibid., Part 2, ch. 6, 226–28.

50. Alexis de Tocqueville, *Democracy in America,* vol. 2, trans. and ed. Harvey C. Mansfield and Delba Winthrop (Chicago: University of Chicago Press, [1840] 2000), Part 3, ch. 22, 622.

51. Ibid., Part 3, ch. 23, 625.

52. Ibid., Part 3, ch. 25, 630.

53. Ibid.

54. Ibid., Part 4, ch. 7, 669.

55. As Sherman notes in "A Fractured Fidelity to Cause" in this volume, David Estlund soberly analyzes tensions between a soldier's moral judgment and the constitutional system that authorizes war, in "On Following Orders in an Unjust War," *Journal of Political Philosophy* 15 (June 2007): 213–34. Unlike Sherman, however, Estlund warns against the "private judgment view" that would effectively incline every soldier toward conscientious objection, at 216, and he defends the broad legitimacy of a constitutional democratic system to make binding decisions—even if some citizens or soldiers find the decision debatable or wrong—about the difficult practical question of whether to use military force, at 223–25.

56. On the need for military institutions and individuals to perpetually learn and adapt, see General David Petraeus, "Beyond the Cloister," *American Interest* (July/August 2007); John A. Nagl, *Learning to Eat Soup with a Knife: Counterinsurgency Lessons from Malaya and Vietnam* (Chicago: University of Chicago Press, 2005); and also Dr. John A. Nagl, Brian Burton, Dr. Don M. Snider, Frank G. Hoffman, Captain Mark R. Hagerott, USN, and Colonel Roderick C. Zastrow, USAF, "Keeping the Edge: Revitalizing America's Military Officer Corps," February 2010, http://www.cnas.org/node/4077; and U.S. House of Representatives, Committee on Armed Services, Subcommittee on Oversight and Investigations, *Another Crossroads? Professional Military Education Two Decades after the Goldwater Nichols Act and the Skelton Panel* (Washington, DC: House Armed Services Committee Print 111–14, 2010), http://armedservices.house.gov/pdfs/PMEReport050610/PMEReport050610.pdf.

57. Huntington, *The Soldier and the State*, 73, and Sherman, "A Fractured Fidelity to Cause"—both referring to Shakespeare, *The Life of Henry V*, Act IV, scene 1, lines 89–190.

58. On these points see respectively (Act, scene, line): I.1, I.2, and II.4.80, "By law of nature and of nations"; III.3.55, "Use mercy to them all"; III.6.105–10 (Henry enforcing the law of war against his old comrade Bardolph); IV, Chorus and scene 3 (St. Crispin's Day speech) on common service outranking rank; and IV.6.36–39, IV.7.1–10 and 52–63 with stage directions (Folio edition) that the English have not killed their prisoners despite the French slaughter of English baggage boys (see also IV.8.75–79 reckoning the many French prisoners after the battle).

59. See Brann, "The Paradox of Obedience"; Wakin's essays in *Integrity First*; Martin L. Cook, *The Moral Warrior: Ethics and Service in the U.S. Military* (Albany: SUNY Press, 2004); and Mark Osiel, *Obeying Orders: Atrocity, Military Discipline, and the Law of War* (New Brunswick, NJ: Transaction, 1999).

60. On recent debates over this issue see Peter D. Feaver and Richard H. Kohn, "The Gap: Soldiers, Civilians, and Their Mutual Misunderstanding," in *American Defense Policy*, 8th ed., ed. Bolt, Coletta, and Shackelford, 338–43. Jean M. Yarbrough defends a moderate gap in "The Role of Military Virtues in Preserving Our Republican Institutions," in *Thomas Jefferson's Military Academy: Founding West Point*, ed. Robert M. S. McDonald (Charlottesville: University of Virginia Press, 2004), 207–21.

61. Eliot Cohen, *Supreme Command: Soldiers, Statesmen, and Leadership in Wartime* (New York: Free Press, 2002); Cohen analyzes Lincoln and Churchill as exemplars of this dialogue.

62. See Sam C. Sarkesian, John Allen Williams, and Stephen J. Cimbala, "The Military Establishment, the President, and Congress," in *American Defense Policy*, 8th ed., ed. Bolt, Coletta, and Shackelford, 139–50, including discussion of the Goldwater-Nichols Act of 1986.

63. One case study is the reaction to General Eric Shinseki's testimony before Congress in early 2002 regarding plans for the invasion of Iraq; most commentary deems his critical answers about the administration plans to be appropriate and even heroic; among the few scholars critical of Shinseki's decision to publicly air such concerns is Damon Coletta, "Courage in the Service of Virtue: The Case of General Shinseki's Testimony before the Iraq War," *Armed Forces & Society* 34 (October 2007): 109–21.

64. Two academic views that clarify the issues but differ on responses to them are Martin Cook, "Revolt of the Generals: A Case Study in Professional Ethics," *Parameters: U.S. Army War College Quarterly* (Spring 2008): 4–15, leaning toward responsibility of generals to dissent in grave cases, and Don M. Snider, *Dissent and Strategic Leadership of the Military Professions* (Carlisle, PA: Strategic Studies Institute, U.S. Army War College, 2008), ar-

guing that generals must limit dissent to sustain trust with civilian leaders, the broader citizenry, and the profession itself.

65. U.S. Marine Corps Lieutenant Colonel Andrew R. Milburn, "Breaking Ranks: Dissent and the Military Professional," *Joint Forces Quarterly* 59 (2010): 101–7. Although he lists "intellectual rigor" as a prerequisite for such moral autonomy, the boldness of his claims is not matched by either rigor or sobriety; the argument rests on a cursory review of the complex literature on civil-military relations, cites no literature on "moral autonomy" for officers, and is marred by other grave errors, such as conflating absence of a congressional declaration of war with absence of legislative authorization for use of force, misstating the just war concept of *jus in bello* for "*jus ad bello,*" misrepresenting the debate in the 1780s and 1790s about the structure and uses of America's armed forces, and mischaracterizing the 1783 Newburgh rebellion as only an effort to "influence Congress" for "financial reimbursement" via a plan to "march on Washington to lobby Congress" decades before Washington, D.C., existed and with no mention of George Washington's grave concerns about the episode.

66. A recent report about the need for officers to undertake continual education in and refinement of strategic and political-military judgment comes from the Center for a New American Security; Nagl et al., "Keeping the Edge." That report, including its proposed reforms, is endorsed in a recent congressional study of all military educational institutions—U.S. House of Representatives, *Another Crossroads?*

67. I draw on a dozen years of teaching at the U.S. Air Force Academy, but further information is available from the website of each service academy and also from independent views of each institution. See, as examples, David Lipsky, *Absolutely American: Four Years at West Point* (New York: Vintage, 2004), or Diana Jean Schemo, *Skies to Conquer: A Year Inside the Air Force Academy* (Hoboken, NJ: Wiley, 2010), and the array of sources cited in these and similar works.

68. For the Officer Development System (ODS) document and a brief description of the program, see the Web pages of the USAFA Superintendent (equivalent to the president), http://www.usafa.edu/superintendent/xp/xpl/ODS.cfm.

PART IV

PARTISAN LOYALTY

9

THE CASE FOR PARTY LOYALTY

RUSSELL MUIRHEAD

Generally, we do not think good citizenship involves party loyalty. Good citizens are expected to think for themselves; they gather information, try to understand public issues, size up candidates, ponder rival programs, and make up their own minds about how to vote. When they vote, good citizens are supposed to deliberate and decide with a view to the common good—not what is advantageous for their party.[1] Perhaps in light of the ideal of nonpartisan independence, most people say, "I vote the person, not the party."[2] What goes for citizens also holds for representatives, who are most celebrated not when they are courageous loyalists but when they are mavericks or when they are willing to "work across the aisle" to form bipartisan coalitions. There are no awards for "Profiles in Partisanship." We admire, for instance, Senators Wayne Morse, of Oregon, and Ernest Gruening, of Alaska, the only two who voted against the Gulf of Tonkin Resolution (which authorized President Johnson to use military force in Southeast Asia), not the eighty-eight senators who voted in favor, caught up in the passion that followed an "attack" that was subsequently shown to be phony.[3] Party loyalty seems less admirable than independence.

Against this ideal of independence, I will try in this essay to defend partisanship as a kind of loyalty. The loyal partisanship I defend is necessary for political action and constitutes one's political identity.[4] This is in contrast to the kind of partisanship that is only incidental or strategic. For instance, a good citizen who understands her devotion as solely to the common good might find that one or another party is most reliably aligned with what she takes the common good to be. As a result, she reliably supports candidates from one party and, in this sense, acts like a loyal partisan. But her underlying motive is not loyalty; it is the contingent assessment that one party more than any other happens to approximate her understanding of the common good. Her loyalty is to justice and the common good, and her connection to the party is only strategic or incidental. It might be fair to call this citizen a partisan, and she might confess a partisan identity if a pollster asked her a question like "Generally speaking, do you usually think of yourself as a Republican, a Democrat, an Independent, or what?" But she would probably not say she is a "strong Democrat" or a "strong Republican" because her partisanship is a secondary commitment, if it is a commitment at all.[5]

What I will try to defend is something more than a strategic association of convenience, where partisanship is part of one's civic identity. It is the posture of those who find it hard to imagine themselves switching parties or who would suffer a loss were they to do so. In the U.S. context, this includes those who say they are "strong Republicans" or "strong Democrats," who might mean to convey by the adjective "strong" that they are loyal. To be a loyal partisan is not merely to be situated in a party by virtue of its alignment with one's own views. For the loyal partisan, partisanship is not only about standing *for* (certain positions) but is also about standing *with* one's political friends across time—perhaps longer than one's own agreement with the party's legislative priorities would alone warrant. *Standing with* establishes a kind of trust or political friendship with one's fellow partisans, as it identifies others—rival partisans—as less trusted adversaries.

In what follows, I first make the case, in brief, for partisan loyalty as an essential posture in politics. Partisan loyalty can be good, I argue, because political action takes memory and patience: we can neither secure the achievements of the past nor realize hopes for the future without loyalty. I then consider the possibility of partisanship without loyalty or strategic partisanship and say something about its defects. In the next section, I discuss party loyalty as a kind of political friendship that constitutes part of one's civic identity. This kind of constitutive loyalty, though crucial for effective political action, also invites serious pathologies. Most important among these is the way loyalty threatens to bring an epistemic closure that insulates loyalists from factual reality—and thus from sharing a political community with their adversaries. Party loyalty, even when it is part of our civic identity, should represent a commitment to behave in certain ways—not to think in certain ways.

THE OCCASION FOR PARTY LOYALTY

In open societies, the common good is always a matter of dispute. For this reason, political action requires more than dispassionate reasoning about the common good or the policies that might serve it. Citizenship engages one in a contest with some citizens and against others. To accomplish something in politics, one has to win in the face of opposition. This contest has a history; it does not start from scratch every morning or with every new election. Party loyalty is about remembrance. Partisans remember the achievements (or defeats) of the past and stand together for the sake of protecting (or undermining) them. Once something is done in politics—the Democrats pass a health care bill, for instance, or the Republicans pass a tax cut—the opposition will continue to oppose. It will impede and obstruct, dilute and diminish, unravel and undo. Politics offers few permanent victories, and today's loser can win in the long run. Supporters therefore need to maintain their support. To secure what one takes to be the achievements of the past requires a group that stands together, remembers together, and strives to protect and cement, to advance and extend, yesterday's success.

Popular mood or crafty legislative machinations might patch together a coalition that, in a moment, gets something done. But, without loyalty, this coalition will soon scatter. It has no memory and no future; *it* is not an *it*. *It* has no identity over time, and, since its members are not connected by political friendship, it cannot stand up to opposition that endures. Whatever it accomplishes will quickly be gutted, stymied, or destroyed. The citizenship of independent judgment, as with partisanship that lacks any loyalty, cannot locate the place in politics where achievements are remembered and therefore protected. This is why independence (loyalty only to your own judgment) is not a genuine political stance. It is a flight from politics, born of the vain expectation that the common good in all of its necessary specifications can command universal assent. So long as people disagree—and so long as they are free, they will disagree—politics will need party, and party will need loyalty.

This is why parties form in the first place. Modern democracy is representative democracy, and parties and partisanship are a natural complement to representative democracy. They begin in the legislature (as "parties-in-government"), where representatives stand to win more as members of a party than as unaffiliated independents.[6] In the first American legislature, in 1790, for instance, representatives had no party affiliation. Very quickly—by the end of the second session of the First Congress—national leaders came to see that the unity of purpose that bound figures like Madison and Hamilton would not survive and that controversies would recur with each new issue that came up. Hamilton's plan for the national government to assume the debts the states had incurred in the Revolutionary War, as well as the question of where to locate the nation's capital, roiled legislators and raised a version of the "great principle" that was decided—but not entirely decided—by the new Constitution: how powerful would the new national government be, and, more deeply, "what sort of nation America was to be"?[7] An unorganized assembly of unaffiliated independent representatives was "unstable, shifting, and chaotic," and the "provisional, issue-specific compromises" that were hammered out left the future of the great principle uncertain.[8] As a result, Hamilton on one side and Jefferson and Madison on the other had reason to form coalitions that would remember the great principle at stake and apply it consistently over time across different issues. By the Second Congress, most representatives were either Federalists or Jeffersonians.[9]

From a wholesome commonsense view of things, politics should be more about solving problems than about winning partisan fights. Pragmatic discussion and compromise seem more constructive than partisan contestation.[10] Ordinary politics is about problem solving, of course—but it is never only that. Political problem solving is not akin to a plumber fixing your leaky sink or a mechanic getting your car to start ("I fixed it—problem solved!"). It is not the application of commonly accepted techniques to commonly identified problems. Nor is it simply forward looking ("Politics: solving the problems of today for a happier tomorrow"). What counts as a problem in politics is itself always a matter of contestation, as is the process of ranking problems according to their relative urgency. When we do agree about how to describe a problem and its urgency, we disagree about how to solve it. So we might agree that 9.6 percent unemployment is a problem but disagree about how much inflation should be tolerated to combat unemployment. In politics, once you get to the problem solving, the fight has already been won (for today).

Speaking of winning, what counts as a success—as "problem solved!"—is often not immediately evident in politics. Policies and programs sometimes take a long time to work themselves out. For instance, the Iraq War failed: its main justification (eliminating Iraq's weapons of mass destruction) turned out to be false and its main goal (establishing a rights-respecting democracy in Iraq) fragile and elusive. Yet, its chief advocate, former President George W. Bush, has insisted that it is too early to judge—only the historians, he says, will be able to fully evaluate whether the war improved governance in the country and the region. To take another example, whether the health care bill passed in President Barack Obama's first term (the Patient Protection and Affordable Care Act of 2010) successfully extends health care coverage while reducing costs can only be dimly appreciated at the time of his reelection; by some estimates, the pilot programs the bill authorizes will take a decade to produce results. Long-term plans require some kind of loyalty from those who are willing to take the risk that those plans will succeed. Politics requires patience, and patience takes loyalty. Independent judgment does not produce patience because the facts one might judge are not yet in. Meanwhile, those who oppose such plans—whether the Iraq War, the health care reform, or, in an earlier day, Social Security or Medicare, civil rights legislation or environmental regulation, or deregulation and tax cuts—will *not* be patient. Against this opposition, any citizen or legislator, any executive or administrator who wants a plan to succeed will need patient support. He or she will need loyalists.

This is the brief for party loyalty. Party loyalty finds its occasion because political action requires remembering the accomplishments of the past and protecting them for the future. Party loyalty is also about looking forward with patience, in anticipation of successes that reveal themselves over time. Those who share political memory and political patience are political friends—fellow partisans. Without this friendship, without the loyalty of fellow partisans, without memory and without patience, nothing can be accomplished in politics.

STRATEGIC LOYALTIES

A prominent understanding of partisanship denies that it contains an element of loyalty—or that whatever loyalty it involves is really just an expression of self-interest. From this "tough-minded" view, partisanship is a strategic thing. It is not merely a tool for realizing some conception of the common good (as discussed earlier) but is even more crudely strategic than that. It is a tool for advancing one's self-interest. The argument claims, first, that it is a mistake to view ordinary citizens as partisans; only office seekers and the political careerists who gather around them (political elites) are real partisans because only they have something real to gain from an election. Second, it claims that the partisanship of political elites is to be understood as simply a strategic tool, designed to advance their ambition and gratify their taste for status and power. Thus, it is a mistake to think that partisanship is about loyalty, at least if loyalty is something that prompts us to go beyond our self-interest. The strategic conception of partisanship might be descriptively accurate in many cases. But it is not entirely accurate; it distorts the phenomenon of partisanship and obscures elements of partisanship that can be admirable—and pathological.

In the tough-minded strategic view of party loyalty, voters are "neither office seekers nor benefit seekers and thus are not part of the political party at all, even if they identify strongly with a party and consistently support its candidates."[11] Voters are merely consumers, on this view. They consume the party's message and, if they like it, buy into its candidates. But they are no more part of the party than loyal Ford drivers are part of the Ford Motor Company. They do not participate in the design, the production, or the marketing of the products; they are not part of the argument about how the party will present its claims or what the party ultimately stands for. If they are loyalists, they are only "brand loyalists"—the lowest form of loyalty.

In contrast to brand loyalists, political elites—office seekers and the careerists who gather around them—are, in this view, the real partisans. They are the ones who craft the party's message and set its direction. More important, they stand to benefit from the party's success. As Anthony Downs says, political elites "act solely to attain the income, prestige, and power that comes from being in office."[12] On this tough-minded appraisal of political motivation, office seekers are not motivated to serve the common good; they are out for their own good. Ideas and policies are not their goals— they just use them to make their ambition palatable to others. Partisans, Downs argues, "do not want office for the sake of policy. . . . They treat policies as a means to the attainment of private ends, which they can reach only by being elected."[13]

For real partisans, party loyalty is a tool to be used to gratify their personal ambitions. Ambitious and self-interested partisans need to act as if they are loyal, just as they need to appear as if they care about policy and the common good for their own sake. No one gets elected by saying, "I have a taste for the perks and recognition that come with public office, and I would be grateful for your vote." Office seekers must mask their private ambition, and party loyalty—sticking with one party through good times and bad—is essential to this mask. Loyalty allays the concern that ambitious people will do anything for power.

This is why party switching is so rare. Since 1890, for example, only twenty-one U.S. senators have switched parties during their Senate service. It usually does not pay to switch, even if your party faces a landslide defeat. No recent example makes this clearer than the case of former senator Arlen Specter, of Pennsylvania, who was elected in 1980 as a Republican and defeated in the primary election of 2010, a year after switching to the Democratic Party (Specter died in October 2012). Specter had never been a perfect fit with the Republican Party; on issues like abortion, hate crime legislation, warrantless wiretapping, and health care funding, Specter had voted with Democrats. The breaking point came in the first year of Obama's presidency, when, in February 2009, Specter voted for President Obama's economic stimulus bill. Specter's standing with Republicans in his home state plummeted, and, facing a likely defeat in the Republican primary, Specter switched parties. "The Republican Party has moved far to the right," he noted. "I now find my political philosophy more in line with Democrats than Republicans."[14]

Gratitude from Senate Democrats and the Obama White House, however, could not protect Specter from a strong primary election challenge by two-term Democratic Congressman Joseph Sestak. Specter led in the polls until a month before the election, when Sestak aired the following devastating ad:

> SESTAK VOICEOVER (video of Sestak talking to voters): "I'm Joe Sestak, the Democrat. I authorized this message."
>
> SPECTER (video of Specter speaking): "My change in party will enable me to be reelected."
>
> NARRATOR (video cuts to photo of Specter standing arm-in-arm with President George W. Bush): "For forty-five years, Arlen Specter has been a Republican politician."
>
> GEORGE W. BUSH (video cuts to President Bush giving a speech): "Arlen Specter is the right man for the United States Senate. I can count on this man. See, that's important. He's a firm ally."
>
> NARRATOR VOICEOVER: "But now . . ."
>
> SPECTER (video cuts to Specter speaking): "My change in party will enable me to be reelected."
>
> NARRATOR VOICEOVER: (video cuts to photo of Specter standing next to Sarah Palin): "Arlen Specter switched parties to save one job . . . his, not yours."

Specter complained that his quotation was taken out of context (and it was; the full quotation emphasized Specter's ability to serve the public, rather than his mere ability to get reelected).[15] But the damage was emphatic. After the ad aired, Sestak pulled into the lead, and, four weeks later, Sestak beat Specter in the primary (he subsequently lost to the Republican candidate, Pat Toomey, in the general election). As one Pittsburgh voter said, "I'm not real comfortable with Specter switching over. I think it was mostly for his own status."[16]

Indeed, Specter was even more vulnerable to the charge of opportunism than many voters in 2010 perhaps knew. When he began his public career, as an assistant district attorney, in 1959, he was a Democrat. In 1965, he challenged the incumbent district attorney (his boss) by running on the Republican ticket, and, after winning the election, he formally registered as a Republican.

At the time, his opponent called him "Specter the Defector" and "Benedict Arlen."[17] The colorful election caught the attention of the venerable *Washington Post* columnist David Broder when he was a cub reporter at the *New York Times*. Broder recalled the incident in a column more than four decades later: "There is one consistency in the history of Arlen Specter," Broder wrote, "his willingness to do whatever will best protect and advance the career of Arlen Specter." Specter's career, Broder observed, shows that "he will stick with you only as long as it serves his own interests—and not a day longer."[18]

On the tough-minded understanding of party loyalty, Specter was not unusual in his craven desire for office, only unskillful in the way he revealed it. His opportunism, in this view, is the norm: political elites pick a party for the sake of winning; they do not try to win for the sake of the party. What singles Specter out is only how clumsily he revealed the self-interested opportunism of political elites; he made obvious what most mask. He forgot that elected officials need to *act* like they are loyal even though they are out to serve themselves, so that voters have confidence that they will reliably serve the policies and ideals they say they care about. Specter's main failing was not that he lacked loyalty but that he made plain how superficial party loyalty always is for political elites. Specter seemed to exemplify the tough-minded explanation of party loyalty: among elites—the real partisans—it is a strategic pose, while, among ordinary voters, it may run deeper but even then constitutes only a brand loyalty.

Politics, in this view, is not really an occasion for serious loyalties. Instead, voters *and* elites are self-interested. If some voters are loyal to a party, it's because in the past the party has benefited them. In some respects, this is probably an accurate account of things: at bottom, self-interest rules. The problem of democratic politics is that the self-interest of ambitious elites (who want status or recognition) is fundamentally different from the self-interest of ordinary citizens (who want security and prosperity). Party loyalty, superficial as it is, functions as a partial solution to this problem, insofar as it tethers political elites to ordinary citizens.

If it captures something of the strategic essence that defines political people, this account also distorts important features of the political world, including party loyalty. Like many modes of explanation that purport to unmask the way things appear in order to show how things really are (for instance, the Marxist explanation of religion as an opiate of the masses), this account of party loyalty undercuts the way many people understand themselves. Many people who take an interest in politics understand themselves to take an interest in *public things*, apart from the way public things bear on their private interests. What makes politics a distinctive and attractive field of interest or endeavor is that it carries our attention beyond the narrow confines of our private lives. From the perspective of a private interest in security and comfort, political people make sacrifices: they give up privacy, wealth, and discretionary time, and they risk their reputations. If we were to ask why political people are willing to sacrifice these things, the answer that they crave the perks of office only restates the question: what is so great about public office that some people are willing to risk so much?

This is not to say that we should always accept people's self-understandings at their face value, but one merit of this naïve self-understanding ("I am in politics to contribute to the common good") is that it gives an account of the goal or object of political ambition. It is perfectly possible that some people—perhaps most people—in politics want public office because they want to pursue policies and ideals that they understand to be for the common good. This does not mean that they are self-effacing or altruistic; they may also want glory, but, if they do, they want to be recognized not for their mere existence (as with a celebrity like Paris Hilton) but for the good things they have done. They have purposes and goals or, more narrowly, policies and programs they want to advance; they do not just want office for its own sake. John Aldrich, who offers an enlarged rational-choice account of party formation in the United States, argues that the people who formed parties in eighteenth- and nineteenth-century America did not aim "merely to win elections and control offices; their goals invariably included achieving policy objectives." Their fights were "struggles over principles." Those principles included the powers of the central government, the principles of Union, and slavery. Partisan loyalists were "self-interested in the narrow sense, but not merely that. They were also actors with broader and richer goals."[19]

The connection between party loyalty and principle accounts for why one cannot imagine Gordon Brown as a Tory and why it strains credulity to imagine that he joined the Labour Party simply because it offered a better path to power than the alternatives. One might say the same about other party leaders, like Dick Armey or Tom DeLay, or Nancy Pelosi: they were ambitious because they were partisans, not partisans because they were ambitious. Unlike Arlen Specter, they could not be the people they were and have switched sides. Their side represented, in some sense, their very identity. The same could be said of those nameless and unrecognized political elites who run and lose, often against nearly hopeless odds. For instance, it seems implausible to say that the Democrats who run in Utah's third congressional district (which in the thirty years since it was created has been represented by a Democrat for only six) chose their party or remain loyal to their party simply because it is necessary for them to win office. It seems more likely that they are loyal to their party in spite of the fact that their party renders it almost impossible for them to win.

The same is also true for many ordinary voters, especially those who consistently say they strongly identify with a particular party. As we have seen, on the rational-choice view, such voters are not really partisans—they are merely brand loyalists. And brand loyalty might be cast as the lowest form of loyalty, since it is passive. Its central power comes through *exit*: it lacks *voice*. A loyal Coke drinker might switch to Pepsi if Coke changes its formula, as a loyal Labour voter might vote Liberal if she is frustrated with the direction of the Labour Party. Yet, part of the claim for loyalty at its best is found in its commitment to voice over exit—to arguing, planning, reforming, even protesting. Those lacking any loyalty can rather easily leave their countries, parties, and friends for better options elsewhere. True loyalists "love it" but cannot so easily "leave it": so they stay and argue. Brand loyalists might argue, if anyone could hear them, but, as disconnected individuals in a mass, they are usually heard only when they exit in large numbers.

But superficial brand loyalty fails to capture the depth of partisan identities, which are highly resistant to change, powerfully influence how people vote, and even shape the way citizens see themselves and the political community.[20] Maybe it is right to categorize ordinary party loyalties as "brand loyalties," but only if we understand that brand loyalties can run deep and generate more action than is typical of consumers in a marketplace. Party loyalties (and maybe some brand loyalties, too) are not just short cuts to the conclusion of a cost-benefit analysis. They also involve deeper moral attitudes, like gratitude and trust. They are a kind of mirror that reveals who we are to ourselves and also presents an image of ourselves to others. Given the untidiness of large parties in a two-party system, we cannot know precisely what it means when someone says, "I am a Democrat," or "I am a Conservative," but it often means more than "On balance, I think the Dems have been better for me than their rivals." Party loyalty implicates one in larger (if also vague) understandings of the social order and justice—as well as an historical view of what from the past should be regarded as an achievement and what goals for the future demand patience. This is not to say that every partisan (or any partisan) has a well-articulated view of all this; unless they happen to give lectures for a living, it is probably inchoate and implicit in their partisan loyalty, rather than detailed and explicit.

Partisan loyalty is more like patriotism than it is like our preference for Hertz over Avis. Perhaps we could call patriotism a brand loyalty, too, but doing so would distort the object of our loyalty: countries are not merely brands. Neither are parties. They are like brands in some respects, but, unlike brands, they involve a struggle and a contest over principle. Partisan identities connect to other social identities rooted in class, region, and religion. They are linked not only to philosophic ideals of social and political life but also to concrete ways of life. The managers of mere brands aspire to this kind of profound connection to their customers but can only simulate it, because brands belong not to social groups but to corporations. Party loyalty connects to identity, to who we are. At its best, it is more noble—and, at its worst, far more dangerous—than self-interest. To grasp the promise and the pathology of party loyalty, we need to understand it not simply as a strategy but also as an identity.

LOYALTY AS IDENTITY

Loyalties can transcend strategy and even reasoning. They are a personal possession that embodies a commitment to a specific person or group, not a universal commitment. The loyal partisan seems to possess a commitment that goes beyond reason:

"Loyalties invariably entail commitments that cannot be grounded in reasons others share," says a recent defender of loyalty. "There comes a point at which the logic runs dry and one must plant one's feet in the simple fact that it is my friend, my club, my alma mater, my nation."[21] Loyalty kicks in when reasons run out. A loyal partisan, by contrast, stands with his or her party even when times are bad: after a landslide election defeat, when morale is low and the future is unclear and no strategic reason can be found to stay with the cause.

This "nonrational component" of loyalty is, one might argue, loyalty's essence. Anyone can be a friend when friendship pays; what distinguishes the loyal friend is the willingness to sacrifice, to pay a price for the friendship, to remain a friend when the reasons run out. Loyalty depends on reasons that are reasons for me or for you but not necessarily for us both. At times, loyalists remain true to the object of their loyalty even when no particular meaning or purpose can be attached to it. This is why group loyalties, notably patriotism but also partisanship, are morally ambiguous. When loyalty is blind, when it is disjoined from judgment, it can prompt people to great sacrifice and great deeds. That loyalty goes beyond strategy is what makes us cherish it: if it is in someone's interest to stand by my side, I do not need his loyalty. It is the way that loyalty prompts us to go beyond ourselves that gives loyalty a kind of nobility. And yet, in transcending self-interested strategic reason, loyalty threatens to become wholly immune to reason and judgment. It can become a form of unthinking stubbornness that brings with it a kind of closure—closure to fact, to principle, and to consequences. This is why loyalty presents a "permanent moral danger."[22]

Both the nobility and something of the crude stubbornness of loyalty can be seen in Robert E. Lee, who loyally insisted on resigning his office in the U.S. Army at the outset of the Civil War and joining the cause of his native South. For many, this exemplifies the tragic dimension of loyalty, which can generate obligations of belonging that conflict with other principles.[23] If loyalty were always principled—if it were always subordinated to moral reasoning about obligation—it could not give rise to this kind of tragic conflict. On the other hand, seeing loyalty as a matter of belongings that do not involve choice gives an inarticulate quality to the obligations it supports. The primitive inarticulacy of such obligations places them beyond explanation or justification—and threatens to close off the reasons at stake in their commitments.

Even General Lee could not seem to really explain his obligation to fight for the South. Who he was—his identity—was sufficient to settle the question. After he was offered the command of the Union army and after his native Virginia had voted to secede from the Union, Lee faced a predicament: side with the North and serve the army to which, as he wrote, "I have devoted all the best years of my life and all the ability I possessed" or make war "against my relatives, my children, my home."[24] Although Lee did not share in the popular elation that followed Virginia's secession, he resigned from the Union army and resolved never again to take up arms "save in defense of my native state."[25] Before long, he did take up arms, accepting a commission from Virginia. For his part, Lee refused to prescribe any course of action to others, including his son Custis, also in the Union army. Custis "must consult his own judgment, reason, and conscience as to the course he may take," Lee wrote. "If I have done wrong, let him do better," Lee said. "The present is a momentous question which every man must settle for himself and upon principle."[26] That he was not willing to prescribe any action to his son suggests that his decision was personal, not principled. He said nothing about the justice of Virginia's cause and offered no principle of justice or gratitude that could apply to others. He mentions his attachments—*his* relatives, *his* children, *his* home. If these attachments constitute a principle, it is an imperative of loyalty: *stand by your own.* Lee's connection to his own dictated his choice, if indeed it was a choice at all. Virginia's course "carried him with her," without resistance.[27]

Lee's example points to a basic problem with loyalty: is it enough to say, "I am standing with my own"? Or must one also say something about why the causes, principles, and purposes that define "one's own" are worthy? Lee does not seem to have felt the need to explain why he thought his own people were engaged in a worthy cause. This has not diminished the sympathy with which he has been treated, even by recent commentators. He is "one of America's few classical heroes . . . because we cannot help recognizing the human tragedy of such a man," wrote Judith Shklar.[28] His predicament can be appreciated "without necessarily approving of the choice he made." But his predicament can be appreciated only if we agree that loyalties can partly constitute our identities in a way that makes certain actions (in Lee's case, standing with the South) almost irresistible. The irresistibility of Lee's action was suggested by the fact that he did not offer reasons and arguments for his decision. It is as if his identity as a Southerner closed his mind to any further arguments or principles at stake in the decision.

Closed Loyalties

Loyalty seems to invite this kind of closure; our loyalties seem to make a claim on what we are willing to consider, even what we believe. Consider, for instance, the personal loyalties that arise in friendship. As Sarah Stroud argues, "the demands of friendship extend into the realm of belief."[29] A good friend does not simply refrain from speaking badly about her friend: "The good friend," Stroud says, "is prepared to take her friend's part both publicly and . . . internally."[30] The claims of friendship weigh most heavily when a friend is the object of criticism and blame. Imagine, for instance, that you are told that a very good friend connived and deceived to outmaneuver another person for a promotion. In a case like this, what does friendship demand? In Stroud's view, we should expect some "epistemic partiality" from our friends. The first thing a good friend should do in encountering this kind of criticism is to look for ways to discredit it: a good friend would scrutinize the evidence and insist on a more convincing level of evidence before drawing negative conclusions. We should question the source (perhaps the person has a stake in the situation that compromises his objectivity?). We should scrutinize the information, looking for weak spots and omissions. Even if the evidence appears incontrovertible, the claims of friendship do not give way. A good friend would imagine alternative explanations ("the person against whom my friend connived had already been conniving against him—my friend had no other choice other than to quit"). And, even if alternative explanations are not credible, a good friend might draw different conclusions and inferences from the evidence, relating it to more positive qualities. Rather than admit a friend is deceptive, we might classify him as effective; rather than cunning, we might say he is able to negotiate the bureaucratic maze.

A similar kind of epistemic partiality characterizes partisan loyalties. This is most obvious when we consult the approval ratings of recent presidents. At the end of George W. Bush's first term, 15 percent of Democrats approved of Bush's performance, while 89 percent of Republicans approved.[31] At the time, it was the "most polarized presidential approval between parties ever measured by Gallup." Yet, the partisan approval gap was mirrored at the end of Obama's first year as president. At the beginning of 2010, 88 percent of Democrats approved of Obama's performance, while only 23 percent of Republicans approved. The epistemic partiality of ordinary friendship seems to map onto political friendship: Democrats are more suspicious of evidence that Obama has done a bad job, construct alternative narratives to interpret negative evidence (like unemployment levels or the size of the federal deficit), and highlight a different set of facts than Republicans in order to paint a more flattering picture of the Obama presidency.

Loyalty makes corresponding cognitive demands on ordinary friendship and partisan friendship. In ordinary friendship, as Stroud says, because we need "to maintain a favorable opinion of our friend's character," it should not be surprising "that we would massage our beliefs about our friend's character in a favorable direction and downplay any information which might threaten that esteem."[32] Similarly, in politics, we need to maintain a belief that our party is more likely to effectively pursue the common good: it makes no more sense to support the worse party than to be friends with a bad person. Our commitment to a party is a kind of constraint on what we can believe about it. For instance, the seminal description of modern partisanship from the first wave of mass survey research in the 1950s—*The American Voter*—showed that party identification powerfully influences the way we perceive and evaluate political things. Party loyalty is a "perceptual screen" that filters information, exaggerating what is favorable to one's own party.[33]

The danger of epistemic loyalty is that it will obscure the reasons that gave rise to the loyalty in the first place. If we are so loyal to our friends that we forget why we originally became friends, we might remain committed to a friend even when the friendship becomes exploitative or destructive—and, if our epistemic partiality is profound enough, we might not even notice that it has become destructive. Similarly, the original reasons for party loyalty ought to have something to with what the party stands for. As a matter of fact, for some partisans, party loyalty might be a thoughtless habit or inheritance (that follows in the partisan identity of a parent, for instance). But party loyalty at its best ought not be quite like an ethnic belonging; it is not an attachment that constitutes one's identity from birth but a commitment that arises from reasons. When the perceptual screen or epistemic loyalty that partisanship entails blinds us to the original reasons that made sense of party loyalty, we are at risk of acting contrary to our own belief, values, and commitments.

For instance, in an experiment where rival partisans are presented with two welfare policies (one more generous than any actual policy in the United States and the other more stringent than any actual policy), liberals are more likely to favor the generous policy and conservatives are more likely to favor the stringent policy. But, liberals *favor the stringent policy* when told that Democrats in Congress also support it and that Republicans oppose it.[34] Conservatives, by contrast, are more likely to *favor the generous policy* when told that Republicans in Congress also support the policy and that Democrats oppose it. In both cases, people insist that the "details of the proposal" and their "philosophy of government" motivate their views, not what Democrats and Republicans typically believe. Loyalty to party trumps loyalty to principle—without loyalists' even noticing it (or, at any rate, without their admitting it). Here, the epistemic partiality that party loyalty involves seems to get the better of good sense and an accurate perception of factual reality. At the extreme, party loyalty threatens to issue in the kind of closure that marked Lee's decision to abandon his post in the Union army and fight for the South. By leaving principle and reason entirely to the side, the loyalty becomes inarticulate, senseless, and self-defeating: it cannot explain itself. Party loyalty is necessary and good because of its connection to political action—but, when it causes one to betray one's foundational principles, even the principles that made sense of party in the first place, it starts to look more like a stubborn prejudice and less like an admirable willingness to stand together for the sake of protecting past achievements and getting something done.

One might interpret the results of the experiment more sympathetically. Democrats might favor *what seems like* the more stringent welfare policy once they are told congressional Republicans oppose it and Democrats favor it because they trust partisan leaders to assess the policy's details more accurately than they could. The implicit reasoning might go like this: "On the surface, the policy looks more stringent. And, ordinarily, I would oppose it for that reason. But the congressional leadership must know something I do not. Perhaps there are implications I don't see or details that aren't present in the summary I consulted. Legislation is complicated. What I do know is that anything the Republican Speaker of the House, John Boehner,[35] supports I generally do not like." In this interpretation, loyal partisans do not follow their party even at the cost of betraying their principles. Rather, they *trust* the party to defend their principles. They put less trust in summary descriptions of legislation: perhaps the description is deceptive? Short of devoting days to understanding the intricacies of the legislation, it might seem more reasonable to put one's trust in the party (or even, more simply, to trust that the party one doesn't like is wrong): if the Republicans support it, I oppose it.

This more sympathetic interpretation of party loyalty is skeptical about the existence of nonpartisan political facts and information. Partisans trust the party leadership; they do not trust avowedly nonpartisan descriptions of legislation. This skepticism, however, invites what is perhaps the most grave pathology associated with party loyalty: an isolation from the terrain of common factuality. The deepest argument for epistemic partiality in friendship might be that, when it comes to the quality of a friend's character, there is no fact of the matter. *All* assessments of character are interpretations, and all interpretations are, at bottom, partisan. When all is partisan, either you're with me or you're against me; there is no ground upon which a neutral observer can stand.

Stroud's defense of epistemic partisanship, for its part, does not require complete closure to "base-level facts and events."[36] The loyalties entailed by friendship do not ask us to create an alternative reality or to ignore, distort, or deny basic facts. Friends interrogate negative facts with more energy and accept positive facts more readily—but they can acknowledge the same facts as a neutral observer would. Yet, at the same time, Stroud betrays a skepticism about the possibility of "base-level" facts. A friend does not need to deny the "purportedly raw data" with which she is presented, she argues. Why are "raw data" always "purportedly raw data"? Perhaps the idea is that, when it comes to the facts and events that bear on our assessment of people's characters, "raw data" are hard to come by. Did John *in fact* deceive in order to get a promotion? In ordinary circumstances, it would require quite an investigation to prove such a thing, and even then the proof would likely rely on people's memories (which are notoriously fallible), on the imputation of intentions (always hazardous), and on the presence of observers who themselves did not have a stake in the matter (always rare). In the world of friendship, perhaps there are very few raw data that are not "purported." This is why, if a good friend is not *required* to deny basic facts and events, still, "she will look for openings that might permit her to do this."[37] Assessments of character almost always involve interpretations that go beyond "raw data"; friendship does not so much sever us from the data a neutral observer might see as it acknowledges that such "data" are very rarely to be encountered in their pure form.

The same might be said of politics and partisanship. As we noted, it is very difficult to describe the successes and failures of politics because it can take many years before the evidence is in. Moreover, because political questions are so complicated and interconnected, it can be hard to isolate facts in a wholly nonpartisan way. When they can be isolated, it is not always clear how to evaluate them in a wholly nonpartisan way: knowing that Medicare is taking an increasing share of the federal budget does not tell you much about what to do about it. At the extreme, loyal partisans might even come to suspect that there is no such thing as a nonpartisan politically relevant "fact." Like the facts of friendship, the raw data are at best "purported." This might explain why rival partisans see the same basic political facts quite differently. For instance, in the period 1980 to 1988, when Ronald Reagan was president, inflation fell precipitously from 13.5 percent to 4.1 percent. Yet, in 1988, more than half of those identifying as "strong Democrats" said that inflation had become worse or much worse over the Reagan years; fewer than 8 percent of those polled said that it had improved.[38]

Again, we might try to interpret a result like this sympathetically: perhaps Democrats felt it was disloyal to admit that inflation had declined (even though they knew it had). Perhaps they did not want to acknowledge the decline in inflation without a corresponding account of the increase in unemployment in Reagan's first term. In short, perhaps they were willing to assert something they knew to be untrue because the "fact" about inflation, isolated and insulated from other related facts, suggested a conclusion they believed unwarranted (like "Reagan did a good job"). But it is also possible that Democrats simply were less likely to grasp that inflation in fact had declined; their loyalty made them impervious to the possibility that anything good might have happened during the Reagan administration.

When party loyalty seems to be the cause, rather than the consequence, of rival perceptions of elemental facts in the political world, political discussion, debate, and deliberation are imperiled; if brute facticity is obliterated, basic political rationality—and, therefore, political action—becomes impossible. Sometimes it is said that rival partisans inhabit "different worlds." When the common terrain of factuality is obliterated, this is no exaggeration: it becomes impossible to share a political community. This specter can be dimly glimpsed in the "controversy" over President Barack Obama's citizenship. Six months after President Obama was elected, 58 percent of Republicans either thought Obama was not born in the United States (and therefore held his office unconstitutionally) or weren't sure. This was in spite of evidence as incontrovertible as could in practice be adduced for any person that he was in fact born in Hawaii.[39] Perhaps some Republicans simply said this to an anonymous pollster out of loyalty—they knew that Obama is a natural-born U.S. citizen, but they got satisfaction in taunting the other side and did not mind weakening the president's stature and sense of legitimacy. But it's also possible that some of them really believed that Obama is not a natural-born citizen and that their partisan loyalty closed them off to the very possibility of encountering evidence that would cause them to believe differently. To the extent that this belief undermines their confidence in the legitimacy of the Obama presidency, it corrodes the legitimacy of government and law more generally.[40] The more this corrosion touches, the more difficult it becomes to share a political community.

Epistemic partiality is one thing—it's part of what being a loyal friend or a loyal partisan means. But epistemic closure is another.

There is such a thing as a politically relevant fact. When a Republican presidential aspirant says that there are more unemployed Americans than employed Canadians, it is either right or wrong (it's wrong).[41] When a Democrat asserts that the Bush tax cuts are the main reason for the federal deficit, it is either right or wrong (it's also wrong).[42] Some facts are "bad facts": they make what we love or what we're part of or what we want look less worthy. Political people try to convert bad facts into mere opinion—and perhaps this is true for people more generally, since it is hard to maintain a loyalty, even to a good friend, in the face of bad facts. But, to succeed too well in converting facts into opinion, to make all facts merely "purported facts," undermines the basis for justified loyalties in the first place. It dissolves the ground of political action and, in the end, makes it impossible to belong to a common community.

Open Loyalties

Our task with regard to political loyalties, and perhaps loyalties more generally, is to maintain them without succumbing to epistemic closure. This requires acknowledging that even the most worthy objects of our loyalties might be—are likely to be—imperfect. It is possible to be loyal without being blind. And it ought to be possible to be a partisan without denying, discounting, or distorting every bad fact. In contrast to the epistemic closure that constitutive loyalties invite, partisan loyalties ought to be epistemically open. It is possible to be a partisan with an open mind.

But it is not easy. There is something about an open mind that threatens to diminish commitment. When we resolve to "keep an open mind about this," we hold off on "making up our minds" until we gather more evidence or take more time to discuss and deliberate. In this respect, an open-minded partisan would seem a contradiction in terms. The open mind would seem to belong to independents—and is part of the reason independents are politically ineffective. To have an open mind is to be unsure of what to do, to favor further study over action. Why fight for something we think might be erroneous? For that matter, why believe something in the first place that, in our skeptical openness, we might think is wrong? Openness, moderation, and skepticism are perhaps more conducive to ambivalence than to partisan loyalty. This is not to say there is anything wrong with ambivalence, which might be the best characterization of the less partisan, centrist part of the electorate.[43] The point is not that everyone should be partisan, only that it is difficult to combine partisan loyalty and openness.

But this combination is, in a more general sense, what liberal democratic politics requires of citizens. Ideally, liberal citizens are capable of both affirming their own loyalties and tolerating other citizens who are loyal to different things in different ways. John Rawls, for instance, argues that liberal citizens who affirm some particular comprehensive conception of life, whether philosophic, moral, or religious, should still recognize that their own judgment is burdened by necessary ambiguities and imperfections. These "burdens of judgment" arise from a recognition that different people will see different sides of the same question, that evidence is hard to adduce and difficult to weigh, and that the human world is hard to describe and predict. Because human judgment is burdened by vague concepts (whose application is hard to specify with exactness) and rival moral claims that are vexing to adjudicate, reasonable people will disagree.[44] To acknowledge this is to understand why it would be wrong (or unreasonable) to settle constitutional essentials according to one comprehensive conception.

Affirming a comprehensive conception and recognizing that our judgment about that conception is so burdened by sources of uncertainty and error that it would be wrong to force it on others is a delicate combination. The same burdens of judgment that support tolerance might erode the strength of our affirmations. And, on the other hand, the strength of our loyalties might cause us to forget that our judgment is burdened. To be capable of affirming some comprehensive conception on one hand and to acknowledge on the other hand that reasonable people might reject what we affirm is the way—the necessary way—of liberal citizens. A similar delicate combination is appropriate for loyal partisans. They affirm a partisan conception of justice and of the direction public policy should take—but they simultaneously recognize that it might be reasonable to reject what they affirm.

The point of this recognition is not to diminish one's partisan commitments or temper one's loyalty. It is only to render partisan loyalists open to the possibility of encountering bad facts. If the bad facts pile up over a long enough duration, then it might be right to modify one's loyalty—even in the case of friendship, a good friend is not obligated to believe the best *no matter what.* If we keep an open mind with respect to bad facts, we run the risk that we may discover that the object of our loyalty is unworthy—even that we have wasted a large part of our life in devotion to the cause. But a few bad facts here and there are to be expected; nothing human is pure, and the loyal should not need to remake the world with a purity it can (and should) never possess. Loyal partisans, like liberal citizens, need to live with dissonance; they can affirm even when what they affirm is imperfect. Perfect people probably would not need loyal friends, and perfect causes probably would not need loyal partisans.

The combination of loyalty and openness should not be interpreted to mean that partisan commitments are, at bottom, rationally indefensible or idiosyncratic. Consider, for instance, how Stuart Hampshire made sense of his commitment to democratic socialism. It is a mistake, he claimed, "to look for a moral theory, or a set of propositions, that could serve as a justification, or foundation, of my political loyalties." He said, "It is difficult to acknowledge the bare contingency of personal feeling as the final stopping point when one is arguing with oneself, or with others, about the ultimate requirements of social justice. But I am now fairly sure that this is the true stopping point."[45] Someone like Hampshire could freely acknowledge that other people have other feelings and thus will embrace different understandings of justice. Presumably, too, he could encounter and recognize bad facts, since his partisan commitment is based in feeling, not on a fact-based theory. A Hampshire-loyalist can tolerate and accept adversaries. But, in the end, he cannot make sense of his own loyalty in terms that might make it compelling to anyone else. He rejects the possibility of reasons that might apply to more than one person. Party loyalty, for Hampshire, is, in the end, a matter of personal feeling. And why should what one person feels persuade anyone else? For Hampshire, all argument and all reasons are frosting on the cake: they are what make a personal and unjustifiable *feeling* more palatable to others, but they are not the real substance of the matter. Hampshire's modesty might seem a model of openness (everyone will have his or her own feelings and thus his or her own loyalties), but really it is another form of epistemic closure. By reducing his partisan loyalty to feeling, Hampshire insulates it from facts—good and bad. His theory is immune to reasons and argument, and, so long as he has the requisite feeling, his mind is closed.

The openness that characterizes party loyalty at its best does not need to reduce partisan commitment to a feeling. It can (and needs to) acknowledge that partisan loyalties involve feelings but ultimately depend on *claims*. In politics, various people and various groups make claims on others and on the community in general. These claims entail an understanding of justice or of the sort of recognition, resources, rights, and opportunities that are deserved. No claim can be complete without an argument; yet, even with the best arguments, no claim can go very far in politics without some connection to a particular social group, some way of life that generates particular needs and aspirations. The claims that arise in particular groups are not mere preferences. They involve arguments about what is deserved and what kind of political community is most worthy of our support.

To recognize that my claims will conflict with the claims of others is to be conscious of inhabiting a political world. To recognize that no political philosophy can eradicate the conflict of claims does not reduce all partisan loyalties and commitments to inexplicable feelings. A permanent conflict of claims is the ineliminable condition of politics; yet, the claims we make in politics are no less true for this reason. Conflict requires us, if we do not wish our claims to be overlooked or denied, to fight for our claims. Yet, the recognition that our claims conflict with the claims of others, claims that may also be in their way valid, commits us to "hearing the other side." More exactly, it commits us to a contestatory procedure by which the other side is heard and might win. This places a limit on partisanship and transforms political enemies into opponents. It does not commit partisans to see their cause as based in idiosyncratic feelings, but it should commit them to reject violence, whose aim can only be to oppress or kill political opponents. And it renounces any party's pretension to constitute the *last party*, whose success would obviate the need for future partisan contestation.

Open loyalties are more oriented to action than to belief. Party loyalists ought to be committed to do certain things (support their party's candidates) and act in certain ways (volunteer, contribute, talk, vote). But party loyalty, ideally, should place very slight constraints on what one thinks or believes. In the most general sense, it should not be necessary to believe that one's party is perfect in order to be loyal to it. Party loyalty—and friendship, too—should be able to contain an awareness of bad facts. Neither our friends nor our parties need to be perfect in order to deserve our loyalty. The basis for loyalty is not that our cause represents the "whole truth." It is that very little of what we accomplish can be sustained—and very little of what we think would be good can be accomplished—unless we stand together. Because every cause, even every imperfect cause, is embattled, we need to stand together to protect and secure the achievements of the past and win something for the future. Political action, imperfect as it always must be, requires memory and patience. And these require standing together in a group—or a party.

NOTES

I would like to thank Mitch Berman, Jane Cohen, Yasmin Dawood, John Deigh, David Estlund, Gary Jacobsohn, Sandy Levinson, Joel Parker, Richard Pildes, Larry Sager, Jeffrey Tulis, and the members of the Philosophy and Law Colloquium at the University of Texas School of Law for their searching criticisms and generous suggestions about an earlier draft of this chapter.

1. Samuel Freeman, "Deliberative Democracy: A Sympathetic Comment," *Philosophy & Public Affairs* 29 (Autumn 2000): 375.

2. Martin P. Wattenberg, *The Decline of American Political Parties, 1952–1988* (Cambridge, MA: Harvard University Press, 1990), 22.

3. The resolution passed 416-0 in the House; see Ezra Y. Siff, *Why the Senate Slept: The Gulf of Tonkin Resolution and the Beginning of America's Vietnam War* (Westport, CT: Praeger, 1999).

4. For a kindred argument that stresses partisanship as a mode of identification—in contrast to the "weightlessness of independence"—see Nancy L. Rosenblum, *On the Side of the Angels: An Appreciation of Parties and Partisanship* (Princeton: Princeton University Press, 2008), 319–68. Rosenblum's account points to the question of this chapter: should partisan identification be understood as a form of loyalty?

5. This is the question the National Election Survey has asked panels of U.S. voters since the 1952 election. It is followed up by: (IF REPUBLICAN OR DEMOCRAT:) "Would you call yourself a strong (REPUBLICAN/ DEMOCRAT) or a not very strong (REPUBLICAN/DEMOCRAT)?" (IF INDEPENDENT, OTHER [1966 and later: OR NO PREFERENCE]:) "Do you think of yourself as closer to the Republican or Democratic party?" This produces the well-known seven-step scale of strong Democrat/weak Democrat/Independent Democrat/Independent Independent/Independent Republican/weak Republican/and strong Republican. See http:// www.electionstudies.org/nesguide/toptable/tab2a_1.htm.

6. John H. Aldrich, *Why Parties? The Origin and Transformation of Political Parties in America* (Chicago: University of Chicago Press, 1995), 29–31.

7. Ibid., 72.

8. Ibid., 76.

9. Ibid., 77 and 68–96 generally.

10. Ronald Brownstein, *The Second Civil War: How Extreme Partisanship Has Paralyzed Washington and Polarized America* (New York: Penguin, 2007); Morris P. Fiorina with Samuel J. Abrams and Jeremy C. Pope, *Culture War? The Myth of a Polarized America* (New York: Pearson Longman, 2005).

11. Aldrich, *Why Parties*, 21.

12. Anthony Downs, *An Economic Theory of Democracy* (Boston: Addison-Wesley, 1957), 28.

13. Ibid.

14. "Specter's Statement on His Decision to Switch Parties," *New York Times* (April, 28 2009), www.nytimes.com/2009/04/28/us/politics/28caucus .specter.html.

15. The full quote, with the excised part in italics, is, "My change in party will enable me to get reelected *and I have heard that again and again and again on the street: 'Senator, we're glad you'll be able to stay in the Senate and help the state and nation.'* From "Specter: Killer Ad out of Context," *Philadelphia Inquirer* (13 May, 2010), http://www.philly.com/philly/blogs/harrisburg_politics/Specter_Killer_ad_out_of_context.html?viewAll=Y&text.

16. Quoted in Marc Levy, "Specter Defeated by Sestak in Bid for 6th term," *Times-Tribune* (19 May, 2010), http://thetimes-tribune.com/news /u-s-senate-specter-defeated-by-sestak-in-bid-for-6th-term-1.794984 #axzz1DZVOhLa4.

17. David S. Broder, "Campaign Bitter in Philadelphia," *New York Times* (30 October, 1965).

18. David S. Broder, "Specter the Defector," *Washington Post* (30 April, 2009), www.washingtonpost.com/wp-dyn/content/article/2009/04/29/ AR2009042904016_pf.html.

19. Aldrich, *Why Parties*, 67.

20. Donald Green, Bradley Palmquist, and Eric Schickler, *Partisan Hearts and Minds: Political Parties and the Social Identities of Voters* (New Haven: Yale University Press, 2002), 78.

21. George P. Fletcher, *Loyalty: An Essay on the Morality of Relationships* (Oxford: Oxford University Press, 1993), 61.

22. Alasdair C. MacIntyre, *Is Patriotism a Virtue?* (Lawrence: Department of Philosophy, University of Kansas, 1984), quoted in Fletcher, *Loyalty*, 34.

23. Michael J. Sandel, *Democracy's Discontent: America in Search of a Public Philosophy* (Cambridge, MA: Belknap Press, 1998), 15.

24. Douglass Southall Freeman, *R. E. Lee, a Biography*, vol. 1 (New York: Charles Scribner's Sons, 1934), 441, 443.

25. Ibid., 444; see discussion in Judith N. Shklar, *Ordinary Vices* (Cambridge, MA: Belknap Press, 1984), 160; and Fletcher, *Loyalty*, 153.

26. Freeman, *Lee*, 444.

27. Ibid., 447.

28. Shklar, *Ordinary Vices*, 160.

29. Sarah Stroud, "Epistemic Partiality in Friendship," *Ethics* 116 (April 2006): 502.

30. Stroud, "Epistemic Partiality," 505.

31. Brownstein, *The Second Civil War*, 16; Jeffrey M. Jones, "Views of Bush Reach New Heights of Polarization," *Gallup News Service* (21 October, 2004), www.gallup.com.

32. Stroud, "Epistemic Partiality," 511.

33. Angus Campbell, Philip E. Converse, Warren E. Miller, and Donald E. Stokes, *The American Voter* (Chicago: University of Chicago Press, 1960), 133.

34. Geoffrey Cohen, "Party over Policy: The Dominating Impact of Group Influence on Political Beliefs," *Journal of Personality and Social Psychology* 85 (November 2003): 811.

35. John Boehner became Speaker of the House in 2011; he has served as a Republican representative from the Eighth District of Ohio since 1991.

36. Stroud, "Epistemic Partiality," 507.

37. Ibid., 508.

38. Larry Bartels, "Beyond the Running Tally Partisan Bias in Political Perceptions," *Political Behavior* 24 (Special Issue: Parties and Partisanship, Part One) (June 2002): 134.

39. "58% of GOP Not Sure/Doubt Obama Born in the U.S.," (31 July, 2009), http://www.politico.com/blogs/glennthrush/0709/58_of_GOP_not_sure_dont_believe_Obama_born_in_US.html. Seventy-seven percent of Americans overall thought he was a citizen, and 93 percent of Democrats thought so.

40. See, for instance, the "citizen grand juries" that have attempted to

charge Obama with treason: U.S. District Court for the District of Columbia, Misc. # 09-346 (RCL) (2 July, 2009), https://ecf.dcd.uscourts.gov/cgi-bin/show_public_doc?2009mc0346-2.

41. This was Mitt Romney at the Conservative Political Action Conference (12–13 February, 2011), http://factcheck.org/2011/02/factchecking-republicans-at-cpac/.

42. See William G. Gale, "Five Myths about the Bush Tax Cuts," *Washington Post* (2 August, 2010), http://www.washingtonpost.com/wp-dyn/content/article/2010/07/30/AR2010073002671.html.

43. Morris P. Fiorina and Samuel J. Abrams, *Disconnect: The Breakdown of Representation in American Politics* (Norman: University of Oklahoma Press, 2009), 22, 36, 49, 168.

44. John Rawls, *Political Liberalism, with a New Introduction and the "Reply to Habermas"* (New York: Columbia University Press, 1996), 54–58, 62.

45. Stuart Hampshire, *Justice Is Conflict* (Princeton: Princeton University Press, 2001), ix, xiii.

10

DEMOCRACY AND THE PROBLEM OF THE PARTISAN STATE

YASMIN DAWOOD

Is partisanship fundamentally antithetical to democratic principles and values? According to traditional democratic theory, the pathologies associated with partisanship—blind loyalty, narrow interests, political polarization, and extremism—pose serious challenges to democratic functioning. Political parties are often viewed as divisive, corrupt, and self-serving. Recent work in democratic theory, however, has invited us to reconsider the conventional wisdom. Nancy Rosenblum and Russell Muirhead argue (separately) for an ethic of partisanship.[1] They contend that partisanship is best understood in light of its considerable and often overlooked virtues rather than solely with respect to its vices. On this view, political parties and partisanship are indispensable for democratic functioning.

INTRODUCTION: THE PARTISAN STATE

Given the debate over the merits of partisanship, this essay raises the following question: when and under what conditions should partisanship play a role in democratic politics? Partisanship might be described as loyalty to the interests of one's political party over the common good (or, less abstractly, as loyalty to the interests of one's political party over what one might believe to be the genuine merits of a program sponsored by the opposing party). I will examine this question by focusing on an undertheorized issue that raises difficulties for both traditional democratic theory and the ethic of partisanship. I shall refer to this issue as the problem of the partisan state.

By the problem of the partisan state, I am referring to the phenomenon that the state, instead of acting as an impartial body committed unequivocally to a Madisonian politics of the "public good," often acts as a partisan entity.[2] Most (if not all) theories of democracy describe the state as an impartial institution that acts on behalf of the whole. At the same time, a basic principle of representative democracy is that the political party that wins at the polls assumes the mantle of government. The fact that the state is controlled at any given time by a political party is treated as an unremarkable feature of democratic government. V. O. Key, for instance, described parties as consisting of three main components: the party in the government, the party in the electorate, and the party organization.[3] Indeed, the transformative process—from political party to state—is so quotidian that it is treated as self-evidently unproblematic within the confines of democratic theory. It is generally assumed, without much elaboration, that the winning party or candidate must act for the people as a whole, not just for those individuals who voted for that party or candidate. The partisan political party is transformed, at least in theory, into an impartial state through the mechanism of electoral victory.

Yet, even a cursory analysis of the political system in the United States, for example, reveals myriad ways in which the state acts as a partisan entity in the processes of democracy. Public officials, such as the president and members of Congress, seek to implement the partisan agenda of their respective parties. As Clinton Rossiter argued almost two generations ago, one of the central "hats" that the president wears is that of "party leader," which means, in the modern world, raising vast sums of money for the party's candidates and supporting those candidates against any and all opponents from other parties.[4] And members of Congress increasingly take their cues for whether to support or to oppose the president's programs from their party affiliation. As Daryl Levinson and Richard Pildes have argued, the Madisonian "separation of powers" has given way to what is better termed "the separation of parties," with significant consequences for the operation of American government.[5] For instance, the selection of Supreme Court justices by the president and the approval process by the Senate are conducted in an openly partisan manner. State legislatures enact election laws that often benefit the political party in power. As Samuel Issacharoff and Richard Pildes have argued, the state in these contexts is often none other than the dominant political party (or, in some cases, a coalition of parties).[6] Even Supreme Court decisions (including one decision that determined the outcome of a presidential election) on occasion appear to have been decided along partisan, and not simply ideological, lines.

At first blush, the partisan state appears to be inherently illegitimate because it violates a basic requirement in democratic theory that the state act as an impartial institution on behalf of the whole. Rather than dismissing the partisan state as a failure of democratic theory, I argue, counterintuitively, that there are arguments within democratic theory to support the partisan state. In particular, I claim that the partisan state has a legitimate role to play in certain aspects of democracy but not in others. One objective of this essay is to develop a normative framework by which the actions of the partisan state can be judged.

Since the state is largely in control of the democratic process, a crucial first question is to determine how the democratic process itself is influenced by partisan loyalty. To simplify the inquiry, suppose we can, as an abstract matter, describe the democratic process as one that selects public policies and public officials. This description is incomplete because the democratic process also selects some of the rules by which public policies and public officials are selected. The democratic process can thus be described as performing the following functions: (1) the selection of public policies; (2) the selection of public officials; (3) the selection of the rules by which public policies are selected; and (4) the selection of the rules by which public officials are selected. I suggest that this functional approach is helpful because it allows us to both identify and distinguish among the four fundamental types of decisions that every democracy must make. These four types of democratic decisions can be influenced by partisan loyalty, and therefore there are four ways in which we can have a partisan state.

The second question is how to distinguish legitimate partisan activity by the state in the democratic process from illegitimate partisan activity by the state in the democratic process. That is, the task is to determine which actions of the partisan state are consistent with democratic ideals and which actions of the partisan state subvert democratic ideals. To this end, I claim that there is a distinction between what I call first-order partisanship and second-order partisanship.[7] First-order partisanship encompasses the selection of public policies and public officials, that is, options (1) and (2). An example of first-order partisanship is the implementation by the president of the partisan agenda of his or her political party. Second-order partisanship encompasses the selection of the rules by which public policies and public officials are selected; that is, options (3) and (4). An example of second-order partisanship is the influence of partisanship on electoral redistricting.

This essay argues that first-order partisanship has a qualified claim to democratic legitimacy, while second-order partisanship has almost no claim to democratic legitimacy. The reason for the difference is that first-order partisanship is largely consistent with the principle of self-government, while second-order partisanship, by contrast, undermines and disrupts self-government. I claim that the distinction between first-order and second-order partisanship can be used to assess and judge the actions of the partisan state.

Although the partisan state is ubiquitous, it has not received a sustained theoretical analysis within democratic theory. In this chapter, I seek to address this conceptual gap by developing an account of when and under what conditions partisan activities by the state are democratically legitimate. In so doing, I also engage with the recent scholarship on the ethic of partisanship by considering how our commitment to state impartiality imposes limits on the legitimate scope of partisanship within a democracy. Under the ethic of partisanship, partisan loyalty is viewed as having a proper place within a democracy. The partisan state, however, embodies a potential clash of loyalties. Public officials arguably face a conflict between their loyalty to the nation and their loyalty to their party. Their loyalty to their party is perfectly compatible with partisan self-interest, while their loyalty to the nation may demand adherence to the public interest. To be sure, these two loyalties often overlap, and, no doubt, some partisans believe that their agenda is in the nation's best interest. That being said, it should be difficult, at least at certain times, for public officials to be both good partisans and good patriots.

As a point of clarification, I should note that my focus is not the legal status of the *political party* but the status of the *state* as a partisan entity. As Nathaniel Persily and Bruce Cain argue, political parties have an ambiguous legal status because they are perceived as being both public institutions and private institutions.[8] If political parties are state actors, they are then subject to various constitutional restraints, such as equal protection, that are routinely applied to states. If, by contrast, political parties are private associations, they may be able to rely upon constitutional protections to defend themselves from exercises of state power.[9] While the legal relationship between the state and the political party has been the subject of considerable scholarly commentary, it is not the topic addressed here.

For the purposes of this essay, I refer to partisan loyalty and partisanship interchangeably. I also draw a distinction between the "ethic of partisanship" (which is a theory of democracy) and "traditional democratic theory" (which refers to those theories of democracy that predate the ethic of partisanship). This terminology is not meant to suggest that the ethic of partisanship is not a democratic theory. Although this article focuses on the democratic system in the United States, the theoretical issues discussed have broader, if not universal, applicability.

This chapter proceeds in four parts. Part I describes the ethic of partisanship. It contends that the ethic of partisanship offers an important corrective to traditional democratic theory because it opens up a conceptual space for the normative appraisal of ethical and nonethical partisanship. Part II argues that the impartial state is a central feature of the two most influential models of democracy. This part also suggests that traditional democratic theory helps to identify the justifiable limits of the partisan activities of the state. Parts III and IV seek to develop an account of when and under what conditions partisan actions by the state are democratically legitimate. Part III contends that first-order partisan activity by the state may be democratically justifiable, while Part IV concludes that second-order partisan activity by the state almost certainly cannot be justified on democratic grounds.

I. THE ETHIC OF PARTISANSHIP

The pathologies associated with partisan loyalty present the most vexing theoretical and practical problems facing democratic politics in the United States today. In recent years, political parties have become increasingly polarized, with the result that political gridlock on a range of issues, such as health care and judicial confirmations, has become a regrettably routine occurrence.[10] Indeed, the empirical evidence shows that political parties have become more internally homogenous and more ideologically polarized from each other than ever before in American history.[11] In addition, there is a vicious cycle of polarization in which partisan elites become polarized, thereby triggering increased polarization among citizens, which in turn fuels further polarization among partisan elites as they react to the demands of their constituents.[12] As Richard Pildes has recently observed, extreme partisan polarization is now the "defining attribute" of the U.S political system.[13]

A. The Democratic Value of Political Parties

Whatever qualms we may harbor about political parties, it is almost inconceivable to imagine a democracy functioning without them. As Russell Muirhead notes, political parties perform a number of indispensable tasks, including, for example, educating and mobilizing voters, giving voice to citizens' needs, simplifying choices, recruiting candidates, organizing the structure of government, establishing the governing majority and the opposition, and enabling citizens to hold the governing party accountable at elections.[14]

Nancy Rosenblum argues that there is a conceptual distinction between political parties and partisanship. Partisanship refers to the advocacy of a cause, while political parties act as the carriers of partisanship.[15] Each is necessary to realize the value of the other. Rosenblum suggests that political parties make three principal contributions to democracy. First, political parties engage in regulated rivalry through which political conflict is channeled and managed. The political party that holds power is checked by the party in opposition; indeed, since the opposition party is brought into the very frame of government, party conflict acts as an internal check on tyranny. Second, political parties organize the business of government, and they recruit individuals for office. Third, political parties create lines of division that allow for meaningful debate in politics. Although the ideological positions of parties may not necessarily add up to a philosophical truth, political parties stage battles by identifying issues and drawing distinctions among rival positions. Parties thus play an indispensable role in democratic politics by regulating rivalries, organizing political involvement and issues, and creating the lines of division through which politics takes place.[16]

B. The Democratic Value of Partisanship

Proponents of the ethic of partisanship have advanced a variety of arguments about the democratic value of partisanship. For Rosenblum, partisanship is "*the* political identity of representative government."[17] Party ID is not merely membership in a political party; instead, it is a profoundly personal identity, a kind of self-conception that, like ethnic or religious identity, shapes attitudes and worldviews. On this account, partisanship is neither derivative of nor reducible to other earlier cultural, ethnic, or religious identities.[18] Rosenblum identifies three main values of partisanship: inclusiveness, comprehensiveness, and a disposition to compromise.[19] Partisan inclusiveness is dictated by the political necessity of winning elections, but partisans also seek to obtain the approval of the people as a whole. Partisan comprehensiveness refers to the need for partisans to present publicly a comprehensive vision of their general approach to social problems. Although partisan identity does not encompass a unified theory of justice, parties must advance a conception of the common good in order to get elected. As such, political parties are vehicles for coherent and comprehensive agenda setting. Third, partisans have the ability to compromise with fellow partisans in order to protect the public interest. Rosenblum focuses on the compromises that occur *within* political parties over the selection of candidates and policy positions.[20] While partisanship does not entail these three values at every point, only partisanship as a type of political identity has the potential to do so.[21]

Critics of partisanship often point to so-called independents, who are lauded for their impartial public spiritedness. Rosenblum argues, contrary to the conventional wisdom, that independents are not necessarily better for democracy than partisans. Independents are less knowledgeable and less engaged with politics than are partisans, and they do not necessarily bring a balanced approach to the issues.[22] Instead of fostering the rise of independents, committed democrats would be further ahead if they worked to foster better partisanship.

Rosenblum's arguments about independents also shed important light on the role that loyalty plays in a constitutional order. Her defense of partial loyalties bears important affinities with certain defenses of federalism. Jacob Levy, for instance, argues that the "separation of loyalties" between the federal center and the states serves to protect the constitutional order.[23] As Levy puts it, "authority can be safely vested in the central government in part because, and perhaps just to the degree that, the people are inclined to be loyal and attached to their states rather than to the center."[24] Rosenblum argues likewise that party loyalty, as well as the conflict it produces, acts as an internal check on tyranny.[25] Because the opposition party is brought into the frame of government, it can check the political party in power.[26]

According to Russell Muirhead, the intrinsic value of partisanship is that "it expresses a willingness to make a good faith effort to stand with a group striving for democratic legitimacy."[27] Partisans are motivated to provide reasons that appeal to as broad an array of voters as possible, and, while their motivation is strategic, it is also, Muirhead suggests, part of a broader aspiration to encompass the people as a whole. Even partisan conflict is valuable because it can produce compromises that leave citizens in a better position than they would have been in without the conflict. Muirhead thus argues for an ethic of partisanship under which partisans stand with others in order to advance their collective understanding of the public interest.[28]

In addition, Muirhead suggests that we should distinguish among different kinds of partisan loyalties. He proposes a theory of loyalty as identity, which, he argues, should be distinguished from strategic loyalty. Strategic loyalty, which refers to self-interested loyalty on the part of political elites and voters, does not capture the ways in which partisan loyalty is a deeply held identity that influences how "citizens define themselves and the political community."[29] Although loyalty-as-identity is a better account than strategic loyalty, it has difficulties of its own. Specifically, loyalty-as-identity confronts the problem that it can become completely detached from reason and judgment. Loyalty inevitably contains a nonrational element; indeed, the essence of loyalty is that it is a commitment that exists even in the absence of reasons. To resolve this problem, Muirhead introduces an important distinction between closed loyalties and open loyalties. Using the analogy of loyalty within friendships, Muirhead argues that partisan loyalties can be characterized as a kind of epistemic partiality. This is so because party loyalty acts as a "perceptual screen" through which the object of loyalty is viewed. At an extreme, however, epistemic partiality can descend into epistemic closure. With epistemic closure, the connection between loyalty and reason is completely ruptured, and loyalty becomes akin to a deep-rooted prejudice. Muirhead argues that partisan loyalty poses a great danger to the political community when the "common terrain of factuality" among citizens no longer exists. The task, therefore, is to preserve loyalty-as-identity without descending into epistemic closure. For this reason, it is crucial that partisan loyalties strive to remain epistemically open. Under Muirhead's account, loyal partisans would remain true to their parties even in the absence of that party's perfection, but, should enough negative evidence present itself over a course of time, then loyal partisans should be able to question their commitments. Loyal partisans would have to negotiate the tension between openness and commitment, but this particular tension, as Muirhead observes, is what liberal democracy already demands of its citizens.

C. Democratic Practice and the Limitations of Partisanship

One of the great strengths of the ethic of partisanship is its nuanced and sensitive treatment of the dangers of partisanship. Nancy Rosenblum offers an extensive account of the virtues and vices of partisanship, and, while it is not possible to canvass the full breadth of her theories, it is worth noting, even if briefly, her reflections on impartiality and political extremism. Rosenblum observes that Hume thought it was possible for partisans to act as impartial observers.[30] By contrast, Rosenblum argues for a "less demanding ethic of partisanship" under which there is no moral requirement for partisans to take the perspective of the impartial observer, provided, however, that certain conditions are met.[31] These conditions are satisfied when "partisans accept regulated rivalry, do not aim at eliminating the opposition, and concede that political authority is partisan and uncontestable."[32] Parties can violate the ethic of partisanship by abdicating responsibility for educating and mobilizing voters, by not responding to the problems that parties are uniquely situated to address, and by refusing to engage in the work of governance.[33] In addition, the ethic of partisanship is violated by extremism. Partisan extremism, according to Rosenblum, is evidenced by a single-minded disinclination to compromise, by a failure to be inclusive, by pandering to the base, and by a lack of concern about the political costs of protracted fights among rival partisans.[34] Hyperpartisanship, which is characterized by a shrill, hostile, and deeply polarizing politics, also subverts the ethic of partisanship.[35]

Muirhead's principal concern about partisan loyalty is that it can descend into epistemic closure. His conceptual distinction between open loyalties and closed loyalties sheds new light on what is wrong with partisanship: it is not the *loyalty* as such that poses a problem so much as the fact that epistemic partiality, taken to an extreme, can sever altogether the connection between loyalty and reason. He demonstrates that partisan loyalty requires a delicate balance between openness and commitment. There is much to be said for his position that the objective is not to diminish partisan loyalty but to cultivate it so that it is in keeping with democracy.

One concern that can be raised with respect to Rosenblum's and Muirhead's theories is whether it is feasible for partisanship to be purged of its various pathologies. For instance, parties may engage in nonethical partisanship in order to win elections. If parties abided by the ethic of partisanship, would they hand a political advantage to their rivals? Is ethical partisanship possible within a competitive electoral system? Andrew Rehfeld argues, for example, that politicians will not be reelected if they strike the open-minded posture that is envisioned by the ethic of partisanship.[36] Given the virulent nature of contemporary partisanship, one wonders if parties are routinely violating the standards of even a less demanding ethic of partisanship. On a related note, ethical partisans are expected to place some limits on the intensity of their partisan attachment. To the extent that partisans must engage in self-limitation, an ethic of partisanship may expect too much of those immersed in the heat of political battle.

In addition, it could be argued that the absence of reason associated with closed loyalties is also a strength, at least in certain circumstances. Blind devotion to a cause is undoubtedly a weakness if one is concerned about judgment, but it may be a strength if one is concerned about political mobilization. Closed loyalties may be more efficacious in mobilizing political support (especially in the face of apparent failure) precisely because of the unreasoned nature of the attachment. If partisanship is purified, then its value to democracy may increase by some measures but decrease by others. Some of what makes partisan loyalty valuable to politics might actually be lost if partisanship were purified of even some of its passion. Unreasoned devotion is what helps parties (and long-shot presidential candidates) win political office.

The response to these concerns is, I think, that the ethic of partisanship is valuable precisely because it allows us to critically assess partisan activities without having to condemn partisanship in its entirety. I understand the ethic of partisanship to establish a standard of realistic idealism under which partisanship is democratically legitimate, provided that it meets certain conditions. When partisan activity fails to meet these conditions, it amounts to nonethical partisanship.

As a species of nonideal theory, the ethic of partisanship seeks to diminish the gap between democratic theory and democratic practice by recasting partisanship as a legitimate attribute of democracy. The ethic of partisanship is thus a valuable corrective to traditional democratic theory, which has tended to either ignore or criticize parties and partisanship. Rosenblum and Muirhead have developed a theoretically rich and highly nuanced account of the ethic of partisanship. Crucially, they have provided democratic theorists with the conceptual tools with which to distinguish ethical and nonethical partisanship.

II. DEMOCRACY AND THE IMPARTIAL STATE

As discussed above in Part I, the ethic of partisanship is valuable because it has opened up a conceptual space within democratic theory for the normative appraisal of partisanship. Rather than assuming that partisanship is contrary to democratic ideals, we must determine which instances of partisanship are consistent with democratic ideals and which instances of partisanship subvert democratic ideals. In this part, I claim that traditional democratic theory is useful because it can help to identify the justifiable limits of partisanship. That is, traditional democratic theory can be used to develop a more nuanced account of when and under what conditions partisanship should play a role in democratic politics.

In this part, I argue that a central feature of democratic theory is the assumption that the state is (or ought to be) an impartial entity. To illustrate the centrality of the impartial state in democratic theory, I consider the two most common models of democracy— the aggregative model and the deliberative model.[37] My purpose is not to provide an exhaustive account of these approaches nor, indeed, of democratic theory; instead, I wish to sketch the outlines of these two models in order to demonstrate the general consensus within traditional democratic theory that the state should be impartial. As discussed in Parts III and IV, the impartial state serves as a useful baseline against which to measure the actions of the partisan state.

A. *The Aggregative Model of Democracy*

According to the aggregative model, democracy is a process by which citizens' preferences are identified, aggregated, and translated into a selection of laws, policies, and public officials.[38] The preferences of citizens are conceived as being largely motivated by self-interest, rather than by a conception of the common good.[39] In addition, such preferences are treated as exogenous to the political process in that they are seen to exist prior to the activity of aggregation.[40] Political parties, which are also advancing their own interest in attaining or retaining power, compete to satisfy as many voter preferences as possible.[41]

The aggregative model is usually, although by no means exclusively, associated with a liberal account of government.[42] On this view, the state must play a neutral role in translating the predetermined interests of the citizens into a set of laws and policies. A key idea is that the democratic process must accord equal consideration to the interests of each citizen.[43] A democratic state is not permitted to skew the revealed preferences of citizens in order to further the partisan interests of the governing party; instead, the state must employ a neutral device, such as majority rule, to transform such preferences into policy. In addition, neutral rules (including, for instance, constitutional rights) are required to protect individuals from one another and against the government.[44] Thus, even under an account of democracy that embraces citizens' private preferences, it is assumed that the state plays an impartial role in the translation of preferences to law.

B. The Deliberative Model of Democracy

The deliberative model of democracy has several variants, all of which emphasize a commitment to reason-giving. Citizens and public officials engage in deliberation about the laws and policies that should be adopted and they seek to persuade fellow participants of the rightness of their ideas. Policies are thus chosen on the basis that they are supported by the best reasons. In contrast to the aggregative model, the deliberative model envisions that citizens' preferences will be transformed by engaging in democratic discussion.[45] That is, preferences are viewed as being endogenous, rather than exogenous, to the political process.[46]

The deliberative account differs from the aggregative account in a crucial respect because it holds that individuals' judgments may not be motivated by self-interest. Thus, the deliberative account is associated with public-regarding judgments, whereas the aggregative account is associated with self-interested preferences. It should be noted that these two models of democracy do not exhaust the universe of possibilities. One could imagine, for instance, that individuals could hold preferences that are public-regarding (in the sense of what is good for society) and that they could also form judgments that are partially selfish (by taking into account what is best for them personally).[47] For the purposes of the discussion, however, I shall focus on the traditional distinctions between the aggregative and the deliberative accounts.

Under the deliberative model, the role of the state is decidedly neutral: the state must ensure that all those affected by the decision making are included in the deliberation on equal terms.[48]

There must be a set of common procedures by which democratic
decision making is conducted. Citizens engage in deliberation
with the objective of reaching an agreement, even though such
agreement may not necessarily come about.[49] Deliberation thus
need not result in consensus, although most deliberative theorists
would hold that decision making should aim for consensus by taking the views of all affected persons into account.[50] Most theories
of deliberation acknowledge that the aggregation of preferences,
through voting and elections, is an inevitable feature of deliberative democracy.[51] Indeed, some theorists would argue that electoral campaigns involve a process of deliberation among citizens
about the common good.[52]

The deliberative model is often associated with a republican
account of government; indeed, for some theorists, the deliberative model is synonymous with (or derivative of) the republican
approach. For the sake of simplicity, I will refer to the deliberative and republican traditions as falling within the "deliberative
model." Under the republican tradition, civic virtue, rather than
self-interest, plays a prominent role. Participation by citizens in
politics is highly valued both because it protects against govern-
mental oppression and because it develops civic virtue and communal loyalty. Virtuous and public-spirited representatives engage
in deliberation about what the common good requires, rather than
engaging in a competitive process of bargaining, as envisioned by
the liberal approach.[53]

In the republican tradition, freedom can exist only under a system of law. As Philip Pettit argues, good laws can protect people
from domination by others without also subjecting them to domination by the state.[54] According to Pettit, domination is the capacity to interfere on an arbitrary basis in certain choices that another person is in a position to make.[55] Arbitrariness occurs when
an agent's actions are subject only to the will or judgment of the
agent; that is, the actions are chosen without reference to the interests of those affected by the acts.[56] The laws create freedom so
long as they protect the people's common interests and are not the
instruments of anyone's arbitrary will. Although the law involves
interference, even coercion, such interference is not arbitrary and
hence nondominating.[57] Pettit argues that if the "state is forced
to track the common good then it won't dominate its citizens."[58]

The state "can interfere in people's affairs and yet not dominate them so far as the interference is forced to track the interests that people are sincerely disposed to avow."[59]

Pettit asserts that freedom as non-domination can be promoted if two constraints are in place. The first constraint is constitutionalist, and it involves a commitment to the rule of law, the division of power, and antimajoritarianism.[60] With respect to the constitutionalist constraint, Pettit emphasizes that "the instruments used by the republican state should be, as far as possible, non-manipulable."[61] This means that institutions and processes must be "maximally resistant to being deployed on an arbitrary, perhaps sectional, basis."[62] In particular, the instrumentalities of the state should not be open to interference by any one individual regardless of whether that person's objective is to secure the public good or his or her private ends.[63] The second constraint is democratic contestability. Pettit argues that the nonarbitrariness of public decisions depends in part on the ability of citizens to contest those decisions that conflict with the public good.[64] The key idea is that, under the republican tradition, the state engages in dominating behavior if it does not advance the common good.

C. The Impartial State: Two Conceptions

The idea of the impartial state is central to both the aggregative and the deliberative models of democracy. I shall argue, however, that there are two main conceptions of state impartiality at work. Under the aggregative account, the state must play a neutral role in translating the interests of the citizens into a set of laws. Neutrality requires that the state not favor any one private interest over another in the process of translating preferences into policy. The democratic process must accord equal consideration to the interests of each citizen.[65] Thus, the state must treat the preferences of citizens in an impartial manner. At the same time, it is acceptable for the final policy outcome to reflect the preferences of the majority, even if this means that the policy favors a particular subset of the citizenry. The state is also neutral with respect to the quality of the policy outcome. As long as the outcome is consistent with the preferences of the majority, then the state has no further obligations.

Under the deliberative account, by contrast, the demands of state impartiality are much more rigorous: the state is not permitted to advance any private preferences at all. Instead, democratic government must aspire to translate the common interests of the people into the governing laws.[66] The state must therefore support the common good instead of the partial interests of only some members of society. The traditional understanding of the common good, associated with Rousseau, is the idea of the general will—only those interests that can be willed generally should be protected by law. Rousseau writes that "[i]t is important, then, that in order to have the general will expressed well, there be no partial society in the State."[67] To determine the general will, individuals must express a judgment about the public interest by viewing the problem from a general, as opposed to a private, perspective. The implication is that the general will cannot be determined in the presence of partial interests or factions, since personal interests destroy the common interest. As Anna Stilz puts it, "where the partial association prevails over all the others, the state is ruled by a private will—the will of this faction—and the general will exists no longer."[68] In addition, the state must ensure that all those affected by the decision making are included in the deliberation on equal terms.[69] There must be a set of common procedures by which democratic decision making is conducted. Under the republican account, the state must be impartial and must promote the public good instead of providing special treatment to certain individuals and groups.[70]

I claim that the differences between these two understandings of state impartiality rest upon a distinction between procedural and substantive impartiality. The aggregative model, I suggest, is based upon a procedural conception of state impartiality. The main role of the impartial state is to translate, in a neutral fashion, the preferences of citizens into policies. By contrast, the deliberative account has a more demanding requirement of state impartiality. Not only must the translation of preferences to policy be conducted in an impartial fashion, but also the substantive content of the resulting laws must be impartial in that these laws advance the common good, rather than the partial interests of only some members of society. The deliberative model thus envisions both procedural and substantive impartiality on the part of the state.

The distinction I am drawing between procedural and substantive impartiality raises a host of issues, not least of which is the inherent difficulty of drawing a distinction between process and substance. This problem is connected to a larger debate between procedural and substantive approaches to democracy. Although it is beyond the scope of this essay to engage in this debate, it is worth noting that there are theoretical approaches to bridging the distinction between process and substance that still allow for the existence of each. Corey Brettschneider's "value theory of democracy," for instance, holds that there are certain core values—political autonomy, equality of interests, and reciprocity—that can be used to evaluate and justify not only democratic procedures but also the policies that are produced by these procedures.[71] Despite the complexities of this debate, I suggest that the distinction between procedural and substantive impartiality captures an important difference between the aggregative and the deliberative accounts of democracy.

To summarize, these models converge on the idea that there must be neutral rules by which the preferences of citizens are translated into laws. Thus, both models share a commitment to procedural impartiality with respect to the translation of preferences to policy. The two models diverge, however, with respect to substantive impartiality. Under the aggregative model, it is acceptable for the content of the laws to reflect the interests of a subset of the citizenry, while, under the deliberative model, the content of the laws may advance only the common good of the people. In the next two sections, I use these general standards to evaluate the democratic legitimacy of first-order and second-order partisanship.

III. First-Order Partisanship

The problem of the partisan state is that the state, instead of acting as an impartial body, often acts as a partisan entity in the processes of democracy. As Rosenblum observes, "parties are doubly partial, for they represent a particular part and they favor it."[72] This double partiality, I suggest, does not disappear once the political party assumes the powers of the state. Under traditional theories of democracy, the partisan state would likely be viewed as violating the ideal of state impartiality. The ethic of partisanship, however, opens the conceptual possibility of distinguishing between ethical and nonethical partisanship. Rather than assuming that partisanship is inherently undemocratic, we must investigate the possible contributions of a specific partisan action to democratic government.

As described in the Introduction, the first question is to determine how the democratic process is influenced by partisan loyalty. I claim that the democratic process can be described as performing four fundamental functions: (1) the selection of public policies; (2) the selection of public officials; (3) the selection of the rules by which public policies are selected; and (4) the selection of the rules by which public officials are selected. These four types of democratic decisions can be influenced by partisan loyalty, and thus, by extension, there are four ways in which we can have a partisan state. Partisan loyalty can affect those decisions that lead to the selection of public policies, the selection of public officials, the selection of the rules by which public policies are selected, and the selection of the rules by which public officials are selected.

The second question is how to distinguish legitimate from illegitimate partisan activity by the state in the democratic process. I argue that there is a distinction between what I refer to as first-order partisanship and second-order partisanship. First-order partisanship encompasses those democratic decisions that involve the selection of public policies and public officials (assuming that these decisions are affected by partisan loyalty). Second-order partisanship, which is discussed in Part IV, encompasses those democratic decisions that involve the selection of the rules by which public policies and public officials are selected (assuming that these decisions are affected by partisan loyalty).

A. *The Selection of Public Policies*

There are many ways in which partisanship affects the selection of public policies in a democracy. Most obviously, the political party that wins the election seeks to implement a specific partisan agenda. In the same way, presidents have certain policy objectives that align, for the most part, with the platform of their political parties. More controversially, Supreme Court justices issue judgments (a kind of public policy) that are often influenced by the justices' partisan identities.[73]

Whether we view the influence of partisanship on the selection of policy to be legitimate or illegitimate depends to a large degree on our preferred theory of democracy. Under the aggregative model of democracy, it would be acceptable for the state to implement a partisan policy (in the sense that it is supported by a party's adherents) provided, however, that the prior process of translating preferences to policy was conducted in a neutral fashion. Another condition is that the democratic process must accord equal consideration to the interests of each citizen.[74] The aggregative view does place some constraints on the level of legitimate partisan influence. Under the aggregative view, the actual aggregation of preferences must be done in a fair and impartial way, as opposed to, for example, a process of aggregation that is governed wholly by the partisan self-interest of those in power.

By contrast, the deliberative model of democracy presents a far greater challenge to the partisan selection of public policies. In addition to the requirement that there be a set of common procedures that provide an equal say to all those affected by the decision making, the state must also advance an impartial conception of the common good. An impartial conception of the common good can be defined as "a conception of the good that does not give any special weight to the interests and concerns of the agent but treats all interests or concerns in the same way."[75] By contrast, a partial conception of the common good "attributes more weight to the interests and concerns of the agent or of those connected to him in some way (his family, his ethnic group, or his fellow country-men, for example) than to those of others."[76] Partiality is the "introduction of private considerations into a judgment that should be made on public grounds."[77] A deliberative model holds that the state engages in domination when it fails to advance the common good. On this view, the partisan selection of public policies violates the requirement that the state act only to further the public interest.

B. The Selection of Public Officials

State-run elections are usually conducted on partisan terms. Political parties, including the incumbent governing party, recruit candidates for office. Voters give support to candidates in large part on the basis of the candidates' partisan affiliations. Elected public officials are almost always selected for public office along partisan lines. That being said, it is important to distinguish between partisan elections and nonpartisan elections. In the United States, for example, most judges (i.e., state judges) are selected by election, rather than by appointment. Some states conduct partisan elections for judges (i.e., the judge's party affiliation is listed on the ballot), whereas other states, at least formally, have nonpartisan elections (i.e., the judge's party affiliation is not listed on the ballot). There is some debate in the literature about whether nonpartisan elections are truly nonpartisan, but recent empirical research by Michael Kang and Joanna Shepherd demonstrates that elected judges are more likely to decide in favor of business interests that have donated money to the judges' electoral campaigns.[78] This finding, however, is true only for judges who have been elected in partisan rather than nonpartisan elections.[79] Kang and Shepherd therefore argue in favor of nonpartisan methods for the selection of judges.[80]

In terms of the appointment of public officials, the president's choices are often (if not always) influenced by partisan considerations. For example, the president's selection of a Supreme Court candidate is a partisan decision, as is the Senate's confirmation process. Jack Balkin and Sanford Levinson advance a theory of partisan entrenchment to explain the propensity of presidents to appoint judges and justices who are ideological allies.[81] By selecting a sufficient number of judges and justices who share the political agenda of the president's party, presidents can thereby shape the direction of the evolution of constitutional doctrines.[82] In sum, much of the selection of public officials in a democracy (at least in the United States) is conducted along partisan lines.

Under an aggregative view of democracy, elections are understood to be conducted along partisan lines. Voters express their preferences for various candidates, and these preferences are translated into electoral outcomes. The selection of public officials by appointment also enjoys a democratic pedigree. To the extent that the president's selection of a federal judge is influenced by whether or not the judge and the president are ideologically like-minded (and assuming that the president is supported by a majority of the population), the president's choice will likely reflect the preferences of the majority. Under a deliberative view of democracy, by contrast, the partisan selection of public officials contravenes the idea that public officials are to be selected for their virtue. Representatives are to be chosen for their ability to engage in deliberation and for their commitment to the common good, not because their ideological viewpoints happen to coincide with the private and partial interests of the citizens.

C. First-Order Partisanship and Democracy

I would like to make the counterintuitive claim that the partisan state, at least with respect to first-order partisan activity, can be partially defended on democratic grounds. Under an aggregative view of democracy, first-order partisanship is generally acceptable, provided that the process of translation (from revealed preferences to either the selection of public policies or public officials) is conducted in a neutral fashion. That is, the substance of decisions can be partisan, provided that the translation methods are impartial from a procedural standpoint.

First-order partisanship is consistent with democratic ideals in other ways, as well. Democratic accountability is brought about when public officers follow through on the promises they made to voters during the election period. By implementing the party's agenda, partisans are promoting democratic accountability. The selection of public officials through elections is clearly consistent with democratic ideals; indeed, for some theorists, this is the very meaning of democracy.[83] It is possible to argue that the selection of public officials via appointment is also consistent with democratic principles. By voting for the president, citizens are expressing a preference about the actions that the president will likely take while in office, and one of those actions is the selection of public officials, such as the justices of the Supreme Court. To the extent, however, that the selection of justices is entrenched beyond the president's term in office, it is not consistent with the ideals of democratic representation and accountability.[84]

By contrast, under the deliberative view of democracy, first-order partisanship poses certain difficulties. The state must advance an impartial conception of the common good, which by definition means that the common good cannot reflect either the private interests of individuals or the interests of groups. To the extent that first-order partisanship results in the implementation of a partisan agenda, it would seem to violate the ideal of the deliberative model of democracy. In a similar manner, the deliberative view would hold that the selection of public officials, whether via election or appointment, should be conducted on the basis of the candidates' virtues, rather than on the basis of the candidates' partisan affiliations.

A possible response to a proponent of the deliberative model of democracy is that there is some ambiguity about how we should view a partisan policy position. On the one hand, we could view the partisan position as inherently partial and perhaps even self-interested. On the other hand, the ethic of partisanship would tell us that partisans aim to present a comprehensive vision of the public good. As Nancy Rosenblum argues, partisanship is valuable because it allows for the articulation of a conception of the common good.[85] Likewise, Russell Muirhead observes that partisans aim to offer reasons that appeal to a wide array of people and therefore "have to form some more or less articulate and better or worse approximation of the common good."[86] Although their motivation may be to secure an electoral advantage, the fact remains that parties have to "speak the language of the common good."[87] Partiality often involves a judgment about what the public interest entails.[88] Thus, it may be too simplistic to oppose partisan self-interest and the public interest as necessarily antagonistic. Although the partisan interest and the public interest conflict at times, it is also conceivable that there is an overlap between the two. In addition, it could be argued that the public interest is inherently contested. Party conflict is based in part on rival understandings of what constitutes the common good.

In sum, first-order partisanship has a qualified claim to democratic legitimacy because it is broadly compatible with what I take to be a fundamental principle of democracy—the principle of self-government. To the extent that the choice of public policies and public officials is largely consistent with popular will, the principle of self-government is not breached. To be sure, the idea of self-government can be understood in various ways, including, for example, as being consistent with aggregative principles or deliberative principles. For this reason, it is important to note that the argument that first-order partisanship is largely consistent with popular will is most likely to coincide with a theory of self-government that emphasizes majoritarian (or aggregative) principles, rather than deliberative principles. It is conceivable for an instance of first-order partisanship to have the support of the entire nation, in which instance it would cohere with a deliberative understanding of self-government.

IV. Second-Order Partisanship

Second-order partisanship refers to those democratic decisions that involve the selection of the rules by which public policies and public officials are selected.

A. *The Selection of the Rules by Which Public Policies Are Selected*

At the federal level, many of the rules by which public policies are selected are constitutionally hard-wired.[89] These hard-wired rules encompass a broad range of items, including the federal structure, the apportionment of voting power among the states in the House and the Senate, and the presidential veto. Because these rules can be changed only through constitutional amendment, they are not subject to being altered by partisan majorities in the ordinary course of the democratic process.

In addition to these hard-wired constitutional rules, there is also an array of statutory rules, regulatory rules, and informal norms that determine the rules by which public policies are selected. The selection (and interpretation) of these rules is often subject to partisan influence. For example, the major parties attempt to select those rules and processes that would best serve their respective political agendas in congressional committees.[90] Another prominent example of partisan influence on the selection of rules that select public policies is the practice of filibustering. The filibuster, which is a right to unlimited debate, is used to stall the passage of legislation. The debate can be brought to an end only when cloture is invoked, which requires sixty votes under Senate rules. It is no longer necessary for the debate to even take place. As Josh Chafetz notes, a filibuster essentially triggers a sixty-vote supermajority requirement to pass a piece of legislation in the Senate.[91] Senators choose to filibuster certain bills, and, although this practice is used to oppose rather than select a specific public policy, there is no question that filibustering is conducted along partisan lines.

There are also rules, such as Supreme Court judgments, that have an indirect effect on the selection of public policies. Some of these rules are selected by the justices because the rules align with the justices' partisan leanings. In addition, these rules often have predictable partisan effects. The Supreme Court decided in the *Chevron* case, for example, that courts should defer to an administrative agency's interpretation of a statute, provided that a two-step test is met.[92] The Court's deference (or lack of deference) to agency interpretation could have an effect on the kinds of public policies that are ultimately adopted by the agency. As Thomas Miles and Cass Sunstein argue, the evidence shows that the *Chevron* rule is applied differently depending on the political preferences of the judges that are applying it.[93] This suggests that courts also engage in the partisan selection of the rules by which public policies are selected.

The partisan selection of the rules by which public policies are selected contravenes the principles of both the aggregative and the deliberative models of democracy. Despite their differences with respect to the common good, these models converge on the idea that there must be neutral rules by which the preferences of citizens are translated into laws. Since the partisan selection of the rules can potentially lead to a different selection of policies, the democratic process is not according equal respect to the interests of each citizen. By manipulating the democratic machinery by which such preferences are translated, partisans are undermining the basic principles of democratic accountability and representation.

B. The Selection of the Rules by Which Public Officials Are Selected

In a democratic system, there are a number of rules that determine the selection of public officials. In the United States, for example, several topics in election law—including electoral redistricting and campaign finance—are concerned with these rules. Politicians routinely select those rules that will best advance their and their party's chances of succeeding at the polls. The partisan selection of the rules by which public officials are selected is often democratically illegitimate for the same reasons that the partisan selection of the rules by which public policies are selected may be illegitimate. Under both the aggregative and the deliberative views of democracy, the process of translation from citizen preferences to an outcome (whether it be a law or a public officeholder) should be conducted in a neutral and fair way. The state must ensure that all those affected by a decision have a say and that equal consideration is accorded to the interests of each citizen. By manipulating the rules to advance their party's interests, partisans are skewing the translation process, in addition to according unequal consideration to the citizens' interests.

Many scholars have examined the problems that arise when public officials select the rules by which they are selected. John Hart Ely argued that the Supreme Court should engage in judicial review when the political market is malfunctioning in a systematic way.[94] One kind of systematic malfunction occurs when public officials use their positions to thwart change to ensure that "they will stay in and the outs will stay out."[95] Michael Klarman refers to the latter behavior as legislative entrenchment.[96] Legislative entrenchment occurs through such practices as incumbency protection, restrictive ballot access laws, and malapportionment.[97] Samuel Issacharoff and Richard Pildes have advanced the "political markets" theory. They argue that democratic politics are "akin in important respects to a robustly competitive market—a market whose vitality depends on both clear rules of engagement and on the ritual cleansing born of competition."[98] Dominant political parties, however, have a propensity to manipulate the rules of the game in order to reduce electoral competition.[99] By locking up political institutions, dominant parties are able to secure permanent partisan advantage. Political markets theorists also emphasize that the state is composed of partisan powerholders.[100] The states' authority to pass election laws means that states have the ability to set the rules of the games for themselves and for their political rivals.[101] Political markets theorists argue that the Supreme Court should therefore intervene to prevent the political self-entrenchment of parties.

There are competing views about the precise harm that is caused when public officials select the rules by which they are selected. Guy Charles argues, for instance, that the "intentional manipulation of democratic institutions by state actors" leads to distortion and a "loss of legitimacy" in a democracy.[102] Dennis Thompson contends that, apart from the inherent conflict of interest, there is the deeper problem that such a system permits current majorities to unduly restrict future majorities. As Thompson puts it, the "mischief is not self-dealing, but self-perpetuation."[103] In addition, Thompson notes that the conflict of interest takes a variety of forms.[104] He points out that, while individual legislators and political parties are all motivated by self-interest, it is important to recognize that the different kinds of self-interested conduct conflict with one another.[105] Thompson also argues that "we should not presume that the conflicts between the interests of politicians and those of the system always represent a choice between self-interest and the general interest."[106]

On a related note, Richard Hasen has developed a nuanced account of how we should view the self-interested conduct of elected officials. Hasen defines "bad legislative intent" as an intent to protect incumbents and political parties from political competition.[107] Not only is bad legislative intent often difficult to prove; Hasen argues that it is also difficult to draw the line between good and bad legislative intent "even among the class of laws that appear to be driven, at least in part, by anticompetitive aims."[108] As Hasen notes, courts have allowed legislators to engage in such anticompetitive conduct as incumbency protection when redrawing electoral districts.[109] The rationale is that there are democratic benefits to having knowledgeable and experienced legislators who can be responsive to voters.[110] That is, incumbency protection may be consistent with democratic principles because voters may be more effectively represented by incumbents.[111] The idea that it may be difficult to draw a distinction between self-interest and the general interest is an important qualifier to the critique of second-order partisanship.

C. Second-Order Partisanship and Democracy

Second-order partisanship encompasses the partisan selection of the rules by which public policies and public officials are selected. Although the aggregative and deliberative models do not speak directly to the issue of second-order partisanship per se, these models do converge on the issue of how citizens' preferences should be translated into policies. Both the aggregative and the deliberative models of democracy hold that the translation process must occur through neutral rather than partisan grounds. The state must ensure that all those affected by a decision have an equal opportunity to participate in the decision-making process. In addition, the democratic process must accord equal consideration to the interests of each citizen.

Second-order partisanship is usually inconsistent with democratic ideals because it interferes with and skews the translation of citizen preferences. If the processes by which public officials and policies are selected are themselves determined in a partisan manner, the outcomes that are produced by such processes are less likely to reflect the public interest however defined. This is particularly true with respect to the selection of the rules by which public officials are selected. Relatedly, second-order partisanship interferes with democratic accountability because democratic processes are biased to favor the interests of public officials over the interests of citizens.[112] As described earlier, a host of democratic pathologies may ensue when public officials select the rules by which they are elected into office. The partisan selection of the rules by which public officials are selected can at times amount to an abusive exercise of public power, one that amounts to domination by the state.[113]

One implication is that a better partisanship would involve the absence of partisanship from certain kinds of democratic decisions. Although it is possible to demand of partisans that they act in an impartial manner for certain decisions, it may be the case that we cannot rely solely on partisans to create a better partisanship. Institutions must also be designed in such a way as to minimize the partisan nature of the state's decisions. One approach is to delegate certain decisions to impartial institutions, such as independent redistricting commissions (although, to be sure, there is some skepticism about whether it is feasible to have institutions that are sufficiently independent).[114] In terms of desirability, redistricting commissions suffer from one significant disadvantage. The characteristic that makes nonpartisan commissions appealing—their insulation from ordinary politics—is also a deficit from a democratic standpoint. As

Michael Kang argues, it is better if the rules of democracy are themselves determined through democratic processes.[115]

Another promising approach is found in Adrian Vermeule's
theory of veil rules. Vermeule's argument is that legal rules can
"promote impartiality by depriving officials of information they
might use in self-interested ways." In essence, the rule creates a
"veil of uncertainty that forces officials to act as though motivated
by impartial considerations."[116] Vermeule distinguishes Rawls's veil
of ignorance from veil rules because the "first type of veil rule suppresses the decisionmaker's knowledge of the actors' identities;
the second type suppresses the decisionmaker's knowledge of the
actors' payoffs."[117] An example of a veil rule is delayed effectiveness.[118] Adam Cox, as Vermeule notes, has proposed that legislatures be required to enact redistricting plans that do not take
effect for up to two to three election cycles. The uncertainty of
not knowing how the plan will benefit the legislators means that
the redistricting plan will likely be more impartial.[119] In addition,
Vermeule's theory of system effects suggests that it is important
to examine whether the overall system of partisan competition is
able to mimic the ideal of impartiality through the use of various
invisible-hand mechanisms.[120] Vermeule's theories are consistent
with the idea that ethical partisanship requires at times that partisans be forced to be impartial.

There are some political moments in which partisans should
assume the pose of an impartial observer. A better partisanship,
in some instances, requires the absence of partisanship. Nancy
Rosenblum, for example, argues that partisans must accept "regulated rivalry."[121] In a like manner, Russell Muirhead observes that
ethical partisans "agree to carry out their contest within certain
boundaries."[122] The ethic of partisanship is consistent with the
idea that the rules of the game must be applied impartially to all
participants. When the processes of translation have become thoroughly captured by partisan manipulation, however, I suggest that
the ethic of partisanship has been breached.

In sum, second-order partisanship is usually inconsistent with
the principle of self-government; indeed, second-order partisanship undermines and disrupts the very mechanisms that ensure
that democratic processes impartially translate citizens' preferences and judgments. Unlike first-order partisanship, which has

some claim to a democratic pedigree, second-order partisanship has almost no claim to democratic legitimacy. A possible exception would occur if the state were to select second-order rules in a way that reflects the interests of the citizens. For the selection of second-order rules to be consistent with democratic principles, however, there must be safeguards against partisan manipulation.

CONCLUSION: DEMOCRACY AND THE PARTISAN STATE

I began this essay by asking when and under what conditions partisanship should play a role in democratic politics. I examined this question by focusing on the problem of the partisan state. The problem of the partisan state is that the state, instead of acting as an impartial body, acts as a partisan entity in the processes of democracy. Rather than viewing the partisan state as a failure of democratic theory, I concluded that the partisan state, at least in some instances, is consistent with democratic principles. First-order partisanship, which refers to the partisan selection of public policies and public officials, has a qualified claim to democratic legitimacy. By contrast, second-order partisanship, which refers to the partisan selection of the rules by which public policies and public officials are selected, has almost no claim to democratic legitimacy. The reason for this distinction is that first-order partisanship is largely consistent with the principle of self-government, whereas second-order partisanship undermines self-government. In conclusion, partisanship has a legitimate, even indispensable, role in certain aspects of democracy, but it should have no place in other aspects of democracy. The challenge for democratic theory is to distinguish between the two in such a way that we can benefit from the virtues but avoid the vices of partisanship.

NOTES

I would like to thank Corey Brettschneider, Bruce Chapman, Anver Emon, Richard Hasen, Sanford Levinson, Ian Lee, Jacob Levy, Russell Muirhead, Joel Parker, Philip Pettit, Andrew Rehfeld, Nancy Rosenblum, and Adrian Vermeule for very helpful comments and conversations. I am also grateful to Mayo Moran for her support and encouragement.

1. Nancy L. Rosenblum, *On the Side of the Angels: An Appreciation of Parties and Partisanship* (Princeton: Princeton University Press, 2008); Russell Muirhead, "A Defense of Party Spirit," *Perspectives on Politics* 4 (December 2006): 713–27.

2. To be sure, the state may be controlled by different political parties depending on which institution or office is the subject of analysis. In a time of divided government, for instance, certain institutions of government may be controlled by one party while other institutions are controlled by the opposing party.

3. V. O. Key, *Politics, Parties and Pressure Groups*, 5th ed. (New York: Crowell, 1964), 163–65.

4. Clinton Rossiter, *The American Presidency* (New York: Harcourt, Brace, 1956).

5. Daryl J. Levinson and Richard H. Pildes, "Separation of Parties, Not Powers," *Harvard Law Review* 119 (June 2006): 2313.

6. Samuel Issacharoff and Richard H. Pildes, "Politics as Markets: Partisan Lockups of the Democratic Process," *Stanford Law Review* 50 (February 1998): 708.

7. The terminology of "first-order partisanship" and "second-order partisanship" is similar to Heather Gerken's important distinction between two types of diversity: first-order diversity and second-order diversity. According to Gerken, first-order diversity (or intraorganizational diversity) refers to the idea that institutions will mirror the polity, while second-order diversity (or interorganizational diversity) refers to the variation that exists among decision-making bodies. See Heather K. Gerken, "Second-Order Diversity," *Harvard Law Review* 118 (February 2005): 1102–3.

8. Nathaniel Persily and Bruce E. Cain, "The Legal Status of Political Parties: A Reassessment of Competing Paradigms," *Columbia Law Review* 100 (Symposium: Law and Political Parties) (April 2000): 777–78.

9. Ibid.

10. This gridlock is a function of the particularities of the American constitutional order, and does not necessarily describe the partisan politics of a parliamentary system. My thanks to Sandy Levinson for this point.

11. Mark D. Brewer, "The Rise of Partisanship and the Expansion of Partisan Conflict within the American Electorate," *Political Research Quarterly* 58 (June 2005): 228–29.

12. Ibid., 219.

13. Richard H. Pildes, "Why the Center Does Not Hold: The Causes of Hyperpolarized Democracy in America," *California Law Review* 99 (April 2011): 273.

14. Muirhead, "A Defense of Party Spirit," 715.

15. Rosenblum, *On the Side of the Angels*, 8.

16. Ibid., 13, 119–21.

17. Ibid., 7.

18. Ibid., 345.

19. Ibid., 358.

20. Ibid., 361.

21. Ibid., 357–62.

22. Ibid., 367.

23. Jacob T. Levy, "Federalism, Liberalism, and the Separation of Loyalties," *American Political Science Review* 101 (August 2007): 464.

24. Ibid., 465.

25. There is also an important disanalogy between Jacob Levy's defense of federalism and Nancy Rosenblum's defense of partisanship. In the case of federalism, no province can ever take the place of the whole. In a partisan democracy, by contrast, the state apparatus can be captured by one party. In this way, partial loyalties in the context of partisanship pose a systemic risk to democracy. My thanks to Jacob Levy for this point.

26. Rosenblum, *On the Side of the Angels*, 13, 119–21.

27. Muirhead, "A Defense of Party Spirit," 719.

28. Ibid., 720.

29. Muirhead, "The Case for Party Loyalty" (this volume).

30. Rosenblum, *On the Side of the Angels*, 142.

31. Ibid.

32. Ibid., 143.

33. Ibid., 456.

34. Ibid., 406.

35. Ibid., 387.

36. Andrew Rehfeld, "Regulated Conflict and a 'Proto-Millian' Defense of Parties or 'Vote for Me, I've *Probably* Got the Right Answers,'" *On the Side of the Angels* symposium, http://jacobtlevy.blogspot.com/2009/01/on-side-of-angels-symposium-15.html.

37. I am using the terminology that is commonly found within the literature. It might be better to call the aggregative model a "preferentialist" model, since both the aggregative and the deliberative models require aggregation. The aggregative model calls for an aggregation of preferences, while the deliberative model calls for an aggregation of judgments. My thanks to Philip Pettit for this observation.

38. Cass R. Sunstein, *Designing Democracy: What Constitutions Do* (Oxford: Oxford University Press, 2001), 7; Iris Marion Young, *Inclusion and Democracy* (Oxford: Oxford University Press, 2000), 19.

39. Robert A. Dahl, *A Preface to Democratic Theory* (Chicago: University of Chicago Press, 1956), 29–31.

40. Cass R. Sunstein, "Preferences and Politics," *Philosophy & Public Affairs* 20 (Winter 1991): 10.

41. Jane Mansbridge, *Beyond Adversary Democracy* (New York: Basic Books, 1980), 17.

42. John S. Dryzek, *Deliberative Democracy and Beyond: Liberals, Critics, Contestations* (New York: Oxford University Press, 2000), 11.

43. Joshua Cohen, "Procedure and Substance in Deliberative Democracy," in *Democracy and Difference: Contesting the Boundaries of the Political,* ed. Seyla Benhabib (Princeton: Princeton University Press, 1996), 98.

44. Dryzek, *Deliberative Democracy,* 9.

45. Benjamin Barber, *Strong Democracy: Participatory Politics for a New Age* (Berkeley: University of California Press, 1984), 136–58; Ian Shapiro, *The State of Democratic Theory* (Princeton: Princeton University Press, 2003), 21.

46. Sunstein, "Preferences and Politics," 10, 17–18.

47. My thanks to Philip Pettit for these points about public-regarding preferences and partially selfish judgments.

48. Young, *Inclusion and Democracy,* 23.

49. Amy Gutmann and Dennis Thompson, *Democracy and Disagreement* (Cambridge, MA: Belknap Press, 1998), 2–12, 52–53. For an argument about the need for consensus, see Jurgen Habermas, *Between Facts and Norms: Contributions to a Discourse Theory of Law and Democracy* (Cambridge, MA: MIT Press, 1996).

50. John Ferejohn, "Instituting Deliberative Democracy," in *NOMOS XLII: Designing Democratic Institutions,* ed. Ian Shapiro and Stephen Macedo (New York: New York University Press, 2000), 76; Cass R. Sunstein, *Democracy and the Problem of Free Speech* (New York: Free Press, 1995), 247.

51. James Johnson, "Arguing for Deliberation: Some Skeptical Considerations," in *Deliberative Democracy,* ed. Jon Elster (Cambridge: Cambridge University Press, 1998), 162.

52. Thomas Christiano, *The Rule of the Many: Fundamental Issues in Democratic Theory* (Boulder: Westview, 1996), 246.

53. Cass R. Sunstein, "Beyond the Republican Revival," *Yale Law Journal* 97 (Symposium: The Republican Civic Tradition) (July 1988): 1548–56.

54. Philip Pettit, *Republicanism: A Theory of Freedom and Government* (Oxford: Oxford University Press, 1997), 36.

55. Ibid., 52.

56. Ibid., 55.

57. Ibid., 36.

58. Philip Pettit, "The Common Good," in *Justice and Democracy: Essays for Brian Barry,* ed. Keith Dowding, Robert E. Goodin, and Carole Pateman (Cambridge: Cambridge University Press, 2004), 150.

59. Ibid., 151.

60. Pettit, *Republicanism*, 174–83.

61. Ibid., 173.

62. Ibid.

63. Ibid.

64. Ibid., 183–200.

65. Cohen, "Procedure and Substance," 98.

66. Philip Pettit, "Democracy, Electoral and Contestatory," in *NOMOS XLII: Designing Democratic Institutions*, ed. Ian Shapiro and Stephen Macedo (New York: New York University Press, 2000), 106.

67. Jean-Jacques Rousseau, *The Social Contract and Other Later Political Writings*, vol. 2, ed. Victor Gourevitch (Cambridge: Cambridge University Press, 1997), 3, 60.

68. Anna Stilz, *Liberal Loyalty: Freedom, Obligation, and the State* (Princeton: Princeton University Press, 2009), 78.

69. Young, *Inclusion and Democracy*, 23.

70. Cass R. Sunstein, *The Partial Constitution* (Cambridge, MA: Harvard University Press, 1993), 17.

71. Corey Brettschneider, "The Value Theory of Democracy," *Politics, Philosophy & Economics* 5 (October 2006): 261, 266, 268; Corey Brettschneider, *Democratic Rights: The Substance of Self-Government* (Princeton: Princeton University Press, 2007).

72. Rosenblum, *On the Side of the Angels*, 106.

73. Jeffrey A. Segal and Harold J. Spaeth, *The Supreme Court and the Attitudinal Model* (New York: Cambridge University Press, 1993).

74. Cohen, "Procedure and Substance," 98.

75. Brian Barry, *Justice as Impartiality* (Oxford: Clarendon, 1999), 20.

76. Ibid.

77. Ibid., 13.

78. Michael S. Kang and Joanna Shepherd, "The Partisan Price of Justice: An Empirical Analysis of Campaign Contributions and Judicial Decisions," *New York University Law Review* 86 (April 2011): 73–74.

79. Ibid.

80. Ibid.

81. Jack M. Balkin and Sanford Levinson, "Understanding the Constitutional Revolution," *Virginia Law Review* 87 (October 2001): 1066–67.

82. Ibid., 1067–68.

83. Joseph Schumpeter, *Capitalism, Socialism and Democracy*, 3rd ed. (New York: Harper Perennial, 1950), 272–73; Adam Przeworski, "Minimalist Conception of Democracy: A Defense," in *Democracy's Value*, ed. Ian Shapiro and Casiano Hacker-Cordon (Cambridge: Cambridge University Press, 1999), 23–25.

84. In any event, most judges in America (i.e., state judges) are selected

by election and, in addition, have, in almost all states, limited terms of office. The federal judges are thus the exception in the American system of government.

85. Rosenblum, *On the Side of the Angels*, 359.

86. Muirhead, "A Defense of Party Spirit," 719.

87. Ibid., 717.

88. Rosenblum, *On the Side of the Angels*, 108.

89. Sanford Levinson, *Our Undemocratic Constitution: Where the Constitution Goes Wrong (and How We the People Can Correct It)* (New York: Oxford University Press, 2006), 6.

90. There is an extended public choice literature on the manipulation of agenda setting through voting rules. For a discussion (and rebuttal), see Gerry Mackie, *Democracy Defended* (Cambridge: Cambridge University Press, 2003).

91. Josh Chafetz, "The Unconstitutionality of the Filibuster," *Connecticut Law Review* 43 (May 2011): 1008–10.

92. Chevron U.S.A. v. Natural Res. Def. Council, 467 U.S. 837, 865 (1984).

93. Thomas J. Miles and Cass R. Sunstein, "Do Judges Make Regulatory Policy?" *University of Chicago Law Review* 73 (Summer 2006): 870–71.

94. John Hart Ely, *Democracy and Distrust: A Theory of Judicial Review* (Cambridge, MA: Harvard University Press, 1980), 103.

95. Ibid.

96. Michael J. Klarman, "Majoritarian Judicial Review: The Entrenchment Problem," *Georgetown Law Journal* 85 (February 1997): 498.

97. Ibid., 502.

98. Issacharoff and Pildes, "Politics as Markets," 646.

99. Ibid., 644.

100. Ibid., 708.

101. Persily and Cain, "Legal Status of Political Parties," 781.

102. Guy-Uriel E. Charles, "Democracy and Distortion," *Cornell Law Review* 92 (May 2007): 607–8.

103. Dennis F. Thompson, *Just Elections: Creating a Fair Electoral Process in the United States* (Chicago: University of Chicago Press, 2002), 179.

104. Ibid., 174–75.

105. Ibid., 175.

106. Ibid., 176.

107. Richard L. Hasen, "Bad Legislative Intent," *Wisconsin Law Review* 2006 (2006): 846.

108. Ibid., 861, 875–76.

109. Ibid., 876.

110. Ibid.

111. Ibid., 846. Hasen argues that proof of bad legislative intent should be neither necessary nor sufficient to challenge the constitutionality of an electoral law. Instead, the existence of such bad intent should trigger courts to take a "hard look" at the election law in question. Ibid., 846, 888. Courts should look at the effects of the contested law on the rights of individuals and groups, in addition to engaging in closer means/end scrutiny in order to redress legislative self-dealing. See also Richard L. Hasen, *The Supreme Court and Election Law: Judging Equality from* Baker v. Carr *to* Bush v. Gore (New York: New York University Press, 2003).

112. It should be noted, however, that second-order partisanship does not encompass such problems as majority tyranny; it addresses only a particular subset of the abuses of public power.

113. Yasmin Dawood, "The Antidomination Model and the Judicial Oversight of Democracy," *Georgetown Law Journal* 96 (June 2008): 1431–33.

114. Richard H. Pildes, "Foreword: The Constitutionalization of Democratic Politics," *Harvard Law Review* 118 (November 2004): 79.

115. Michael S. Kang, "De-Rigging Elections: Direct Democracy and the Future of Redistricting Reform," *Washington University Law Review* 84 (2006): 669. In addition, Kang argues that increasing democratic contestation *within* the major parties would serve to reduce the overall level of partisan polarization. See Michael S. Kang, "Sore Loser Laws and Democratic Contestation," *Georgetown Law Journal* 99 (April 2011): 1030–36; see also Michael S. Kang, "The Hydraulics and Politics of Party Regulation," *Iowa Law Review* 91 (October 2005): 131–87.

116. Adrian Vermeule, *Mechanisms of Democracy: Institutional Design Writ Small* (New York: Oxford University Press, 2007), 8.

117. Ibid., 32.

118. Ibid., 49.

119. Ibid., 66 (discussing Adam B. Cox, "Designing Redistricting Institutions," *Election Law Journal: Rules, Politics, and Policy* 5 (2006): 412–24).

120. Adrian Vermeule, "Foreword: System Effects and the Constitution," *Harvard Law Review* 123 (November 2009): 33–36; Adrian Vermeule, "The Invisible Hand in Legal and Political Theory," *Virginia Law Review* 96 (October 2010): 1433, 1438–39.

121. Rosenblum, *On the Side of the Angels*, 143. Rosenblum notes that "redistricting for partisan gain is an expected part of the system," at 223.

122. Muirhead, "A Defense of Party Spirit," 722.

INDEX

293